Miscarriage

Women's experiences and needs

Christine Moulder

An Imprint of HarperCollins*Publishers*

Pandora
An Imprint of HarperCollins*Publishers*
77–85 Fulham Palace Road,
Hammersmith, London W6 8JB
1160 Battery Street,
San Francisco, California 94111–1213

Published by Pandora 1990
This edition revised and updated 1995
3   5   7   9   10   8   6   4   2

© Christine Moulder 1990

Christine Moulder asserts the moral right to
be identified as the author of this work

A catalogue record for this book
is available from the British Library

ISBN 0 04 440941 9

Typeset by Harper Phototypesetters Limited
Northampton, England
Printed in Great Britain by
HarperCollinsManufacturing Glasgow

For Tom & Ellie

Contents

SECTION SIX · THE WAY FORWARD

Acknowledgements

In many ways this book is a collective effort. Although the responsibility for the final manuscript is mine, many people have contributed and I would like to thank them. Most of all I would like to thank the women who shared their experiences so openly – many said how helpful it was to talk or write. I hope they feel I have done them justice. I am grateful to the members of the Miscarriage Association who completed the questionnaire, to the Brighton and Worthing branches of the N.C.T., the Moulescombe and St Gabriel's women's health groups in Brighton, and the Sheffield Miscarriage Support Group.

I would also like to thank Kathryn Ladley of the Miscarriage Association, who was very encouraging at the beginning and who suggested the questionnaire, and Jenny Waterhouse and Ethel Hemmingway who coped with sending it out with the newsletter, when they had so many other things to do; David Hitchin, Chief Programmer, Research Data Analysis Unit, University of Sussex, for his advice and computer analysis of the questionnaires, and Alison Lyner for her help in coding them; and the staff at The Library, The Post Graduate Medical Centre, Brighton General Hospital, for so efficiently getting all the literature together with such good humour.

Many people have contributed their time and expertise. I would particularly like to thank: Dr Ann Browne, Dr Dubbins, Freedom Fields Hospital, Plymouth; Dr C. Everett, Alton Health Centre; Dr T. Friedman, University of

Nottingham Medical School; Dr P. Gill, Northern General Hospital, Sheffield; Joy Hardy, Health Visitor; Dr E. Morrison, Royal Sussex County Hospital; Liz Preece, Midwife, Alton Health Centre; Liz Pinczewski, The Miscarriage Support Group of Australia; Dr Helen Roberts, University of Glasgow; Wendy Savage, The London Hospital; Dr W. Vlaanderen, Lukas Hospital, Apeldoorn, The Netherlands.

I am particularly grateful to John Jacobs, University of Sussex, for his advice, support and encouragement throughout the entire project and his patient and careful reading of the manuscript.

Throughout the time I have been working on this book, I have represented the Miscarriage Association at the SANDS working party on pre-stillbirth. I have learnt a lot from the discussions and am grateful for the opportunity it has provided to share information and develop ideas.

I am grateful to the many women, friends and acquaintances, who have read the manuscript and shared their ideas, but especially to Ros Kane from the Miscarriage Association, Mary Davies from the National Childbirth Trust and Dr Lesley Morrison, Consultant in Women's Health, The Elisabeth Garrett Anderson Hospital, who all carefully read the manuscript and made constructive comments and suggestions. I have valued their encouragement.

My husband, Richard Pemberton, and children have all, in different ways, been affected by miscarriage and have contributed to my understanding of the effects it can have. I am grateful to them for what I have learnt from them and for their support and tolerance in coping with a busy and preoccupied wife and mother.

Introduction

My illusion, common to so many women, that all pregnancies inevitably end in a healthy baby, was shattered. Very few people are ready to acknowledge what can go wrong. Like so many I was unaware of how widespread miscarriage is. I had long been aware of societal pressures to have children, but had not appreciated how strongly the 'ability' to bear children is linked to your own self-image as a woman. Your definition of success and confidence depends far more on biology than is ever realised.

Pam, who wrote this, miscarried when she was eight weeks pregnant. Like most of us she was ignorant about miscarriage and shocked by the impact it had. This book is about her and many other women's experiences; it is about the depth, range and diversity of feelings that miscarriage engenders. And in addressing issues like the physical process of the miscarriage, the nature of the loss and disposal, I have attempted to demystify the experience of miscarriage.

The book is based on the experience of more than 350 women. I interviewed at length 30 women from different walks of life and their experience was varied. Specific topics were covered in the interviews which were tape recorded and transcribed. All had miscarried within the last two years but for some the miscarriage was more significant than others. They were referred to me by doctors and health visitors, or they heard of this project through the National Childbirth Trust or by word of mouth. I made specific approaches to a couple of women's health groups. Many other women have contributed either by writing or talking at length about their experiences.

In addition 320 women from the Miscarriage Association completed a questionnaire about specific issues, health care, the impact of the miscarriage on their relationship with their partner, how they handled it with their children, and their feelings about the miscarriage if they had previously had a termination. Over a third also wrote lengthy accounts of their experiences. They are not a representative group of women – they all felt strongly enough about their miscarriage to join the association and they were motivated enough to complete a fairly lengthy questionnaire – but in other respects there is no reason to think their experience is significantly different from other women who have miscarriages.

I have used the information from both sources throughout the book. It is the words of these women that tell the story of miscarriage. For the sake of privacy none of the contributors' real names has been used. In the few instances where it has seemed helpful to quantify the responses to the questionnaire, I have done so and referred to it as 'the survey', for the sake of brevity.

Medical care is a prominent part of most women's experience of miscarriage. I have attempted to understand women's needs when they miscarry and assess how far current medical practice meets them. The 'Guidelines for Good Practice' on page 253 summarises all the practical implications that are made throughout the text of the book. I hope they will be useful to women and health workers alike who want to improve the quality of service that is offered.

I have not attempted to review all the relevant literature or to give detailed medical information – this has been done elsewhere. Where it is helpful I have referred to relevant research and given details of where to find out more. I have tried to avoid using complicated terms but where it is unavoidable, or useful to have the medical term, I have explained it; there is a glossary of terms on page 264. I have also listed organisations that might be useful in providing further help and information on page 273.

I have attempted to portray a wide range of experience. If you have miscarried, or someone close to you has, I hope you will be able to find something in the book that rings bells, that will help you feel that you are not alone. If you work in the health service or you are reading this to learn more about miscarriage, I hope you will gain some insight into the experience and feel better equipped to respond to women who miscarry.

Introduction to 1995 Edition

Much has changed in the few years since this book was first published. Miscarriage is increasingly recognised as a significant event and is no longer the hidden experience it once was. As a society it seems we are more open about these issues, making it easier for women who want to share their experiences to do so, and there is greater awareness among health professionals of the meaning the experience may have and the care women need. So miscarriage may not necessarily be the isolating experience it once was, and women are less likely to encounter the ignorant 'never mind, try again' response that used to be so common and caused so much distress.

The women who have spoken out about their experiences have broken the silence about miscarriage, although a mixture of events has, in my view, contributed to the change in understanding. The self-help movement, the Miscarriage Association and SANDS (Stillbirth and Neonatal Death Society) have continued to promote pregnancy loss as an issue of public concern as well as offering support, information and advice to women and health professionals. Scientific developments in assisted reproduction have increased medical and research interest in early pregnancy and made it an acceptable area of study. More research has been published which establishes the psychological consequences of miscarriage. In response to public and professional pressure about the lower gestational age of viability, the legal definition of stillbirth was changed in 1992 from twenty-eight to twenty-four weeks of pregnancy. Discussions around this issue focused on the arbitrary nature of the division between miscarriage and stillbirth.

The House of Commons Health Committee's 1992 Report on Maternity Services recognised the value of appropriate training for staff and also acknowledged the importance of the development of good practice and sensitive policy to meet the needs of those who experience miscarriage as well as stillbirth and neonatal death. Whatever one's views about the recent changes in the Health Service and despite the pressure on resources and the rhetoric about a consumer-led service, it is clear that patients' views are increasingly taken into account and attempts are being made to organise services around women's needs.

Putting ideas into practice is a different matter, but there have been tangible improvements in care. The boundary between maternity and gynaecological services appears to be more fluid, enabling women to be cared for on maternity wards where this is appropriate. There is much greater awareness of the value for women of knowing about the loss as well as the importance of sensitive disposal practices. There is recognition of the need for follow-up care of some kind, although it may not be provided. Many hospitals are now establishing Early Pregnancy Assessment Units or Clinics in order to respond more quickly and effectively to women who bleed in early pregnancy. The medical management of miscarriage is now being offered in a few units. In the future, all other things being equal, women may be able to choose the management most suited to them: an ERPC (Evacuation of the Retained Products of Conception), medical management or allowing nature to take its course.

Despite the progress that has been made, however, women's needs do not change. Miscarriages will always occur and, while perfection and normality in pregnancy are mistakenly taken for granted, they will continue to cause distress. A miscarriage is an inherently confusing and contradictory experience. After a miscarriage many women face the task of making sense of what has happened to them. I hope this book will continue to help women in this process as well as guiding those who care for women – family, friends and health professionals alike – to understand how a woman may be feeling and the sort of help she may need.

Christine Moulder
November 1994

Section one

THE MISCARRIAGE

Jean's story – part one

'**W**hen I was eight weeks pregnant I stopped feeling pregnant, the changes were very subtle and at first I hardly noticed. Suddenly I realised that I hadn't felt sick for ten days, my breasts no longer hurt. I was reassured by the doctor at my antenatal appointment at ten weeks, this was nothing to worry about, everything was normal. Six days later the small spots of blood started. I was so calm about it, my husband was worried and sent me to bed. The next morning the GP was reassuring, it was probably nothing to worry about, many women bleed in early pregnancy. He didn't recommend bed rest, but said I should take it easy but otherwise carry on life as normal. I felt well and still confident that all would be fine, despite the small spots of brownish blood. Three days later the first small clot appeared, from that moment onward I was sure I would lose the baby. By the next day the bleeding got worse. I felt awful, faint, lifeless, and I had developed period-like pains which stretched right down into my thighs. My GP sent me to casualty. A female doctor examined me, she was very sympathetic and explained that the cervix was open and nothing they could do could save the pregnancy. I felt a certain amount of relief, knowing exactly what was happening after all the uncertainty of the past few days. If I had to lose the baby at least it was early in the pregnancy, I hadn't let myself become attached emotionally. I knew the D and C needed doing and accepted it philosophically. It was as though I was working on automatic pilot, I hardly

1

showed any emotion. Time dragged by as I waited for the D and C. I fought the tears, I was determined to fight all this emotion and be strong and not cry.

'Two and a half months after the miscarriage I felt mentally ready to try again. My body immediately seemed to torment me, by first making me feel I was pregnant and then came another period. Moods of excitement were immediately followed by moods of depression. Eventually my missed period was followed by a positive pregnancy test. I was concerned by the fact that I didn't feel as pregnant as previously. I didn't feel as sick, I longed to feel sick. I convinced myself everything was OK, and it was due to nerves. I didn't want to tell anyone I was pregnant. I was six weeks pregnant, I went to the loo and on the toilet paper appeared a light pinkish mucus, not very much, but without doubt blood stained! I just couldn't believe it, it couldn't be happening to me again. I was almost hysterical, I wanted to scream "No" at the top of my voice and I was so close to tears. My GP explained that there was little I could do but wait and see. It was a little early for a scan, although he did arrange one for a few days' time. He felt an internal was advisable and there was little merit in doing another pregnancy test yet, because it would stay positive for several days after a miscarriage. That left me to sit at home and hope. The bleeding was very light, it didn't even stain the sanitary towel but every time I went to the loo there was the tell tale spots of blood.

'It was two days later when the bleeding started properly and the clots started to appear. Again I knew that I had lost the baby, and I just wanted the miscarriage to be over as quickly as possible. More bleeding followed, with more clots and some pinkish grey tissue coming away. I wasn't in any pain and it was more like a bad period. The bleeding seemed to have virtually stopped for two days and I thought the miscarriage was over. My GP had said that, if I did miscarry, because it was so early, I was unlikely to need a D and C. My husband had to go out of town to an important business meeting and I insisted he went since the bleeding had stopped and I felt physically fine. That afternoon the bleeding started again, I felt scared and lonely.

When I went to the loo blood seemed to be everywhere. I lay on the bed terrified to move. Finally, when lying down the bleeding stopped, only to restart if I got up. I really don't know why I didn't call the doctor.

'The next morning I went back to the GP who sent me to casualty. The SHO said I needed a D and C, I was insistent that I didn't want one. I was forced to agree once the registrar also confirmed that I needed it. Yet again I was cool and calm. My husband was still away, all my messages seemed to have missed him. I phoned some friends and explained where I was and I am grateful to them for coming to keep me company. The hardest thing was phoning my mother and telling her that I had had another miscarriage. My husband didn't get back in time to see me before I went in for the op and I felt so lonely during those hours. I had never realised before how much I need him to give me support. Physically, apart from feeling tired after the anaesthetic, I was fine but mentally I was exhausted.'

Jean was particularly unlucky having two miscarriages. Most women who miscarry will be successful in their next pregnancy. But they were very ordinary, straightforward miscarriages. She vividly describes the phases she went through; her initial awareness that things were not right, and the progression to thinking that something was definitely wrong. She was reassured, but a turning point was reached when it became clear to her that the pregnancy had ended, the baby was lost. Her feelings of helplessness during that period of uncertainty, and the relief she felt when it became clear to her that she was miscarrying, are common to many women. It is frightening because there is absolutely nothing you can do to prevent it happening – it is beyond your control. She did not know what to expect. It's unclear exactly what is going to happen and when; the pattern of bleeding and pain is unknown. She remained outwardly calm at the time, only letting her feelings surface when she reached home. In the first section of the book we will explore further the wide range of experience and the issues to do with the physical nature of miscarriage.

'Then I knew it was all over': Realising you are miscarrying

The Phase of Uncertainty

The symptoms of miscarriage are also the symptoms of other problems in pregnancy, many of which right themselves and do not result in the pregnancy ending. Many women, it is unknown how many, bleed in pregnancy. You may bleed a little, even a lot, and experience cramps – the symptoms of miscarriage – and yet still go on to have a perfectly healthy baby. It is estimated that among women who bleed enough to be admitted to hospital 50-60 per cent will miscarry[1]. So when you first get some indication that the pregnancy may be going wrong, you will not know if you are going to miscarry or not.

A miscarriage is not a clear cut event. It is often only in retrospect that you realise when it started and that the symptoms were to do with the miscarriage and nothing else. At the time the possibility of miscarriage may not have occurred to you or you may worry, but keep reassuring yourself. 'I'm bleeding, I'm going to miscarry – It's stopped, I'm all right – It's started again, I'm worried – But the doctor said my cervix is closed, there's still hope – I'm going to – I'm not going to'. A phase of uncertainty, of being 'in limbo' is common for many women and this contributes to the stress and anxiety you may feel.

Often there is a phase of thinking it might happen but not knowing if it will, of perhaps ignoring the symptoms in the hope that they will go away, of worrying and waiting for your worst fears to be confirmed, of having your hopes raised only to be dashed later, and of eventually realising or facing up to the fact that the pregnancy has ended. It may be only well after the physical drama of the miscarriage is over that you fully realise the pregnancy has ended. It is a process of what one American researcher has called 'coming to know'.[2] A difficult time, of recognising the symptoms for what they are and balancing the physical evidence against your hopes that the pregnancy will continue. This can take a matter of a few hours or it may drag on for days or weeks. At this time the support and reassurance of others, both those close to you and the professionals you consult is critical. If you have children, you may need help in looking after them. If you work, you may be unable to do so.

ॐ

Realising You Have Miscarried After It Has Happened

You may not know you have miscarried. Many early miscarriages, before or around the time the first period is missed, are not experienced as one because you may not have known you were pregnant. Slightly later miscarriages also go undetected and are experienced as being like a period but a bit later and a bit heavier than usual. Susan only realised that she had miscarried in retrospect.

> At the time it seemed like a late, bad period which took a long time to start properly and was in the end very heavy but now, having been pregnant again, I realise that I had all the symptoms of very early pregnancy. I have not had a period like that since, and I am sure I was pregnant.

With the increased availability of early pregnancy tests, it is possible to know of a pregnancy very early on, if you wish. But you may not want to know and sometimes very early miscarriage is easier to deal with by treating it as if it is a late period. Loraine had had a heavy, very late period, but her periods had been very erratic and she thought nothing of it. However she was bleeding every few days and was sent for a scan. She was told she had been pregnant.

> It would have been much nicer not to know. I didn't know I was pregnant and I didn't think about it as a baby at all.

Her approach works as long as the miscarriage is early, and straightforward. If it is later and more complicated and the reasons for the symptoms are unknown, it can be a very frightening experience.

꒰

What Should I Do?

When you threaten to miscarry you are faced not only with the uncertainty but also with your ignorance about what you should do. Many women are advised, with the onset of bleeding, to rest in bed. There is no evidence that, for the majority of women who threaten to miscarry early in pregnancy, this is of any help. If the pregnancy has gone wrong from the start, there is nothing that you can do to save it. It only makes sense to rest in bed if you feel unwell, or if it is the place where you feel most comfortable. Bed rest may be impossible because of your family responsibilities, and it can be a depressing and isolating experience, especially when it may not be necessary. Many women say that once they rest the bleeding lessens or it stops and their hopes are raised that the pregnancy will continue, only for the bleeding to start again once they get up. You can end up feeling that you have prolonged the miscarriage. As one health visitor said:

> Some people feel that bed rest is at least doing all you can and that's fine, if it makes them feel better. Most women I

have spoken to found it seemed to make them more depressed, and indicated that the miscarriage was preventable and avoidable – placing the blame with them.

A few women have told me that they feel resting at the vulnerable time in their pregnancy has helped them a lot. It may be appropriate, for example, for women who threaten to miscarry later in pregnancy and who have been told they have an incompetent cervix.[3] But the general use of ultrasound in clarifying whether a pregnancy is viable or not, has brought to an end long periods of bed rest for no valid reason.

ॐ

Recognising the Symptoms

You may intuitively know you have miscarried or your symptoms, after a short time, make it abundantly clear. The possibility of miscarriage had not crossed Jan's mind until she got up to go to work and discovered she was spotting. She was nine weeks into her first pregnancy.

> As I spotted more I rested more. On Monday night I was in pain all night. It's amazing how you fool yourself – I thought I had terrible wind. Eight am on the Tuesday morning I went to the loo and really strained and I think I passed the fetus. I couldn't see anything but I visualised my cervix opening. That's when the pain stopped. Clearly something had happened. I started bleeding an awful lot which frightened me. Once I started bleeding a lot, I knew it was all over.

Linda thought she was miscarrying when the bleeding started when she was between ten and eleven weeks pregnant, but she was then reassured by her GP and by her friends, many of whom seemed to have bled during pregnancy. She bled for three days before she was admitted to hospital.

When I look back, about a week before it happened, I felt very fit and energetic. I didn't feel like going to bed early. I didn't feel at all sick and was actually feeling very uneasy about that. That was the beginning. Then I had some bleeding. It was quite slight to start with. I was quite panicky about it and just lay on the sofa, sort of rigid and felt quite gloomy about it all. The bleeding carried on and I started to get a bit of pain as well. I examined myself and felt quite sure that I could feel the cervix open. The GP examined me and said it was closed so I didn't have to panic. But then the bleeding carried on all the next day. I was losing big clots. It didn't seem right to me. How could it survive this? I was convinced I was miscarrying. My GP examined me the next day and said I definitely had and sent me to hospital.

Kim had miscarried before but felt positive about this pregnancy – all was going well apart from slight spotting which she and her GP had dismissed as nothing to worry about. Her miscarriage at fourteen and a half weeks was very sudden.

I felt grotty the day before it happened and initially thought I was just overtired. That afternoon I started to get crampy feelings in the pit of my stomach, like in period pains. The possibility of miscarrying suddenly flashed through my mind. I began to feel dreadful, both physically and mentally, and took to my bed. I eventually woke at 4.30am to discover that my bed was wet. I realised later that my waters had broken. I went to the loo and discovered a little bleeding. I wiped myself and there in my hand was my baby – tiny but complete and incredibly beautiful.

Kim was deeply shocked by her miscarriage, it was over so quickly. Her experience was more unusual. In contrast some women feel anxious about the pregnancy from the beginning and worry that they will miscarry.

From day one of my pregnancy something in the back of my mind told me that something was wrong, but I couldn't explain exactly what. I was just waiting for it to happen.

It's hard to know at the time if this anxiety is unfounded or whether it is a form of instinctive understanding and preparation for what is going to happen. If you feel something is wrong but you have no physical signs that cause sufficient concern, it can be very confusing, as Mandy discovered.

When I was about eleven weeks pregnant I became ill with a particularly vicious virus infection. I lost a lot of weight and found it difficult to regain my strength. I was worried about my baby but was reassured by my GP and the staff at the antenatal clinic, that all was well. I kept hoping I would soon feel better, but I didn't and eventually began to feel worse. This lasted for a couple of weeks before I started bleeding and had a blinding headache that lasted three days. When the bleeding became heavier it was clear that I was miscarrying and I went to casualty. By then I was nearly twenty weeks pregnant.

⟳

Raised Hopes

Even if you realise you are miscarrying it is easy for your hopes to be raised, if your symptoms abate, only to be dashed later. Caroline had been anxious throughout the pregnancy, almost waiting for things to go wrong. She instinctively knew she was miscarrying as soon as she started bleeding, although her hopes were raised at one point. She was twelve weeks pregnant.

When I went to the loo I saw all this blood like, lots of it, and because you haven't seen it for some time, it's a terrible shock. My first reaction was it's blood, but you're pregnant – you shouldn't have blood. I'm having a period but I'm not. Then the baby's gone. They took me to hospital. In the ambulance I kept saying it doesn't matter, it's gone. But the next morning the bleeding had stopped and I felt more hopeful. I thought I'd got it wrong. That afternoon they took me down for a scan in the X-ray department. The thing was they turned the screen away from me when they did it. And I thought, right – if there was anything there, they'd turn the screen round and say, there it is, everything's all right, and they didn't. Then I knew for definite. I didn't ask the woman doing the scan. I think I knew all the time. I just didn't want to admit it.

She was quite clear she was miscarrying but with the first sign that her pregnancy would continue her hopes were raised. Eileen miscarried at eleven weeks. She had been bleeding on and off for nine days but she didn't give up hope until it became very heavy.

During the time of not knowing, I had no stomach pains and kept thinking it was all right as long as I hadn't. I kept feeding the baby so much attention, feeling my stomach and thinking, stay with us, stay with us, we want you so much. The irony of it was that, all that time I was lying in bed taking things easy and beaming protective love inwards, it was already no longer there, but I didn't have any inkling of that.

ॐ

The Need for the Miscarriage to be Confirmed

While you may be able to listen to the signs your body is giving with confidence, hanging on in hope makes it hard to be completely objective. Your body can play tricks on you, and i the pattern of symptoms is muddled or if you ignore or misinterpret the signs, you continue to believe that the pregnancy will be successful long after it is clear that you have miscarried. It is not always possible to judge for yourself. Many women will turn to a doctor to confirm, either by clinical assessment or with the technological assistance of an ultrasound scan, whether the pregnancy has ended or not.

Sarah started spotting nine days before a scan eventually confirmed that she had miscarried. During that time she swayed between thinking she was miscarrying and remaining optimistic. She was not helped by not knowing what to expect in a miscarriage and therefore what she was waiting for.

I was eight and half weeks pregnant. The day after I had some bleeding, a little fresh blood, no pain, and immediately I thought, I'm going to miscarry, but then the bleeding stopped. The next day there was a murky, darker discharge but it was only slight so it didn't alarm me. There was no heavy bleeding and I assumed that there would be some. So I carried on over the next few days. There'd be no bleeding during the day then in the evening, I'd get some, then none during the night and when I awoke I assumed things were OK. Then I'd be bleeding again in the evening and I'd go to bed saying to my husband that I was going to miscarry in the night. I kept thinking I'd literally wake up in the night in a pool of blood and that would be it, it would be over. That was my assumption but it didn't happen. After four days of this I continued with my plans to visit my mother. When I got to my parents the bleeding became heavier and more continual, like a normal period. I felt I had to do something as I'd neither had a miscarriage, nor had the bleeding stopped. But the longer it hadn't happened the more optimistic I'd become. I saw a GP who referred me immediately to hospital for a scan. I assumed it would happen that day but I was finally scanned three days later. A doctor came and told me after I had the scan that I had lost the baby. That day the bleeding had stopped and I still felt very well. I hadn't had any pains and was therefore thinking things were looking good. I was on bed rest and I felt the assumption was, if you rest properly all will be well. I think I actually miscarried the second day in hospital because I lost a particularly large clot and a lot of thick red blood. I feel foolish, really stupid, that I had lost a baby then and didn't know.

Alice felt she wasted time in hospital waiting for a scan. She first thought she was miscarrying when she started bleeding at eleven weeks but clung on to the good signs until she was scanned nearly a week later, although the bleeding had increased and she was in a considerable amount of pain. She needed someone else to confirm the miscarriage for her.

I was very scared and confused by the conflicting messages I was getting. I was told my cervix was closed so it was still hopeful, yet I was bleeding, having contractions and by this time feeling very unwell. When I had the scan the operator wouldn't discuss it with me. The miscarriage was confirmed when I went back up to the ward and they'd moved my bed in with the women who had had miscarriages and ectopic pregnancies!

Dependence on a scan can prolong the anxious period of not knowing. There is often a long wait for a scan appointment when a diagnosis could probably be made earlier on the basis of clinical evidence, expectations of an ongoing pregnancy are raised – you seize on anything positive, in the hope that it will not happen. Doctors sometimes compound this by ignoring the evidence you bring and failing to listen to the extent of pain or cramp and blood loss that you report. You may feel confused if medical opinion conflicts with your own under-standing of what is happening. You may misinterpret neutral statements positively and feel very resentful when it becomes clear that your pregnancy has gone wrong.

৵

Discovering You Are Miscarrying at a Scan

Scans have quietly revolutionised the experience of miscarriage and most women who are admitted to hospital threatening to miscarry, will have an ultrasound scan. The most sophisticated equipment can detect a heartbeat as early as five weeks of pregnancy , less sophisticated equipment at seven or eight weeks. This, of course, does not necessarily mean that the baby will not be lost at a later stage, but finding a living embryo on ultrasound means, in the majority of cases, an ongoing pregnancy. Long periods of time anxiously waiting to see what is going to happen are, on the whole, no longer necessary.

A scan can confirm what you already feared – the negative result is not news to you. In confirming the miscarriage, a scan enables action to be taken earlier and means that you do not have to spend physical and emotional energy on a pregnancy that has failed, but it can also deprive you of the opportunity of gradually coming to terms with what has happened. Diana found the scan very helpful in enabling her to understand what was happening. She had feared things might not be right as she had spotted on and off for several weeks, and at one point she had had contractions. She had begun to feel she was no longer pregnant but had pushed these worries to the back of her mind. She felt her GP had not taken her seriously.

Because of my symptoms I was scanned in the antenatal clinic at my booking-in appointment when I was fourteen weeks pregnant, and it was discovered that I had a blighted ovum. It confirmed the worries I had been hiding from myself. The doctor explained clearly what a blighted ovum was and showed me the scan. The scan was also checked by a second doctor. They really helped me to understand.

Claire had miscarried at nine weeks in her previous pregnancy and was anxious about it happening again. She had been feeling very sick and tired and her GP arranged an early scan to confirm the viability of this pregnancy to reassure her.

They started scanning and kept going round and round my tummy not finding anything. They kept saying it was too early. I was about seven and a half weeks. They gave me an appointment to come back in a week. I felt really upset about that, partly because I thought it was a non-viable fetus and partly because I felt so ill. By the time I spoke to my GP, she had arranged for me to be scanned on a more sophisticated machine. My husband came with me. They scanned and found an empty embryonic sac but no fetal heartbeat. Their advice was that I should go straight in for a D and C, that I could wait and see what happened but that I would miscarry at some point. So I went in that day. It was worse finding out from the scan because it was a great shock, having had no physical indications from my body that things had gone wrong, but I'd certainly do the same again. There's no way I'd want to feel sick for a couple of months to no avail. It did avert all that. Also I hadn't lost any blood or anything. It was much less physically traumatic. I felt quite well again straight away. I have wondered since if it was a bit early to be so sure. When I had a scan in my next pregnancy the bloke said to me he wouldn't ever advise anyone to have a D and C between seven and eight weeks, because you can't be conclusive at that stage. It made me wonder if that one had been viable. I can't believe they'd have advised a D and C if there'd been any chance, but who knows?

Sometimes a pregnancy can come to an end with little or no indication that anything is wrong. It is called a 'missed abortion'. The baby has died or failed to develop but your body has not expelled it. When you have assumed the pregnancy is healthy, a scan can be a particularly abrupt and shocking way to discover a miscarriage. It is hard to grasp what is happening, even to believe that it is happening at all. Many women say that because they have had inadequate warning signs, they feel conned by their body.

The possibility of a miscarriage had never occurred to Pat until she had a routine scan in the antenatal clinic. She was sixteen weeks pregnant and it was her third pregnancy.

As he was doing the scan his eyes started watering, they all filled up, and I thought, what is the matter with him? Then he called in someone else and she did it for ages. Then the auxiliary came in. Then they left me on the couch and all three of them went in the other room and left me on my own for ages. I knew something was wrong. What they normally do is give you a sealed brown envelope with the scan results to give to the doctor in the antenatal. They didn't do that. They told me to wait outside and that a sister from the antenatal was coming to see me. I know they don't do that. I went outside to my husband and burst into tears, because I knew something was wrong.

The Sister told her that there was no heartbeat and that the baby had died and Pat chose to go home and pack her things rather than be admitted straight away. Like many women she needed time for the information to sink in and so chose to delay her admission to hospital. She went home to pack and felt quite high. By the time she returned to hospital her spirits had plummeted.

I wish now that I'd asked for another scan, and to see it, just to make sure. I had had no bleeding. I didn't really know what a D and C was – I had some idea but I was really frightened. And I was frightened they thought I was having an abortion. After the D and C I bled heavily. I went home the next day and felt OK but that evening I started having contractions. I thought this is like being in labour, maybe there's still a baby there. I went back to the hospital. They examined me and removed a large piece of placenta. I had another D and C at midnight. I came home the next day feeling very tired.

Feelings of disbelief are common. You may feel stunned and convinced that there must be a reason; you may think there has been a mistake or wonder how they can be so sure and expect them to repeat the scan to check the result. In a way this is quite rational, after all, machines do go wrong and human beings do make mistakes, but it is also to do with the difficulty of accepting bad news – we don't want to believe it. After any form of loss it is often difficult to believe that it has happened. You may be particularly vulnerable to this when you discover you have miscarried at a scan.

꒜

The Management of Scans

While ultrasound is used extensively, some would say professionals rely too heavily on technology to the detriment of the development and use of clinical skills. There are informed critics who question the safety aspects of ultrasound, not because it has been conclusively shown to have detrimental effects, but because there have been no long-term studies to show that it is completely safe. There are other concerns with its use. The skill, training and expertise of the operator varies as does the quality of the equipment, all of which affect the quality of the result. Some scans will be ambiguous and will have to be repeated, and it is not impossible for mistakes to be made.

However, handed well, a scan can ease the difficult task of facing up to the fact that you are no longer pregnant. Madelaine, unusually, was scanned at her local health centre by her community midwife. She appreciated the service offered by both the midwife and the GP.

The sac was a funny shape and there was no heartbeat. The midwife explained what it meant. I didn't want to talk too much in case I broke down and cried. My GP came in and answered my questions. There no pressure of time. Then my husband came in and he saw the scan and they explained it all to him. They wanted to scan me again in a week to check. The midwife said it would take its course and prepared me for what might happen. They were very, very helpful.

Unfortunately many women do not have such a positive experience as Madelaine. There are not many health centres with these facilities, so most women will be scanned in hospital, in either the ultrasound department, the antenatal clinic, in casualty or on a ward, and the way the scans are handed leaves many women who miscarry distressed or dissatisfied. There are frequently long delays for a scan appointment or a wait in hospital until one can be arranged. Sarah waited three days in hospital to be scanned.

I was forced into a difficult situation because of the delay with the scan and was given false hope. I could part with this pregnancy if it wasn't right. I was quite happy for nature to take its course if that's what had to be. But I needed to know whether that was going to be the case. Worrying about not knowing put everyone under a great deal of strain, and it was all so unnecessary.

When a scan only takes a few minutes it seems hard to believe it could not have been arranged earlier. The delay in appointments stems partly from the current difficulties within the NHS: pressure of work, lack of resources, inappropriate facilities and the sheer lack of time to do everything properly. It is difficult, but not impossible, to organise a decent service under these circumstances, but miscarriage patients come near the bottom of the priority list.

There are also problems of access to scans. GPs vary in their willingness to refer women who are threatening to miscarry for a scan, and hospitals vary in their ability to offer prompt appointments. It is, of course, always easy to be wise after the event, but some women are not referred for a scan when it would appear to have been appropriate. Diana was very resentful that she had wasted time trying to cope with her pregnancy when a scan would have shown that it had ended.

> I felt very angry that the miscarriage had not been diagnosed earlier. I had been to see the doctor several weeks before, with bleeding and cramps, but was basically fobbed off. If I'd been scanned then I would have known where I was. As it was I struggled on, feeling awful. My friend, who's married to a doctor, had similar symptoms and was scanned straight away.

But the biggest source of criticism is the way the scan procedure itself is handed, and the way that the results are communicated. It is perhaps easy for the professionals involved to forger how overwhelming a scan can be. Tracey was only eighteen when she first miscarried. She had never been in hospital before and she did not know what a scan was.

> I was so frightened what they were going to do to me and my baby. I was in a wheelchair with only a green overall thing on. My turn finally came. I went in and it was dark and full of televisions. I lay on the bed and the man put some kind of jelly on my stomach, than a thing that looked like a shaver. I kept asking him what was happening and he said, the doctor will tell you when you get back to the ward. I was shaking and crying and he kept asking me how many weeks I was.

As the woman whose baby it is, or was, you can feel you have no part to play. Monica described being scanned in a room which seemed full of medical staff staring at the screen but without saying anything to her. At its worst the scan can become a purely technical exercise for the benefit of the staff; you are not allowed to see the screen, communicate with the scan operator or have your partner present, and you are told that you will be given the results later – and it may be much later – by a doctor. All a far cry from Madelaine's experience.

The reasons for this are understandable. Ultrasound is a developing field and there have been rapid technological changes in recent years. It is as if the necessary human skills have not kept up with the technological expertise. Scan operators are often, but not always, radiographers, who have been governed by a charter which does not allow them to communicate information to the patient. So there is a tradition of 'not telling'. This policy places both women and staff in a very awkward position.

Many women know that if all is well they will be shown the heartbeat, the spine or anything that can be clearly seen. When this does not happen, or when routine procedures are changed, you know that something is wrong. Kaitlin saw the screen herself and realised that there was no heartbeat, but she was sent home without being told the result. Or you may pick up other indications that things are not right – the expression on the faces of the staff, the complete silence in the room.

Unless there is a good reason, for example, if the scan needs to be checked by a more senior person who is unavailable, in which case this should be explained, it seems uncaring to deliberately withhold the scan result and farcical if the women has worked it out for herself. Some hospitals are developing a more liberal policy that allows the sonographer to give limited information and allows partners or a close friend to be present. Amy was told very gently by the scan operator that there was not a heartbeat any more and that he was very sorry. Her husband was with her and they were both shown the screen.

But telling someone their baby is dead, or doesn't exist any more or even that it has never existed, is a difficult job for anyone, especially if you only met five minutes earlier, and are in a darkened room, watching a television screen. Many sonographers have little training and preparation for this task, opting for a more technical job in the first place. Doctors are sometimes not that good at it either. When Margot questioned the result of her scan, she was told that it was absolutely certain, the baby was just like a 'blob of jelly'. The scan operator told Gina there was nothing there.

> He was very abrupt, just saying there were fuzzy bits. Neither he nor the doctor looked me in the eye. I felt they couldn't get rid of me fast enough.

Sometimes it is the most junior staff who have to break the bad news. Liz was told that she was miscarrying by a student nurse as she was being wheeled down the corridor after her scan.

As if to add insult to injury, many women find themselves in the midst of apparently healthy pregnant women before and after their scan. Limited facilities may make it difficult to organise things in any other way, but this does not take away the additional pain this can cause.

> In the waiting room – happy faces, a pregnant mum with her husband and two children. The whole family come to see the unborn child, while mine was dead inside me. I didn't begrudge them their happiness, but I didn't want to see them.

Telling someone that they are miscarrying is never easy, but it does help if you are not surrounded by successfully pregnant women and if there is an agreed policy on communicating the result of the scan. It is also helpful if the person who tells you has some understanding of what a miscarriage may mean, is clear and direct in what they say, but sensitive to your reaction, and not preoccupied with defending themselves from the uncomfortable feelings that miscarriage can arouse.

You may welcome the opportunity for a scan and accept the procedures involved, or you may feel it is intrusive and destroys the instinctive knowledge you have about the workings of your own body. Your feelings about a scan often reflect the way it was handled and how sensitively you were told the result. Handled badly it can be a distressing experience. Handled well, a scan can bring enormous benefits in clarifying if your pregnancy has ended and helping you to understand what has been going on in your body. But technological intervention, as in other areas of pregnancy and childbirth, can induce a sense of powerlessness and helplessness which takes time to overcome. Nevertheless, with these provisos, the development of ultrasound has, on the whole, brought great benefit to women who miscarry.

๖ 2 ๖

'Where's all the blood coming from?': The physical process

๖

Every miscarriage is unique but is characterised by the pattern of bleeding, cramps, and pain, the medical intervention and the nature of the loss: blood clots and tissue, an embryo, fetus or baby. Even if you have the same symptoms as someone you know, it is unlikely that you will experience them in the same way. But there are important physical processes at work which will influence the sort of miscarriage you have. In this chapter we will focus on the physical aspects of earlier miscarriage (up to sixteen weeks of pregnancy) although there is no hard and fast dividing line. Later miscarriage will be discussed in Chapter 4 on page 48.

๖

The Physical Facts

The causes of miscarriage are complex and a lot is still not understood. Although a detailed discussion is beyond the scope of this book (see page 268 for books which go into the causes of miscarriage in more detail), it is important to have some grasp of what can go wrong, in order to understand what your body is doing.

It is thought that about 50–60 per cent of early miscarriages are due to chromosomal abnormalities;[1] some research suggests the proportion may be much higher.[2] Fertilization is a complex and miraculous business so it is hardly surprising that it does not always work perfectly. A defect in the sperm or ovum (egg) will result in an abnormal conception and, if the pregnancy continues, the baby will be abnormal in some way. Some ova and sperm will, by chance, be imperfect, but they are also vulnerable to damage by outside factors – radiation, certain chemicals and drugs, and some virus infections, for example. The baby is also vulnerable to these hazards as it develops, particularly in the early stages. So things can go wrong before, during and after conception, and the miscarriage is a healthy response to these abnormalities.

When there is an abnormality either there may be no fetus (only the placenta and membranes will have developed – a blighted ovum), or the fetus may have died at an early stage but the placenta and membranes continue to develop for a while so that you still feel pregnant. You lose blood, clots and tissue – the products of conception – in varying amounts, over a period of time, and it is likely that you will feel some pain. If there is a fetus, it is usually much smaller than would be expected, and if it has been dead for some time, it will have started to disintegrate (maceration is the medical term). It is unusual to lose a recognizable fetus that died prior to the miscarriage.

But this does not account for all miscarriages. Many are largely unexplained. It is thought that in some cases the baby does not implant securely in the womb, but it is not really understood why this may be. Although you may worry that there is something wrong with you that has caused your miscarriage, this is unlikely. The majority of women will be successful in their next pregnancy and, for this reason, most obstetricians will not do any tests or investigations until you have had three consecutive miscarriages. It is very unusual to lose a fetus that was living until it was born in early pregnancy and, for this reason, some obstetricians would argue, warrants further investigations that are not considered appropriate for most early miscarriages.

༶

Not Knowing What to Expect

Unless you have miscarried before you are unlikely to know what to expect. If it is your first pregnancy you will not have had the experience of birth and the familiarity with your body that this can bring. For the women I talked to for this book it was those miscarrying their first pregnancy who found it generally more physically devastating in terms of pain and blood loss. But even if you have been pregnant before you may know little about miscarriage and if you don't know what your body is going to do, should do or is doing, you can feel powerless, helpless and quite frightened.

The professionals are, on the whole, not very good at preparing you for what is to come. When Rebecca was five and half weeks pregnant she was scanned and it was discovered that her long-awaited pregnancy had miscarried.

> He advised me to let it come out naturally, but he didn't give me any clear picture of what to expect. I felt very depressed and longed for some bleeding as a sign it was coming out of me and I could return to normal as soon as possible. Signs of pregnancy began to diminish and then, at about nine weeks, I noticed a large blob of pinky white congealed mucus when I went to the loo. This was quite alarming, even though I had been expecting something. A few days later another blob appeared but still no blood. I went for my third scan at nine weeks and was kept in for a D and C.

Although it is difficult to know the exact pattern of an individual miscarriage, there is an enormous amount of ignorance about the physical process, and there is a lack of openness and discussion about it, even among women who have miscarried. The assumption that having a miscarriage is 'just like a bad period' is widespread and, on the whole, inaccurate. Eileen was eleven weeks pregnant when she realized she was miscarrying.

> The GP said it would be nothing, just like a heavy period. I remember lying there thinking, what will I do if this little recognizable thing comes out, what will we do with it? There I was lying in bed, swathed in sanitary towels. And we lay there waiting and it just never happened. By 8 am the next morning after a sleepless night, I'd stopped bleeding. I didn't feel hopeful – I just felt angry. I so wanted it to happen cleanly and easily.

Eileen was admitted to hospital for a scan and later, an ERPC (evacuation of the retained products of conception). Just as there is normally nothing you can do to prevent a miscarriage, little can be done to make it happen either. Once the miscarriage has been confirmed, the only course of action, if it does not happen naturally, is for an ERPC which will remove what remains of the pregnancy.

෨

Bleeding

The bleeding you experience will vary over the duration of the miscarriage. It may start with slight spotting of darker, old blood, and, as it gets heavier, the blood may become bright red and you may pass clots and tissue. Or it may be heavy and fresh from the beginning. It may stop and you may think the pregnancy will continue, only for it to start again. If your miscarriage is confirmed early and an ERPC is done fairly quickly, you may experience relatively little blood loss.

For some women the bleeding is extremely heavy. Apart from the shock, the sheer volume can be overwhelming – it is difficult to understand where it is all coming from. Not only is it frightening, it is also extremely messy and undignified and can arouse deep feelings of utter helplessness, of being out of control, incontinent, no longer adult, unclean and polluting.

Women describe their fears of making a mess, of leaving a pool of blood behind on the waiting room chair in casualty, of bleeding all over the hospital bed. It is a fear of getting blood in the wrong place, of breaking a taboo.

On arrival at hospital, Helen said she was afraid to stand up as she felt she would 'gush' all over the floor. Caroline started to miscarry at work. She was bleeding heavily and a colleague sat her down and phoned the doctor. She said, 'I was sitting in the director's chair and I thought, what's he going to do tomorrow when he comes in and there's my blood all over it!' Jan was nine weeks pregnant and felt ill-equipped to deal with the heavy bleeding she experienced.

> I phoned my GP who asked me to go to the surgery, which I did. If you don't use sanitary towels, you don't have them around, so I had an ordinary towel folded up and I was wearing these baggy leggings which I could pack things into. I went down to the surgery and sat there for twenty minutes, but it was hurting and I was bleeding so much, so I asked to go in. I told the doctor I was bleeding an awful lot and would make a terrible mess everywhere. They couldn't find anything for me to lie on when he felt my tummy. They found a plastic bag in the end. After that I went straight to casualty.

Mary was twelve weeks pregnant. She had been bleeding for three days but had been trying to ignore it as she was organizing a family celebration and she was determined it would go ahead. Looking back she is sure that if she had known what her miscarriage was going to be like, she would not have left the house.

> The bleeding was getting worse but we went to the restaurant. I managed to eat my soup, then I needed to go to the loo. I just about made it. My shoes were full of blood and I was trailing blood across the carpet. I didn't know what to do – no one had come with me. I had to go into the kitchen to ask the cook to ask the waitress to get

my mother. There was an awful lot of blood. I felt it all bubbling up and coming out – lots and lots of clots, big lumps, and dark red. I think there was a sac coming away because I felt the movement. There was no pain. My mum was trying to clean me up. And there was my poor mother dressed up to the nines scrubbing the carpet in the restaurant. My mother had come equipped with sanitary towels so I walked home with eight sanitary towels and sort of sprinted up the road as best I could. I had a bath and I was still bleeding. I went to bed with black bin liners everywhere so as not to make a mess. It was all so undignified. The physical side bothered me a great deal.

I got taken to hospital by ambulance. When they transferred trolleys that shocked me. There was this pool of blood. When it's going down the loo and being flushed away you don't realize how much you're losing. It shook me up that I was still losing so much when I'd lost so much already. I started to feel all whoosey and I said to my husband 'I'm going to die,' and I passed out. I fainted again that night when I was on the commode. I was still bleeding that evening but it was like a period. I was scanned the next day and had a D and C.

౨

Miscarriages that Become Medical Emergencies

If you bleed heavily it is usually because the miscarriage is incomplete. Severe blood loss can be treated with an injection of Ergometrine or Syntocinon which help the womb to contract and therefore, the blood loss to lessen. The drugs may make you feel sick, in which case an anti-emetic injection may be given to reduce this. It may be necessary for you to have an intravenous drip and sometimes a blood transfusion. If tissue is keeping the neck of the womb open, and increasing the pain and bleeding, a doctor may remove it manually.

For some women a miscarriage is physically traumatic and, for a small number of women, it can turn into a medical crisis, requiring prompt intervention. As Heather found, the medical intervention can dominate the experience.

I was thirteen weeks pregnant when I started my first miscarriage. Each day, for the previous seven days, I had a minute blood loss which my GP assumed were traces of the menstrual cycle, but I then began to lose blood at the rate of a light period. I had bed rest, but three days later started passing clots and was admitted to hospital in the late afternoon. I had no pain but I wanted to empty my bladder. Twice I was given a bed pan and lost blood and clots which was so off-putting that I was unable to urinate. I was given a saline drip because of the heavy loss and an injection to reduce the bleeding. A D and C was planned but had to wait until sufficient time had elapsed from my last meal. I asked for a bed pan a third time and this time a very large quantity of blood [¾ or 1 pint] flopped out of me and I felt very faint. The student nurse helping me summoned several nurses and two doctors and I discovered later that the subsequent treatment was a resuscitation. I had a plasma drip attached to one arm, in addition to the saline. My bladder was drained with a catheter to relieve pressure on my womb, and a senior doctor manually emptied my womb as far as possible. This enabled me to recover sufficiently to have the D and C a few hours later. My initial feelings after the miscarriage were relief at having survived the ordeal.

ॐ

Pain

Pain is a very individual experience and, as with blood loss, the amount of pain women describe varies enormously. Sarah, as we saw on page 11, miscarried at ten weeks and experienced no pain at all. She found it difficult to take the bleeding seriously without any pain and she felt almost conned by her body. Some pain would have made her realize the implications of the bleeding. Mary who bled so heavily in the restaurant had very little pain at the time.

On the other hand, Pauline, who has two children, described the pain of her miscarriage at fourteen weeks as the same as mid-labour pains and much worse than period pains. It was Val's first pregnancy and she also experienced a lot of pain. She described her miscarriage at twelve weeks as 'extremely painful contractions, probably because I was frightened.' When she reached hospital she was given Pethidine to relieve the pain. Many women say that their complaints about the pain, and requests for pain relief, are not taken seriously. Perhaps this is because it is commonly assumed that miscarriage is not painful.

Sometimes the medical intervention that is necessary to remove the pregnancy is painful. Theresa had a missed abortion (her pregnancy had ended some weeks before she had any symptoms that it had gone wrong) and her miscarriage was eventually diagnosed at fifteen weeks. It was agreed that she would have a D and C. As her pregnancy had progressed so far, it was necessary for a pessary to be inserted to dilate the cervix enough for the fetus to be suctioned through. The pessary soon caused contractions which she found very painful.

> I wanted something for the pain. I was in so much agony. It was all so distressing because I was in so much pain. I have never had a baby to compare it with, but I think it must be worse because you're getting nothing at the end of it.

Coping with the pain may dominate your experience and blot out everything else that's going on. It may dull the emotional pain so that you just feel immensely relieved when it's all over.

ৡ

ERPC

Nearly all women admitted to hospital for a miscarriage will have an ERPC (evacuation of the retained products of conception). You may have referred to this as a D and C (dilation and curettage), often called 'the scrape', but strictly speaking an ERPC is correct when a D and C is needed after you have been pregnant. Early miscarriages are not usually complete, in that not all that remains of the fetus, sac and placenta is expelled. An ERPC is done to remove the products of conception which have not been passed. If any products are left you can get an infection which could damage your fallopian tubes and make it difficult to get pregnant in the future. Without an ERPC there is also a slight risk that you may haemorrhage.

It is generally accepted by obstetricians and gynaecologists that with pregnancies lost between six and sixteen weeks, it is difficult to tell if the miscarriage is complete. You are usually advised to keep the products to show the doctor, but it can be very difficult to do this, and, even if you do, they may not always be inspected properly when you get to hospital. Although some hospitals use ultrasound to confirm whether the womb is empty, doctors disagree if this gives an adequate assessment or not. So it has become routine practice that an ERPC is performed. Like many routine procedures, while the implications for them seem clear, inevitably not everyone needs one. An inflexible policy means that some women will have one unnecessarily

In Britain an ERPC will be performed in hospital under general anaesthetic. In other places, in parts of America, for example, where services are organized differently, a full general anaesthetic is not used and women are treated as day patients at a clinic. Hospital admission adds an extra dimension to a miscarriage. You may feel safe and protected in hospital at a time when you feel vulnerable and grateful for being in a place where you will be looked after and emergencies will be taken care of. Or you may find admission to hospital more difficult; they can be very frightening and over-whelming places, and you may resent your loss of autonomy and lack of privacy.

Feelings about the ERPC

While the ERPC is a minor surgical procedure from the health professionals' point of view, it may not seem at all minor to you. You may feel that the ERPC is an immense intrusion and only reluctantly agree to it. Elaine describes how she felt when she was told she was to have a D and C.

> I was in a state. I was frightened because it was the first gynaecological intervention I had had. I hadn't thought about being violated medically before. I wasn't sure what a D and C meant. I was protective of the baby and didn't want them to do anything that might harm the baby if it could be saved.

It can be particularly overwhelming if you are rushed into an ERPC before you have accepted that the pregnancy has ended. As one woman said, 'I was still busy trying to hang on to my baby whilst the doctor was busy organizing a D and C.' She needed time to take in what was happening to her and it is important that this is recognized.

You may be given a choice between going into hospital straight away or in a few days' time and you may welcome the opportunity to go home and think it over, to tell those people close to you and to compose yourself. Or, once you know something is wrong, you may find the idea of waiting very difficult. One woman said she felt like a 'walking coffin' and another that she was horrified at having to carry her dead babies (twins) in her belly for two to three whole days. Helen could not be admitted to hospital for two days and said she found it very hard knowing her baby was inside her, but that it would never be born.

Although generally speaking an ERPC is an extremely safe procedure, with few after-effects, you may worry that it will cause some damage. It is more likely that the ERPC will be done too gently and tissue will remain in the womb than that any damage will be done. These anxieties are quite under-standable when such a precious place is invaded, and you cannot see for yourself exactly what has been done.

Some women feel very positive about an ERPC and say how they feel 'properly cleaned out' and ready to try again. One described how she had 'engineered' her way into an ERPC for her own peace of mind. Bryony, in comparing her experiences of two early miscarriages, one with and one without an ERPC, clearly saw the advantages.

> I recovered much more quickly because of the D and C which returned my body to normal. Psychologically it was good to feel that I had been cleaned out and tidied up, an actual event had taken place and I could say I've had a D and C and expect to be treated as a patient for a few days.

The ERPC serves a ritual, as well as a physical function. It marks the end of a pregnancy and clearly establishes that the miscarriage happened. You may experience a profound sense of loss and disappointment as soon as you come round from the anaesthetic; there is no hope of the pregnancy continuing and the baby has gone.

When an ERPC Can Be Avoided

Ruth's miscarriage was relatively straightforward in physical terms. She was not admitted to hospital and she did not have an ERPC.

> At eight weeks I started getting painless bleeding – not very much, so I ignored it. The next evening it was accom-panied by a very bad ache; the next morning I passed a large clot which I assumed was the child. I managed to get

an appointment to see the doctor that morning. After that I went to work, seeing little point in staying at home. On reflection I probably would have felt better if I had spent at least part of the day in bed.

Ruth did not need an ERPC. Anthea did not want one because of the disruption she feared hospitalization would cause her family. She was nine weeks pregnant when she miscarried at home. After several days' bleeding she experienced cramps and then, for a short while, quite strong contractions. She passed the fetal sac, which she kept to show the midwife who visited her at home. She was scanned at her local health centre which revealed that her womb was empty and an ERPC unnecessary. She bled for a couple of weeks afterwards, the amount gradually decreasing.

Jill did not want to go to hospital because she wanted to minimize the upset her miscarriage caused.

At eleven weeks I started to miscarry. I didn't rest, I changed the beds, did housework until, in pain, I had to stop. I lost it [the complete fetus]. I stayed in bed and the doctor called to check me over. I was bleeding heavily. Not all the placenta had come away, that was why I was bleeding so much. Three days later the rest came away and I started to improve. Perhaps I was unwise, the doctor had suggested I go into hospital for a D and C but I wouldn't hear of it.

For Anthea and Jill the loss was very clear. Both expelled the fetus or fetal sac, and they were confident about handling the process themselves. Both had children and Diana had miscarried before. They had sympathetic and supportive GPs who were prepared to visit them at home and Anthea had a midwife who was involved and offered a lot of help.

In practice many GPs seem to offer a choice to women who miscarry early in pregnancy and are not bleeding very heavily, suggesting that they stay at home to monitor the bleeding over a few days but contact them if it gets heavy. This may feel as though you are not being taken seriously, when in fact you are being offered the opportunity to let your body work naturally without unnecessary intervention and a general anaesthetic. Deirdre miscarried at nine weeks and was anxious that she did not know exactly what she would be losing. She felt tired and unwell, and worried by the extent of the bleeding which continued for several weeks, in diminishing amounts, but in the end she avoided hospitalization and an ERPC. Unfortunately for Claire, who was nine weeks pregnant, it did not work out this way and she had to go into hospital in the end.

> I was advised to stay at home by the GP and not to have a D and C. So the bleeding carried on quite heavily for about four days and I felt really unwell, at which point I decided there really was no point in carrying on and I did go in for a D and C. In the end I had a blood transfusion because I had lost so much.

If the bleeding is severe or if there is a risk of haemorrhage, an ERPC is essential. Because it is difficult to predict how extensive the bleeding will be and it is difficult to tell when one will not be needed, doctors tend to err on the side of caution. An ERPC is a way of controlling the uncertainty. But it does seem that for some women the decision is fairly arbitrary. Without an ERPC you will probably bleed more heavily, over a longer period of time, and you will feel unwell and lacking in energy. You also risk infection, but this is probably overrated. It is a matter of weighing this against the costs of having one – hospitalization, a general anaesthetic, the medical intervention, and the feelings you may have of a loss of control.

ॐ

Pregnancy Loss with Longer-term Implications

Hydatidiform Mole – Molar Pregnancy

Molar pregnancy is unusual in the West (one in 2,000 pregnancies), but, because of the longer-term implications it is important to know about. In a molar pregnancy, an abnormal placenta develops made up of small, grape-like blobs, some of which may be passed in the bleeding prior to the miscarriage. There is usually no fetus and the abnormally high levels of hormones associated with a molar pregnancy may make you feel very sick. If any tissue from a molar pregnancy is left in the womb it may become cancerous, so whenever it is detected it is necessary for the womb to be emptied as soon as possible. As long as it is detected in time it is normally completely curable.

It is routine in most hospitals that placental tissue from all women who miscarry is tested to exclude the possibility of a molar pregnancy. If you are diagnosed as having had one you will have regular blood and urine tests to make sure that the molar tissue is not continuing to develop. Helen, who miscarried at ten weeks, describes what happened to her.

> I have had a year's follow-up. I had fortnightly blood and urine tests until my hormone levels returned to normal [approximately five months]. I then had monthly tests. I now have been given the 'all clear' to try again. I still need another year's follow-up, and I have to have three monthly tests.

Monitoring over a period of two years used to be the norm, but now some doctors advise women that they may try for another pregnancy before this, provided their test results have been clear. In Britain, the tests are usually organized from one of the three regional centres.

As molar pregnancy is so unusual, and has such potentially serious consequences, you may feel quite isolated and desperately in need of information. Jenny was both worried and frustrated waiting for the necessary appointments.

A week after the miscarriage it was confirmed that I do have a hydatidiform mole, and now three weeks later, although I'm still waiting to hear from the regional centre to start doing the tests and still waiting to see the consultant again, so that I can ask the many queries that now occur to me, I feel more human again. I now want to find out as much as I can about the mole so that I can put it all behind me and plan for the future.

Ectopic Pregnancy

Ectopic pregnancy also has longer-term implications and it has serious effects if it is untreated. In an ectopic pregnancy, which is most common between six and ten weeks of pregnancy, the fertilized cells implant outside the womb, generally in the fallopian tube. Pain and bleeding are the most common symptoms, as they are with other forms of miscarriage, but the pain can be very severe and it can be confused with surgical emergencies – like appendicitis. It is difficult to diagnose because urine pregnancy tests may not confirm an ectopic pregnancy and an internal examination will not reveal it either. A scan will only show an empty womb and cannot show what is going on outside of the uterus. Thelma describes her experience:

When I suddenly developed what I can only describe as a severe stitch in my right side I knew something was wrong. The pain didn't lessen but thankfully I slept through the night. However, when I awoke the following morning to go to work, I could barely get out of bed. By now the pain was excruciating and I had been sick. My doctor gave me an internal examination, asked a few questions and then confirmed what I had already been thinking – that it looked like a tubal/ectopic pregnancy. I went straight to casualty and was examined by a gynaecologist. She gave me an internal and anal examination to check for appendicitis. By now I had started to bleed, only very watery though.

Thelma stayed in hospital for a couple of days but nothing was done, so she asked to go home. The next evening she was in severe pain again and felt hot, cold and sick. She returned to hospital and was investigated under general anaesthetic (a laparoscopy) – it was discovered that the pregnancy was ectopic so it was removed through an incision in the lower abdomen (laparotomy).

By the time they actually got me to theatre, my right fallopian tube had burst and had to be removed, and in addition, I was found to have a cyst the size of a small orange on my right ovary which was also removed. I now had to recover not only from losing a pregnancy, but also quite a substantial operation. I remained in hospital for a further week and was discharged with a follow-up appointment for six weeks' time.

About a third of all ectopic pregnancies burst in the tube, usually those that have implanted in the narrow part of the fallopian tube. This is a life-threatening medical emergency and it needs prompt treatment. If the pregnancy is embedded in the wider part of the tube, it may rupture more slowly and you will experience intermittent bleeding, symptoms common to a threatened miscarriage. The embryo will die when the tube bursts.

Although attempts are usually made to save the tube, it is often too damaged and it is necessary to remove it (salpingectomy). As Thelma found, she was then faced not only with recovering from major surgery and the fact that she was no longer pregnant, but with the loss of part of herself and was worried about future pregnancies. There is an increased risk that the next pregnancy will be ectopic and therefore it is advisable to have an early scan to confirm that the pregnancy is intrauterine. However most women will be successful in their next pregnancy.

ॐ 3 ॐ

'What did I lose?'

Understanding What is Lost

Knowing about the loss can be central to your understanding of the process of the miscarriage and help you to make sense of the experience. It may help you to piece together the sort of miscarriage you have had. If you didn't examine the loss, if you were told not to look or felt you weren't allowed to, or if your miscarriage ended in an ERPC, it is unlikely that you will know about the nature of the loss. Even if you asked about it, you may have been given little information. This may not bother you a great deal or you may find it a bit gruesome. But it may be something that troubles you deeply and raises difficult issues. Helen, who miscarried at ten weeks, was very concerned.

> Some questions I don't think can be answered – eg what did I lose – a clump of cells that wasn't quite right, a clump of cells that was grossly abnormal, possibly at an enzyme level, as well as at an obvious level, a baby that died in the same way that children and adults die? Had it got to the point where it had some kind of soul? Where is it now? Is it all right there? Will I know it or see it at some later point like after life?

Some of these questions could not have been answered, but some could. Often you are left in ignorance because it is not considered to be of any consequence but if you are struggling to make sense of what has happened to you this is essential information, and the fact that the questions remain unanswered is a source of concern, if not worry. Linda miscarried when she was eleven weeks pregnant. Six months later she had this to say:

> Afterwards I would really like them to have said what they'd found. What I kept wanting to know is, was it a real baby or was it just a sac without a baby. I'll always wonder that.

It was something Linda went on to think about for a long time. For Pat it was more deeply and actively troubling. Her miscarriage had been discovered at a routine scan. She had had no warning symptoms at all.

> I had terrible dreams of what they found. I wished I'd asked to see what they'd taken out. I know it sounds morbid and everything but I had such dreams about it – it couldn't have been worse had I seen. I kept thinking they've thrown it in the bin. I was frightened it was alive.

It would have helped Pat to see the baby, however macerated it was. Other women say they would just like to have been told about what was removed. It does, on the face of it, seem morbid and gruesome and breaks a taboo, which makes it hard to talk about and to ask questions. You may feel stupid not knowing the precise nature of the loss from your own body, but it is easy to understand why it causes such confusion and natural to worry about what was taken from you and to wonder if there was a baby or not.

❧

Asking about the Loss

It may be difficult to find out about the loss. When Kathy asked what they had found at the D and C she was told 'only products', which did not mean anything to her. Pauline was confused by the long words the houseman used.

> I said, oh for goodness sake, just tell me what you mean. All right, he said, to be blunt, there's still bits of the fetus in there, we're going to have to do a D and C to scrape out the womb. I imagined bits of arms and legs and toes in there.

It is not easy to talk about. Lay terms seem too direct and almost impolite, and medical language seems impersonal and distancing, which is part of its purpose, meaningless, unless you understand its code. At the time you may not think about or feel like asking and when you do there may not be the opportunity.

Pat, after persistence on her part, managed to find out about her baby, much to her relief. She had been told in hospital that there were no 'fetal parts' but she thought there had been a baby and she was very troubled by this. At her follow-up appointment she had the opportunity to get the information she wanted – asking the reluctant houseman questions and reading her notes over his shoulder while he was reading her file.

> The histology report said – a fetus of approx. 14 weeks, probably died two weeks before with it's head sunken in because it had died. They couldn't tell the sex because it hadn't developed as it should. I was relieved because I wasn't going mad, there was something there, and annoyed with him because he'd told me something different when I was in hospital. I was disappointed they

couldn't tell me the sex, but relieved there was probably something wrong with it.

She experienced a great sense of relief when she found all this out. Other women want to know but lack either the opportunity or persistence that Pat had. Theoretically if the recording is accurate it should be possible to find out from the notes about the nature of the loss and what was removed at an ERPC. If your GP does not have this information you can write direct to the hospital. Often it seems that this information gets 'lost'. It either is not recorded in sufficient detail or nobody bothers to tell you – a reflection perhaps of the lack of importance given to miscarriage.

ॐ

When There Is No Fetus

You assume because you have been pregnant there will be a fetus, but this is not necessarily so (see previous chapter, page 23 and 'missed abortion' page 14). This can be a shock and it may make you question the whole nature of the pregnancy. Kim had a missed abortion at twenty weeks.

It was as if the whole pregnancy had not really existed – there was no fetus, when examined I was told it was as if I was fourteen weeks, not nearly twenty. I couldn't understand what my body had been doing. I later pieced together that the baby had died a few weeks earlier but that I had not miscarried till later. This was difficult to grasp and took months to fully understand.

With a missed abortion like this, the baby dies and is reabsorbed in your body, then when you miscarry you lose clots and blood and possibly some tissue. Again, it may help to see this. When Jane came round from the anaesthetic after the ERPC, she asked to see what had been removed. She said,

'They showed me a small dish. But I was very groggy and all I could see was blood and clots, but it was helpful to know.' Celia miscarried at three months, at home, and had been told by her GP to keep anything that came away.

> We had not been able to identify anything remotely fetus-like, although we thought we could identify a placenta. I found the fact that there was no tiny baby 'lost' very hard to come to terms with. During those three months of pregnancy I had read about each stage of development of the fetus and had visualized the baby as complete. We had talked of our babies inside the bump, welcoming them into our family long before their birth. I think I could have grieved more easily if I'd seen a tiny baby.[1]

Initially it may be very confusing. The physical experience is out of tune with the emotional reality. Like Celia, you may find it difficult and feel tricked by your own body. She thought that there was a baby and she had been behaving as if there was one. Although at one point there may have been, by the time she miscarried there was not and she was unaware of this. Or the absence of a fetus may make it easier for you; if you didn't think about the pregnancy as a real baby the miscarriage will have confirmed these feelings. You may also feel relieved that there is not a fetus which you feel responsible for and worry about.

ॐ

When There Is a Fetus

If there is a fetus, however tiny, it can be a tremendous shock to see it – it really brings home the nature of what has been lost. Karen went to the bathroom and miscarried her baby onto the bathroom floor. She had been twelve weeks pregnant.

> An unborn baby in a little sac, all curled up with dark eyes and fingers. I couldn't believe it would be like that but it

was. That's what upset me the most. I thought it would be like a piece of liver, a clot of some kind. But because I could see what it was, it hit home what I'd lost, it was human.

Pam miscarried at ten weeks.

I passed another large clot and saw my tiny baby. I can picture it to this day and even writing this down fills me with emotion as I think back. The hardest thing to do was to let that 'clot' go and flush the toilet. I felt I'd flushed my baby down the loo. Eventually after a lot of prayer I managed to do it.

It is difficult to know what to do with the fetus if there is one. It usually isn't something you have thought about until it happens to you. Often there is no choice – if the miscarried fetus is in the loo, that's where it will stay unless you fish it out. You may flush the loo before realizing what you have done and on reflection will be very distressed. Karen felt very unprepared for such an eventuality.

The next worse thing was I didn't know what to do with it. To flush it down the loo was just not right. I phoned up my aunty who lives down the road and she phoned my husband, who wouldn't come home, not because he didn't love me or didn't care, but he just couldn't face it. In the end we flushed it down the loo. I couldn't save it. I wanted to show my husband but I couldn't keep it in the end.

Jill also miscarried at home when she was eleven weeks pregnant but she solved the problem in a different way.

I was on my own, no one knew I'd miscarried; my parents were too old now to know about my condition. I was alone and frightened. Although I felt very weak I got myself downstairs to the lounge and made a fire to burn the baby and placenta. It was very distressing for me. I cried. I went back to bed.

Kim describes what she did.

> I miscarried a tiny fetus at home when I was fourteen and
> a half weeks pregnant. We didn't know what to do with it
> so we put it in a jar and kept it. When the GP came he
> looked at it, and was very sensitive and compassionate,
> and said how sorry he was. I was very much aware it was
> there and kept going to look at it. In lots of ways I just
> wanted to be with it. There is no way I could have just got
> rid of it – I felt terribly sad but at least there was an oppor-
> tunity to say goodbye. We took it to the hospital.

The time to say goodbye can be very important. Kim went on
to describe vividly how the memory of that baby would always
be with her.

ى

Taking the Loss to the Hospital

It often seems that the right and responsible thing to do is to
take the fetus to hospital so that tests can be done and questions answered. You may feel terribly let down if this does not
happen. Beth describes how cheated she felt when she miscarried twins.

> I saved the placentas and fetuses and the GP took them for
> analysis. I felt as if we were doing the right thing at the
> time, we wanted to know why. The fact that we have had
> no answers almost makes me wish we had kept them, to
> bury their tiny, perfect forms in the garden, close to us.
> The hospital took everything and gave nothing in return.

There is no reason why Beth could not have buried her babies
in the garden, if that is what she wanted to do (see page 70).
Like Beth, Julie also had expectations of what the hospital
would offer when she miscarried at eleven weeks.

I thought they'd do an examination of the fetus but it went straight in the hospital incinerator. Thinking of that makes me terribly upset.

At the time of the miscarriage there is often talk of 'tests', and perhaps the advances of high-tech modern medicine in many fields have fuelled these expectations. It seems common that junior hospital doctors, in their anxiety to help, make promises that cannot be fulfilled. Anxious to know why you miscarried you believe the experts can give answers, so you may feel very disillusioned and disappointed when your expectations are not met.

There are two tests that are routinely performed in most hospitals: firstly, tissue is examined to confirm the pregnancy, this can seem like a bit of an insult at the time but it is important to confirm that the bleeding is not due to any other cause; secondly, the possibility of a molar pregnancy (see page 35) will be excluded. If there is a fetus, it will be looked at to see if there are any obvious abnormalities which should be recorded. It is not routine for there to be further examination, although in some hospitals there might be.

Some units will be better resourced and more able to undertake tests for infection and for chromosomal abnormalities, but it is a complicated, expensive and fairly problematic business. It is often difficult to separate out fetal and maternal tissue, and certain tests can only be done on fresh tissue. If the baby has been dead for a while, or if it has been put in a formalin solution (a preservative), these tests will not be possible. Often when they are done little is discovered. These practical complications, plus limited resources and the pressure of work in many units and the attitude that early miscarriage is a one-off event, explain why little is normally done. Although on a rational level this all makes sense, it is not common knowledge and it is easy to see why women feel let down.

This is often compounded by the apparent lack of respect and dignity with which the dead fetus is treated. Its unimportance and lack of status seems to be confirmed. It is as if it has never existed or that it never should have existed, and nobody has thought out what to do with it when it does. This is in total opposition to the significance it has for you, and it is a source of deep anguish. Kim describes what happened when she arrived at the hospital.

> It was in the jar in my bag. The SHO greeted me with 'So you think you've had a miscarriage' which was a bit unfortunate. We showed her the baby and she put it in a kidney bowl on the table behind me. And then a bit later I realized she'd just taken it away without saying anything to me. It must have been very difficult for her – she didn't really know what to say to me.

You may worry about what will happen to the fetus and where it will go, and you may be left wondering if there was any point in taking it to the hospital at all. It is only a decision you can make yourself. Most doctors will advise that you do take the fetus with you, otherwise any possibility of tests or investigations is excluded. (See also Chapter 5.)

✂ 4 ✂

'I gave birth':
Late miscarriage

Physically, late miscarriage, after sixteen weeks, is different from a loss earlier in pregnancy. It is much more unusual and will be generally because the baby died in the womb or because labour started too early. A much smaller proportion of late miscarriages are due to abnormalities in conception. In this chapter we will focus on the issues that later miscarriage raises.

The longer you are pregnant the more time you have to adjust to the idea of becoming a mother, to think about the baby within you as separate from yourself. The physical changes will be more apparent – you are more visibly pregnant, the baby is bigger and you may have felt the baby move. More people will know of your pregnancy and, like you, will be expecting a baby in due course. You will have made plans and changes to your life to accommodate the new baby.

Ultrasound has done a lot to outwardly confirm the inner experience of the baby. It makes the baby seem even more of a reality. Jenny had a scan and saw her baby moving about and was given a picture of him. When she miscarried at eighteen weeks she was devastated. Mairie was monitored in hospital for ten days before she miscarried at twenty-one weeks.

During the time I'd seen the baby alive on the scan several times, and heard her heartbeat every four hours, and felt her move well. As you can imagine, all this was like *torture*.

48

⨺

Missing the Symptoms

Because you are not expecting to go into labour and you are in what is traditionally thought of as the comfortable, happy and glowing state of pregnancy, the warning signs that things are going wrong are often missed. You may feel quite guilty afterwards because you misinterpreted the signs and did not take the appropriate action to save the pregnancy but there is usually little that could have been done. Sylvie miscarried at seventeen weeks.

> I was losing water for about three weeks before, on and off, and I increasingly felt as if I did not want to walk anywhere – I didn't know there was anything wrong with this, as there was no blood – I wish I had known. I kept thinking I should 'pull myself together' and not lie down all the time.

You are not normally ready for labour in mid-pregnancy and if it is your first pregnancy you may feel very ill-prepared. Veronica miscarried her first pregnancy at twenty-five weeks.

> Then two days before I was due to leave work I went to the loo and there was this sudden gush of water: I thought I had a urine infection, I felt quite achey. The next day I felt faint and then in the evening I had some bleeding. I went into hospital. During the night I had pains but I thought it was cramp. I was obviously having heavy contractions but nobody realized it and I didn't piece it all together till afterwards.

Hilary had been only too aware of her symptoms throughout her pregnancy and had almost been waiting to miscarry. But the longer she was pregnant, the more it seemed that she would have her baby. She was over twenty-two weeks pregnant when she miscarried.

I felt dreadful right from the beginning. I had been bleeding on and off since I was eight weeks pregnant and losing quite a lot of bright red blood. At twenty-two weeks my waters broke, they sort of seeped, but I thought I had a urinary infection, until my mother suggested I might be leaking amniotic fluid. Then one morning I woke up and I lost this huge lump of grey mucus. I was still leaking water and bleeding a bit. My GP didn't seem to realize how serious it was. Then I started having contractions. By the time I got to the hospital and was scanned there was no amniotic fluid left.

౷

Giving Birth

Most women miscarrying after about eighteen weeks of pregnancy, and some before, feel they have given birth. It is almost always experienced and described in such terms and needs to be recognized as such. As one woman who miscarried at twenty weeks said:

Although I had a miscarriage technically, I don't feel this. I went through labour. It was incredibly painful but my husband was with me and it was almost a happy occasion.

With the exception of women who have a late missed abortion there will be a baby that has to be born. The baby may or may not have died prior to the miscarriage. As with full-term birth, the waters must break, there will be pains and contractions and the cervix must dilate for the baby to leave the womb. Of course the baby will be smaller, in some cases much smaller, but it is essentially the same process and this comes as a great shock to many women. Sylvie was not prepared for this.

One night after I had walked a lot during the day I started to cry, and then I started to get pains, like period pains. A few hours later I was doubled up in pain. Then my waters broke. By now I was terrified I was losing the baby. Some friends took me into hospital in the back of their van. I delivered the baby in hospital while I was still standing up – I couldn't bear to see it on the floor. Then I was taken up to the ward after I had delivered the placenta. I think I was in terrible shock because I was either numb or in terrible pain.

There may be less pain if you have an incompetent cervix because the neck of the womb is weak and unable to hold the pregnancy and so opens before the baby is fully developed. Becky miscarried at seventeen weeks and was diagnosed as having an incompetent cervix.

I felt a bit ill but didn't think anything about it. A few days later I passed something which I think might have been the plug. Then some waters trickled. I went into hospital where I lost the baby two days later. I felt very little pain, certainly nothing approaching the pains of labour. They gave me Omnopom which would have dulled the pain and a drip, and the delivery itself happened while the doctor 'examined' me. There was no blood till afterwards.

Women who have a late missed abortion will have a different experience. There will be no baby and, as with some earlier miscarriages, the bleeding may be profuse. When Kim started bleeding heavily she went to casualty.

I started to lose very large clots. It was very uncomfortable and I was in some pain. I couldn't have a D and C straight away as the pregnancy was too advanced, so I was left for a while. But in the few hours I was in hospital I lost a large amount of blood and a lot of clots. At one point the registrar examined me and cleared out a lot of clots. They told me not to look and I don't know what they took away, but I was much more comfortable after that. Later I had a D and C. I had been twenty weeks pregnant.

Worrying about what you will lose adds to the stress of the experience. It seems that this is rarely adequately explained at the time, and it is something that it is difficult to ask about especially if you feel ill, frightened, in a state of shock and very upset. You may be uncertain about how much you want to know and the staff caring for you may go along with this, so it becomes something that is avoided and 'fudged'. The professionals generally do not feel comfortable with it themselves, and it is difficult for them to find the right words, but you are dependent on them for the information, so that you can make informed choices about what you want to do.

꒱

Induced Labour

If it is discovered that your baby has died but you do not go into labour naturally, it will be induced artificially using synthetic hormones, in a drip or pessaries. It is not possible for an ERPC to be performed to remove the baby after about sixteen weeks of pregnancy because of the size of the fetus. The labour may take up to twelve hours, or even longer, and this turns the miscarriage into more of a medical event. Rose discovered that she had miscarried when she was scanned at seventeen weeks. She was admitted to hospital.

Almost immediately I was put on a Prostin drip to start off the labour. They did explain what would happen but couldn't tell me how long. The cramps started after a short while, like period pains and then gradually got very strong. Towards the evening I asked for some pain relief and was given some pills, they said Pethidine would delay everything. At 10 pm my husband had to leave to catch the last bus home. After I'd been in labour about eleven hours, I felt the baby slide out. The nurses were with me and told me not to look. I wanted to ask what it was but didn't dare. The next morning I had a D and C, and went home the following day.

Sandra had a similar experience except that it took much longer. She was in labour about thirty-six hours. She had not realized it would be like going into labour nor that it would be so painful.

> Evening came and with it another doctor who decided that I would need another injection as 'it hadn't come away'. In the early hours of the following morning my waters broke but 'it' still hadn't 'come away'. I wasn't certain what they meant and hadn't the courage to ask.

You may have to be induced if, once in labour, your contractions stop. Trish who miscarried at twenty-two weeks found this difficult to cope with.

> I went into labour at about 5 pm and had regular contractions until 6 am the next morning. When the midwife came round I told her I felt something wriggling at the top of my vagina. She said that my contractions had stopped and I'd know if the baby was coming out. I wasn't allowed an internal because of the risk of infection. After a painful day and feeling very sick and confused, the registrar finally arrived. He gave me an internal and felt her bottom and legs. By this time she was dead. They finally managed to get me on a drip about midnight and she was born at 8.35 the next morning.

ﺯ

It's a Difficult Labour

It can be hard to co-operate with the labour when it starts before you are ready and there is no chance of the baby surviving. You may feel you want to put all your energy into holding on to your baby, when in fact you have to let go – as Sheila so accurately describes. She was over seventeen weeks pregnant when she miscarried.

The nurses were changing pads under me constantly – the blood started in dribbles, then flowed. I knew my baby's time had come. The nurses, one midwife and a trainee were at either side. Push, they said, but I didn't want to – I wanted to hold on to my precious baby. I didn't want it taken away and destroyed like an amputated limb. I would have loved it, taken care of it and my husband and I would have given it a perfect life. That was not to be. After seven hours and one last push, my baby was brought into the world.

Hilary felt it was implied that she was not co-operating and was making her labour worse for herself.

My contractions stopped and I had to be induced. In the end I had six pessaries. They didn't work, they told me I was too tense. It was all so painful and I was so weak.

Women miscarrying at this stage of pregnancy invariably find it a very painful experience. Lisa miscarried at twenty-three weeks.

By the next morning the pains had stopped but at night they started again. By 1.30 am they were really bad. Although I have had two children previously, I have never experienced pains like those. Afterwards a midwife tried to tell me it was all in the mind.

Lack of preparation for labour combined with the emotional pain of losing your baby often seems to make it harder. At twenty-six weeks Veronica miscarried.

Then when they realized I was in labour it turned into a medical crisis. It was an acutely painful breech delivery. They tried to turn the baby but it hurt so much. I didn't know what would happen, I was totally unprepared.

Pain relief is normally given for later miscarriages – often an epidural or pain killers by injection. Some women do not tolerate these drugs very well, as Hilary discovered. She said the pain killers made her sick and gave her dreadful hallucinations. You may not react like this but many women describe the pain killers as making them feel so drugged that they do not know what is going on.

When you finally give birth you may have to have an ERPC to remove the remains of the placenta, but often this is not necessary as the baby and placenta come away intact after a late miscarriage. With an epidural, the remains of the placenta can be removed manually by the doctor.

Most women seem to be discharged from hospital the day after the ERPC if they have one. There is no reason to be in hospital – you do not fit any of the hospital's categories of patient: there is no baby, you are not seen as a mother and you are not ill. You may feel ready to go but Hilary felt she was discharged from hospital too quickly.

I wasn't ready to come home. I'd been in labour for two days and had all those awful drugs and a D and C. I was in pain and had terrible headaches, and then my milk came in. It was awful.

$\sim$

Knowing Your Baby

Knowing as much as possible about your baby can make the pregnancy and the baby more tangible and real. Many women say how important it is to have time with their baby, an opportunity to say hello and goodbye, a time to remember. Seeing your baby also removes the fear of the unknown. You may have fears, probably unfounded, that the baby is deformed in some way. This occasionally happens but it is unusual and the baby can be wrapped in a shawl. What you imagine is usually far worse than the reality. You may not want to see your baby and it would be wrong for anyone to make you, but most women who do see their babies however early they were born, seem to find it immensely helpful and they have no regrets.

> We made the decision to see Ruth. We are both so thankful for this, and proud. I wish I had a photograph. *20 weeks.*

> The midwives were lovely. I was allowed to see and hold my baby. They took a photo of my baby for me and left me alone with him for as long as I wanted. We called him Thomas. *20 weeks*

> The hospital was very helpful and the nurses were fantastic. They encouraged me to see the baby – it was a boy. I feel so terribly sad that he could never have become to be alive. I miss him terribly and always will. He was perfect and had beautiful hands. He was skeletal, not like a baby. *17 weeks*

It can be a great comfort to hold and touch your baby as well.

> It was nice to be able to hold David in my arms and say goodbye to him. *19 weeks*

> We both held Adam. I can't explain how I felt when I saw my husband hold our son. At least he was ours and not somebody else's baby. The midwives had dressed Adam in baby clothes and brought him in a cot. They made the time we had with our son so very special, we will never forget. *25 weeks*

If you do not see your baby it may be helpful to know its sex as this is a crucial part of your baby's identity. You will then be able to refer to the baby as he or she and this can give you something to focus on. The sex of your baby, if it was possible to tell, should always be recorded in your medical notes.

ॐ

The Importance of Good Management

The management of late miscarriage can be crucial in making a bad experience worse or in making it an occasion that has some dignity, and is both bearable at the time and can then be remembered in a positive way. Laura miscarried at twenty-five weeks.

> The staff gave us a lot of comfort and support. I had two lovely midwives with us all the time I was in labour. I had an epidural, so that the pain wasn't that bad; my consultant didn't want me to have any unnecessary suffering. Adam came into the world and into our lives at 3.15 pm – a perfect baby boy. The hospital chaplain was with us by then. He gave us great comfort and said prayers.

Unfortunately it doesn't always work out as well as this. Perhaps the hospital does not have a policy on handling such issues; the staff are working very much on their own and they may not be comfortable with being so open about what has happened. Jo, who miscarried at seventeen weeks, did not want to see her baby, but the behaviour of the staff served to compound her own fears rather than help her to overcome them.

> The young midwife [a trainee] jumped back in shock as the older one wrapped my baby in a paper sheet and took it away to be destroyed. I would not let my husband look at our baby.

Alison's experience demonstrates clearly how with a different approach from the staff she might have felt much better about her experience. She lost her baby at twenty-two weeks.

> I wasn't shown my baby, who was perfect, and to this day I feel very bitter about this. At the time I was too drugged

and upset to ask. I feel that the midwife could have asked me, after say an hour or so, did I want to see my baby. My husband, who was with me was also too upset to ask.

Or perhaps offers are made which at the time you turn down and later regret. Hilary did not feel in a state to cope with very much.

I regret now that I didn't see the baby. They asked me but at the time I was heavily drugged, the miscarriage had been going on for two days. My husband didn't want to see it and he didn't want to force me. So I just said, take it away. My mother told my husband to make sure he knew the sex as she thought I'd want to know. It was a boy. There was no offer of anything, no photo. I would have liked that.

Veronica turned down the offer of a photo which she regretted later. She was twenty-five weeks pregnant when she went into labour.

I saw his bottom and feet but not his face. I hadn't known what to expect in terms of the baby. His heart was beating but he didn't breathe. They asked me if I wanted a photo but I said no. I wished later we had, so that we could have had one if we wanted. When he wasn't breathing it all went deadly quiet – there were all these people. There was no real upset then, I was just relieved the pain had gone. They whisked the baby away and everyone filed out.

Again Veronica's experience could have been very different if she had been prepared for what was to happen and the staff had felt comfortable in helping her. Many hospitals do adopt a policy of asking the mother sometime after the birth if she would like to see the baby, and some will routinely take a photo which will be kept with the mother's notes until she wants it. This should be standard practice.

✌

Follow-up Care

It may only be later that you realize what you want to know and then you are dependent on the quality of your medical notes and the willingness of the staff to give you the information. If you miscarry later in pregnancy, follow-up appointments are normally offered four to six weeks after the birth. The results of the post-mortem, and any tests that were done, should be given to you and it should be an opportunity to discuss the reason for the loss of the baby, although for many, if not most, women this may not be clear. It can be an opportunity to find out more about your baby and ask the questions you did not think of or were not able to ask at the time. You can also write to the hospital if you need further information (see page 94 for discussion on follow-up care).

✌

Special Care

Although twenty-eight weeks is recognized as the gestational age when it is possible for a baby to survive without medical intervention, babies are surviving below this age because of developments in medical technology and expertise. For some babies born before twenty-eight weeks attempts will be made to give them the medical care they need. This invariably means high-tech intervention in a special care baby unit and it will only be available at some specialist hospitals. The issues around special care are complex and beyond the scope of this book, but it is something that you may have to face if you miscarry at this late stage.

The staff tried to find a hospital with a special care baby unit for Veronica's baby but they were unable to find one in time. They are increasingly scarce resources. Hilary had faced the possibility.

My baby was alive all the time but too young to live. I didn't want him to survive. I don't think it is fair on them, at that stage, to be all tubed up.

In the event her baby was born at twenty-two and a half weeks – too early for special care – so it was something she did not have to face. However Sheila did. Her baby was born at twenty-five weeks, his heart was beating when he was born. She describes what happened.

My baby was born and he went to special care. I came late that night and saw him, it was as if he wasn't mine. I couldn't see the baby for tubes. I didn't want to get attached, in case anything happened, yet I wanted to spend as much time with him as possible. The doctors came and said he wasn't going to live and his death was being prolonged. They put him in my arms. He was breathing and he died in my arms. I saw him again before I left hospital. I didn't want to go home. I screamed. They said I could stay as long as I liked. I have his photo on the mantelpiece.

Sheila appreciated the approach of the staff in the special care baby unit, they treated her like a mother, which she felt she was, and her baby as a baby, and not the statusless product of a miscarriage.

ᷣ 5 ᷣ

'It was a baby to me'

> Such life, I'm told, is not
>   life
> And grief unreasonable.
> But I felt that lie
> Within.

Sharon, who wrote this poem, miscarried at thirteen weeks. She clearly perceived her loss as a baby and the fact that it was not treated as one was distressing for her. Tracey miscarried at twenty-four weeks; she also felt she had lost a baby and was deeply troubled that her very real baby was not defined as such.

> He wasn't classed as a baby. He was still classed as a miscarriage and that really upsets me because he was my baby. He was like any other human being – he had tiny little hands and finger nails. I still can't accept he was a miscarriage.

However, there is a lot of difference between Tracey's experience and Sharon's. Tracey gave birth to a baby and Sharon clearly experienced her loss much earlier on in the pregnancy, in these terms. Yet in the eyes of the law neither of them had produced a baby. Tracey may, or may not, have been treated as a mother whose baby had died by those around her. Sharon almost certainly was not.

ᘓ

Definitions

There are various ways of defining when a fetus becomes a baby, but no definition is uniformly used. These definitions influence how those around us, and we ourselves, define our experience. There is a biological definition – a fetus is a baby when it is capable of maintaining life. There are definitions based on criteria of gestational age, size and weight. In some American states a fetus is considered a baby when it is at twenty weeks' gestation, 25cm long and 250 grams in weight. The legal definition in Britain is based on the number of weeks' gestation (reduced from twenty-eight to twenty-four weeks in 1992), and whether the baby shows signs of life. A legal definition has implications for registration and 'disposal' (see page 68) and some women feel very strongly about the lack of legal status of the fetus or baby and significance of the event. In so far as these procedures confirm the baby's existence and the lack of them negates it, they are important.

There are religious definitions – for example Roman Catholics consider that life begins at conception and a baby is a baby from the beginning. There are cultural definitions – in some societies babies are not granted human status until well into their infancy. There are also the practical working definitions of hospital staff which may influence how they relate to their patients, and which are based on some of the criteria outlined above and may encompass their feelings and those of the mother.

What became increasingly clear as I wrote this book is that these external definitions do not take into account women's perceptions and feelings about what has happened. Legal or cultural definitions bear little relation to women's actual experience.

The Use of Language

There is no concensus on when a fetus becomes a baby. It is difficult to know when to use the word fetus and when baby, when it should be mother rather than woman. For some women the word baby overstates the case but not using it will deny the meaning of others' experience. These difficulties reflect our confusion about the significance of what has happened. But language defines experience as these women discovered.

> It was something my mother-in-law said that really hurt me, she asked me if I'd had a bad time when I lost the baby. The words echoed in my brain for days. Although I had accepted the miscarriage until that moment I had not let myself believe that I had lost another baby.

> I found it easier to talk about having miscarried than to say that I lost the baby.

Once you define the loss as a baby, the loss takes on greater proportions, and these women were perhaps trying to protect themselves from that or they experienced it differently. The significance of the miscarriage may not be immediately apparent, instead it may be something that you have to work out for yourself – one of the emotional tasks in the aftermath of the miscarriage.

Early Pregnancy

It is interesting that it is only after a miscarriage that there seems to be the dilemma about using the word baby. In early pregnancy you talk about being pregnant rather than about the embryo or the fetus. It seems quite natural and comfortable to use the word baby – 'This baby's making me sick', 'When the baby's born', 'I'm putting on a lot of weight with this baby' and to young children, 'Mummy's got a baby in her tummy'. This clearly reflects women's perceptions of what is happening to them. It is only after you have miscarried that the words fetus and embryo are used, perhaps because they are less emotive.

Once you are pregnant the process of involvement and attachment with your unborn child begins. For some women this can start even before conception because plans and preparations make the baby a reality before it exists in any form. Modern pregnancy tests can confirm a pregnancy as soon as a period is missed, and scans can make the baby a reality a few weeks into the pregnancy. Other women find the baby takes on a reality of its own when they feel it move, but for many this just confirms a process that is well underway. But, at whatever point the attachment starts, initially you have to accept that the baby is part of you before allowing it to be separate from you. Women get attached to their babies much earlier than used to be thought and you will be somewhere along this path of involvement when you miscarry. Caroline felt it was a baby to her as soon as she knew she was pregnant. Elaine felt so too.

> I was fascinated by the embryonic growth stages, and excited by the idea of creating a new being. I was very possessive about it.

Eileen's pregnancy was unplanned and she had considered an abortion, but, after a lot of thought, she decided to go ahead. This naturally focused her thinking on what was happening to her.

> I was aware of it as a little being in there. I used to direct my thoughts to it and talk to it. I was extremely aware of us being three.

Early pregnancy is a time of adjustment and change. Many women make plans for their baby from a very early stage. There may be practical circumstances which force the reality of the pregnancy upon you – as there were for Linda.

After a couple of weeks of knowing I was pregnant, I definitely started thinking in terms of a baby. I started telling people I was pregnant and discussing it with them, and making plans about work and thinking how it was going to fit in with the boys. We'd fixed to go on holiday with my parents and we were already enquiring of the airline whether we had to book a seat or get a name on a passport. My sister had given me a load of clothes when she went abroad, and my mother was trying to track down wheels for the carrycot. I definitely thought there was a baby there.

Or, like Teresa, you may concentrate on the physical changes in your body and what it is like to be pregnant, which can detract from the reality of the baby.

I was obsessed with my body and the changes. I wanted to be fat and couldn't wait to be waddling about.

For those women who do think of their pregnancy in terms of a baby, from a very early stage, it stands to reason that when the pregnancy ends they feel they have lost their baby, regardless of what they have lost physically, or of what anyone else tells them. The emotional experience is not necessarily in tune with the physical reality. The length of your pregnancy may influence how close you feel to your baby, or the extent to which you perceive your baby as separate from yourself, but not necessarily that you think in terms of a baby and feel emotionally attached.

The Emotional Reality

Frances and Caroline both miscarried at eleven weeks. They both were clear in their own minds about the nature of the loss and their feelings about it.

I don't ever feel it was a properly formed baby. It was a

bunch of goo that never looked like a baby. But emotionally I had a baby and it died.

The baby didn't die. I lost it. It wasn't actually here. It wasn't here to go. But in my mind it was a baby.

Jenny was clear about her feelings about her miscarriage and they were very different to how those around her attempted to define what was happening.

The old clichés appeared, 'never mind, you're young, there'll be other babies, it wasn't a baby anyway'. I may not have ever felt it move, but it certainly was a baby to me and more precious than I could ever explain.

Diana was more confused by the fact that there was not a fetus. For her the emotional experience was out of key with the physical reality and she was finding it hard to understand what had happened and why she felt so upset. She talked of her confusion at a miscarriage support group meeting and she was helped by another woman in the group.

You think there is a child inside you and there never really was one. And this woman said 'well, there was to you, it was a real person to you regardless of what was going on physically, and you have a right to grieve for it'. And I thought well, thank God for that, and felt tremendously relieved.

Where there is discrepancy between expectation and reality, like this, the shock and confusion are greater. Karen in Chapter 3 was shocked when contrary to her expectations, she miscarried a complete fetus. She was faced with the reality of a tiny baby.

When It Is Not a Baby

Clearly not all women relate to their pregnancy in such a way. Some women focus on the fact that there will be a baby in so many months' time, but not that one exists now. Plans and preparations are not made until much later. This was how it was for Claire and Sarah.

> I thought of it as a potential baby. It's not one for me until I can feel it move. I've been like that with all my pregnancies.

> I didn't think of it as a baby but as a pregnancy that was hopefully going to develop into a baby in the end. I'm not very good at thinking about babies before they are born. I didn't think about my children as real live healthy babies until we knew they were.

There may be something about a particular pregnancy that makes you feel differently about it. Sue had not invested in her pregnancy because she felt something was wrong and did not feel well herself. She felt she was 'going through the motions' of pregnancy rather than being actively involved in it.

> I thought there'd be a baby at the end. I couldn't relate to it as a baby at the time. I wasn't aware that I was carrying a baby.

When, at seventeen weeks, she had a missed abortion, she was relieved that there was no fetus. It confirmed the emptiness she had felt about the pregnancy all the way through, and it seemed to echo the meaning it had had for her: the emotional experience reflected the physical reality. She was quite down to earth about it. There was no baby and therefore nothing to grieve over. She had felt unwell for a lot of the pregnancy and now she felt much better and able to get on with life.

Amy felt differently from many women. She had miscarried twice and had three children.

> One point about my reaction to miscarriage is that I don't have the problem that many women seem to have of regarding the lost fetus as a child. Now that I have had my

third I feel she is the one I wanted. I don't see the others as lost children.

The emotional reality of a child for her matched the physical presence of a living baby. It might well have been different for her if she did not already have children or if she had not been successful in having a third child.

Implications

I do not want to suggest that a miscarriage at ten or twelve weeks is the same as losing a baby at twenty-two weeks. It obviously is not. Nor am I suggesting that all women who miscarry at eight or ten weeks are devastated by the experience. Some clearly are, but the loss of a baby at any stage of pregnancy is an experience with a unique meaning for that woman and her partner. All pregnancy loss is part of the same continuum, of experience. There is no natural divide when a fetus magically and conveniently becomes a baby to all concerned, from the mother to the doctor and the lady next door as well.

What is important is that women are able to define the meaning of their own experience and that those around them enable them to do so, without prejudging the nature of the loss. The fact that the individual meaning of the miscarriage goes unrecognized and, moreover, that it is publicly denied, is at the root of the difficulties that many women have with those who are close to them and with those who are supposed to be there to help them (see Chapters 6 and 9).

༆

Disposal

I always had this thing about what did they do with the body. But I was scared to ask as I thought they'd tell me things I didn't want to hear. So I didn't ask but I used to think, I wonder where he is. And that used to play on my mind.

Veronica (who miscarried at twenty-five weeks) is not alone in her thoughts. Characteristically this occurred to her afterwards, it was not something she thought about at the time. But it is not just knowing about what has happened that is important as Denise, who miscarried at eleven weeks, explains:

> One of the saddest aspects I've experienced with a miscarriage, is the disposal of it. One is left in a state of utter disappointment and sort of cut off in mid-air – it is just unfinished.

The question of disposal, a horrible word but there really is no other, is a difficult and sensitive one. It is not something you think about until you need to and it is not easy to talk about, yet it is an issue that bothers a lot of women who miscarry. In practice it is likely that most babies will be incinerated by the hospital. Some hospitals will separate the fetus or the products from other hospital waste, and a few will have a separate incinerator purely for this purpose. A few hospitals organize a weekly service in the hospital chapel after which the fetuses are cremated in the hospital incinerator. The ashes are scattered on a plot which has been set aside at the local crematorium. Unfortunately however, this is not yet common practice. Disposal arrangements vary between hospitals and areas and seem to hinge on the extent to which the loss is perceived as a baby which should be handled with appropriate respect and dignity.

In Britain, a baby does not exist in the eyes of the law until twenty-four weeks' gestation, unless it has shown signs of life outside the womb, when, if it dies, a birth and death certificate must be issued and a burial or cremation arranged. For miscarriages there are no legal requirements. But there is no reason why the baby cannot be buried or cremated and some hospitals will organize this on your behalf or they will help you to arrange this yourselves. It is necessary to have a statement from a doctor or midwife to say that your baby was under twenty-four weeks gestation and showed no signs of life. You will also be expected, as the applicant, to give a few details about yourself, your name, age and address. It is also important to understand that, if you choose cremation, it is unlikely there will be any ashes as the baby is very small. If you wish you can bury a fetus in your garden although it is important to remember that you might move house.

Time is of the essence. It is all too easy, after the event, to decide what you would have liked to have done, which is why it is important hospitals have an agreed policy. Some hospitals keep all recognizable fetuses for six weeks, to allow parents to decide what arrangements, if any, they wish to make. This should be standard practice.

Jane arranged for her baby, who was miscarried at nineteen weeks, to be buried in her local graveyard. Lynda miscarried at twenty-five weeks. Her first baby was stillborn and so her babies were buried next to each other and it gave her and her husband great comfort to know they were together, and that they could visit the grave.

Paula had to arrange a funeral because her baby, who was born at twenty-two weeks, lived for a short while.

Because she was born alive we had to register (or my husband did) her birth and death. Only we attended her funeral and our vicar officiated. My mother was slightly upset not to be included but I couldn't bear my family to see me so upset. I remember holding hands with my husband, as we bravely walked to the hearse to see the tiny white coffin lying there. Afterwards, we collected her ashes and still have them in the cupboard upstairs, even though I have bought a china box to put them in and bury under her three rose bushes in the garden.

Arranging a funeral is a way of acknowledging your loss, of paying respects, and of saying goodbye with some dignity. It does not have to be a religious ceremony – a funeral can take many forms.

You may find the hospital is reluctant to release the remains but there is no good reason why this should be. Vanessa, who miscarried at fifteen weeks, describes the problem she had:

> One of the most difficult aspects of the miscarriage for me was that although I miscarried at home, the ambulance men insisted I take all the 'contents of the womb' into the hospital. I suddenly felt very strongly that this was 'my baby' and wanted to bring it home and bury it. I had to fight very hard at 3.00 am in the morning, against a very unsympathetic night nurse who said that burial was 'impossible'. My partner had to run around trying to find out from the council and local cemeteries early the next morning whether burial of a miscarried child was possible. We discovered that it was, in a communal grave, without a marking, and we were able to bury the child the day after I had the D and C and left the hospital. But the fight with the hospital over 'possession' of the baby was one of the worst aspects of the whole business.

This happened in 1985; ideas are changing and hospitals are becoming more flexible on these issues. If you wish it is within your rights and it is perfectly acceptable for you to make arrangements for the burial or cremation of your baby. Not every woman wants to go to these lengths but you may feel more at peace if you know your baby has been handled and disposed of with dignity and respect.

༄

Creating Memories: Naming and Writing

For many women it is important to mark the pregnancy and the loss of the baby in some way. In later miscarriages, where there is a baby to see and hold and maybe a funeral is organized, there are often memories to cherish. Many women say this helps in signifying what has happened, in making it seem real in a more open and public way. For earlier miscarriages, and some later ones, this doesn't happen, but there are other ways of marking the event, of saying something important happened, of creating memories.

Naming can help. It means you no longer have to talk about it, or the baby. It doesn't matter if you don't know the sex; Frances named her baby at the time of the miscarriage.

> I had a couple of hours after the scan and before the D and C when the loss slackened considerably and I went into a gentle mini-labour, when I felt very close to the little person I would never meet. I chose two names, one for a boy and one for a girl, which had the softest sounds I could think of. I needed that time to be alone with my baby.

For Lesley the time to name came much later.

> I was on my own at home exactly ten weeks after I lost the baby and suddenly knew beyond doubt that the baby was a boy and that he wanted to be called Joshua. We'd planned to call him Ben and yet I never felt, deep down inside, that he was a Ben. Joshua was a far more appropriate name and felt right somehow.

Writing can also help. You don't have to be particularly good at writing or for it to be something that comes naturally to you. The important thing is to express what you feel and to acknowledge what has happened for you. If you feel strongly about something, it is often easier to express your feelings by writing them down than by talking about them. Some women find it easiest to write an account of what has happened to them, others to write poems. Mandy describes what happened for her.

> My children are very precious to me and yet I'll always remember the one I lost. I've even written a poem to 'her', helping to pour out the hurt I still feel. I felt that I would

like to write a poem but could never find the right words. Eventually it was really strange, I went to bed one night and while I was drifting off to sleep, the words came to me. I got up the next day and wrote out the poem straight away. I've never done anything like that before or will again, I expect.

Memorial Service and Memorial Book

As I have already mentioned, a few hospitals organize a memorial service in the hospital chapel each week or month, at a set time. All parents who have suffered a miscarriage are welcome to attend. There is also a book of remembrance in which parents can write if they want to. Lesley found this helpful.

> It's been a bit easier since I've at last plucked up the courage to write something for the hospital's memorial book, in memory of Joshua. After months of agonizing about what to write, I suddenly woke up at 5 am knowing clearly in my mind what to write. I never wake up at 5 am, and I wondered whether Joshua would have in fact been born then.

Nicola's baby was born when she was twenty weeks pregnant. These are the things she found helpful.

> We called her Elspeth and we found it helpful to put a notice in the paper 'in memory', just her name, and the date of her birth, and a short sentence taken from the SANDS book, *Saying goodbye to your baby*.[1] And we put an entry in the memorial book in the hospital chapel.

Even if the hospital does not do it in your area, there is no reason why a memorial service cannot be organized if you would find that helpful. One woman devised her own short memorial service which included prayers, readings and visualizations of the child and of saying goodbye.[2]

> I have had two miscarriages at twelve weeks. I think one of the questions we all ask is 'Why me, why has God done this to me?' I don't have an answer to this but we did find a large measure of comfort in putting together a short memorial service. At the time I think I found the most helpful aspects of the service to be the visualizations. To imagine my children playing, happy and free; to know that they would be loved for ever; and to know that I could see them like that whenever I wanted to, that I had not lost everything of them. It helped to ease the aching of empty arms.

Of course visualizations do not have to be organized in the context of a religious service. They are very good ways of creating memories, of having something positive to hold on to. Evelyn miscarried at ten weeks.

> I often imagine having the baby, the stages of pregnancy I'd be at. I have given the child a name; and had a small private ritual burial service for it which my mother suggested – I put a flower in a small box with a little card inside with the child's name on, which I buried in my parent's garden. I found that very helpful at the time, and it also helps me to think about it now.

Other Memorials

There are more tangible ways of remembering. One woman planted three rose bushes in memory of her miscarried baby. She phoned the Rose Growers' Association to find the rose bush nearest to the name she had chosen for her miscarried daughter. Pat also had something to remember by.

> My parents go to this church and they were planting trees and people were putting plaques on them. They asked us

how we felt but said they'd like to plant one for 'all unborn babies'. It's not just for us. It's for other people as well. At one point I thought one of the trees had died and it was ours. I was so upset when I got home. But I don't think it has. It would be so ironic if it had.

Shirley, who miscarried at eighteen weeks, named her baby Peter.

We have had a bench made with a plaque for Peter and it is placed in a wildfowl reserve, not far from where we live. This is a great comfort to us and we go to see the bench quite often.

It is sometimes helpful to keep all the things to do with the pregnancy together, to make them a bit special. Sarah kept the few cards she had been sent when she was in hospital in a drawer together with an account she wrote of what had happened to her and she said she knew she'd always keep them. Helen put together a scrapbook of her ten-week pregnancy.

I included the positive pregnancy test, the congratulations cards and letters we'd received, photos of me, gloatingly happy about being pregnant; then the 'after' photos of the forsythia in the garden, which I could see as I sat writing in the dining room and staring into middle space, photos of the flowers I was sent, the house as it was that week or so (a mess) and the cards and letters friends sent when they heard.

Sheila, who miscarried her baby at twenty-five weeks, also made a scrapbook of photos and her baby's things. She found it was very helpful to be able to show it to her older child who had difficulty in understanding what had happened to his mother.

It is not always possible to do these things – you may not have any papers or things to put in a special book, you may find writing difficult, you may not want to do anything more public. And not everyone finds these things helpful. You may feel it is inappropriate and are content with the images and memories you have. But if you do think it would be helpful, you should find a way of doing it; it doesn't matter if you do not do it around the time you lost your baby. It is never too late to mark the loss.

THE MEDICAL RESPONSE

༄ 6 ༄

Miscarriage on the NHS

The way you feel about your miscarriage will be shaped not only by the physical experience but by the care you receive. Health professionals have a vital role to play in offering good physical and medical care and also in helping you to understand what has happened. Many women who miscarry feel vulnerable and ignorant, dependent on health workers for care, information and advice. Health professionals cannot take away the sadness you may feel but good care enables you to begin to accept what has happened and does not add to your troubles.

Many women appreciate the care they receive. Half the women in the survey said that overall their care in hospital was helpful, under a fifth said it was unhelpful. Over two-thirds of women who saw their GP after the miscarriage found it helpful, and only a tenth unhelpful. However, there are many women who qualify their appreciation of the help they receive, who explain away inadequate care in terms of the pressures the Health Service is under, and there are many who complain outright about the insensitive and neglectful treatment which made a bad experience worse. Over two-fifths of women in the survey named a health professional as one of the three least helpful people at the time of their miscarriage, under a fifth said they were one of the three most helpful.

This chapter explores the issues around the help that is provided at different stages of a miscarriage – the first symptoms, in hospital and the follow-up care afterwards – and asks what is helpful, what is not, what are women's needs and what should be provided. More specific recommendations for the service that should be offered to meet the needs of miscarrying women are outlined in the 'Guidelines for Good Practice' on page 253.

⁓

The Problems in Context

The crux of the dissatisfaction many women have with their health care is that miscarriage is dismissed as a minor physical event, the potential emotional significance is denied and the meaning ignored. To view miscarriage as the loss of a baby, as many women experience it, rather than some sort of physical mishap has implications. The patient then becomes a woman with emotional needs and the loss becomes something that has to be treated and disposed of with respect. The emotional demands on staff become much more far reaching. Denying the meaning may be their way of coping with painful situations.

The lack of good psychological care is also prevalent in other areas of medicine. Inevitably and necessarily, staff develop defences in order to cope with the suffering and tragedy they encounter. But if the defensiveness becomes all-pervasive there is little room for the recognition and acceptance of the emotional dimension of the patient's experience, which women who miscarry need badly.

The use of language confirms the way women feel that the meaning and significance of their experience is denied. The use of the term 'abortion', even if 'spontaneous' is remembered, seems to lump you too closely together with women who have chosen to end their pregnancy. Referring to the 'products of conception' as 'bits and pieces' and minimizing the significance of the ERPC – the 'scrape' or the young houseman saying it's his job to 'hoover you out' or 'clean you up' – are all part of this. There is often no mention of a pregnancy, or a baby, just language that confirms you as unclean, dirty and out of place.

In a wider context, the tensions surrounding induced abortion may colour attitudes to miscarriage. In the past medical students were trained to consider the possibility of induced abortion when a woman presented with a threatened miscarriage. One doctor explained to his patient that he had to check whether her cervix was dilated or not because some women pretend to have miscarriages in order to have abortions (an example of how thinking about abortion, spontaneous and induced, can be linked). Some medical and nursing staff may find it necessary to deny the status of the fetus in order to enable them to accept and cope with abortion. I am not arguing against abortion, merely that the dilemmas that abortion raises have implications for attitudes to miscarriage, and may encourage people to minimise the meaning of miscarriage.

The specific complaints women have about the way they are treated, the lack of information they are given, the lack of understanding for their feelings and that they are not listened to, stem from these attitudes to miscarriage. They are similar to those made about antenatal care and the treatment of other, specifically female problems. The medical establishment is traditionally male, with male values and stereotypical ideas about women and women's needs, despite the inroads made by some women in recent years, and the fact that most of the caring in the system is done by women. As a woman patient you are relatively powerless and you come face to face with the control men can have over women's lives, over fertility and childbirth. If you question your treatment you run the risk that you may be perceived as difficult or neurotic.

Treatments for threatened miscarriage have come in and out of fashion based on methodologically-weak research, and most have now been proved of little value which means that a doctor has little to offer women who threaten to miscarry. When a woman miscarries there is a double failure – the failure of the woman to produce a healthy baby and the failure of the doctor to be able to do anything about it. The task is therefore to care rather than to cure and this is far less interesting.

Women feel they are treated for a routine, insignificant medical event, and doctors feel they are faced with over-emotional women who have expectations of treatment and explanation which they are unable to meet. It is hardly surprising with this potential conflict of perspectives and expectations that problems arise between women and their professional helpers.

⁓

Help from Your GP When a Miscarriage Threatens

Many women first approach their GP when it seems that their pregnancy may be going wrong. Most women are worried about their symptoms of bleeding, cramps, or that they no longer feel pregnant. For most early miscarriages there is nothing that can be done to prevent the miscarriage but the advice GPs give and the action they take varies. A recent survey showed great diversity in GPs' responses to particular symptoms.[1] For the woman it is a time of anxiety and uncertainty and it is the task of the GP to deal with this. Most women, when they start to miscarry, do not understand what is happening or why. An explanation of their symptoms and preparation for what may happen next is invaluable. Linda phoned her GP when she first started bleeding. She valued the support he gave.

He called in a couple of hours later and said there was nothing he could do, but that he'd come to see how I was. He explained things a bit and he was very nice and very kind. He called a couple of times over the weekend, until the bleeding got so heavy that I was admitted to hospital. He was there if I needed him.

Those GPs who recognize the anxiety that a threatened miscarriage can arouse and provide support and information are greatly appreciated. However many women find their GPs are reluctant to come out to visit, or to talk to them on the phone, that they are dismissive of the problems and give false reassurance that the pregnancy will succeed.

For many women it is unclear what the outcome is going to be. There may be a considerable time of uncertainty before an accurate diagnosis is made – two or three weeks or longer, an ultrasound scan at the local hospital may be necessary. Without knowing if the pregnancy is viable or not, the GP cannot offer effective help. Most women find this time of uncertainty difficult and doctors who tell you that you are over-anxious and neurotic and fail to deal with natural anxiety and uncertainty, are being extremely unhelpful.

꒜

In Hospital

From the medical point of view miscarriage is routine, and boring routine at that. A busy general hospital is likely to have at least four miscarriage patients at any one time. The medical intervention required is minor; miscarriage cannot be prevented or cured or made better; it can only be dealt with and many women end up feeling that they are being 'dealt' with or processed in a fairly perfunctory manner.

I turned up in casualty the same time as another woman. They put us in these little cubicles with the curtains round. They examined us and then sent us up to the ward. By that time there were four of us. We went down to theatre one after the other like on a conveyor belt.

Sue was taken by ambulance to casualty. She felt relieved that, after a difficult time of heavy bleeding, she was in a safe place where she would be well looked after, but she soon understood her lowly place in the hierarchy of importance.

> It was just like on telly. I quickly realized I wasn't going to be treated wonderfully. It was just going to be when they could fit me in.

Often when women are admitted to hospital their hopes are raised only to be dashed later. A lack of trust between the two systems of health care becomes clear when a woman transfers to hospital from the community. At worst there is a refusal to accept the GP's assessment of the miscarriage or to listen to the evidence of the woman herself. Comments like 'the cervix is closed – there's no evidence that you've lost the pregnancy', when a woman has bled heavily at home and her GP has confirmed the miscarriage, serve only to raise expectations unnecessarily and to prolong the agony.

Which Ward?

Where you are placed in the hospital will influence how you feel about your stay there. Some hospitals operate a policy of admitting women through casualty, even if they have gone through their GP. This often means a wait in the waiting room, a long wait in a casualty cubicle for the appropriate doctor, and then a wait for either a bed on a ward or a place in the queue for theatre. Casualty is not the best place to be when you are miscarrying; it is usually too busy and you feel neglected. Women invariably feel more satisfied with their care when they are admitted to a ward that is geared to accept them.

As miscarriage doesn't fit very well in the hospital classification of experience there is no obvious place for women to go when it happens. Hilary felt this keenly when she was admitted to the maternity ward when she miscarried at twenty-two weeks.

The staff were very kindly but I felt marginal. You don't fit in anywhere when you miscarry. There isn't a place for you.

It is easy to feel marginal and a failure because miscarriage is not what is supposed to happen and in some way it is unacceptable – women should be producing healthy babies, not losing them. As a consequence, you may feel that you shouldn't really be there, that your experience is being denied, that the staff are unsympathetic and don't have time for you and that you are unimportant. Particularly in early miscarriage, the contrast between the personal significance and the medical significance could hardly be greater.

In practice women are admitted to a variety of wards within a hospital. It is usual that women losing a baby later in pregnancy (sixteen to twenty weeks plus, but it varies) will be admitted to a maternity ward, to the care of midwives, for the delivery. After the birth they may be returned to a postnatal or a gynaecology ward. While the rationale for this is understandable and probably in the best interests of the woman, being shunted about as your status changes is symptomatic of the fact that you don't fit in.

Women with earlier miscarriages will be admitted to either a gynaecology ward or an emergency ward. Inevitably some women will end up wherever there is a spare bed. Emergency wards are apparently more neutral places but they are geared to medical emergencies, which miscarriage usually is not. On a gynaecology ward you can feel equally out of place.

I found it hard being on a gynae ward with older ladies, some having hysterectomies and complaining about their children and others being sterilized when I so longed for another baby.

There are advantages and disadvantages to the various locations, but women usually do not want to be with other pregnant women who are trying, and apparently succeeding, in maintaining their pregnancies. One woman described the

distress she felt when she woke up the morning after her
ERPC, in a ward with heavily pregnant women in the beds
around her, and another how she was in a ward with pregnant
women who were suffering from bad nausea, with whom she
had to take her meals. Both found it insensitive and unhelpful.
Nor do women who have miscarried want to be with women
who have chosen to terminate their pregnancy.

Likewise they almost certainly do not want to be with
women with newborn babies or within hearing of them – the
crying of a newborn baby is an acutely upsetting reminder of
what you have lost. When Linda was admitted to casualty she
was put in a cubicle next to a woman with a newborn baby.

> You can hear everything that's going on and you wait there
> for ages. And this baby was crying and crying – a real new-
> born baby cry. I remember that being such a sad thing to
> listen to because in my head it became my own baby
> crying. I found it excruciating and felt very distressed.

Elizabeth miscarried when she was twenty-three weeks pregnant.

> I remember while I was in labour, I heard babies crying
> and I was hoping and praying that they were all wrong and
> that my baby too would be born crying.

After the birth of her baby at twenty-two weeks, Gillian was
taken to the postnatal ward and wheeled down the length of it,
past all the mothers and babies.

> I told my husband that no way would I stay in that ward.
> He told the nurses and they put me in a room of my own.
> But I could still hear the babies crying and had to put
> cotton wool in my ears to shut out the noise.

Many women need privacy from other patients at the time of
the miscarriage. This may be difficult to organize but it should
not be the case that a woman who is twelve weeks pregnant,

and bleeding heavily, experiences her miscarriage on a trolley in a busy casualty department, or that a woman who is sixteen weeks pregnant loses her baby into a bedpan in a curtained-off section of the gynae or emergency ward, at visiting time, while the woman who has made it to twenty weeks qualifies for a single room on the maternity ward, with a midwife in attendance.

Women vary in the amount of privacy they want after the miscarriage. Some prefer to be alone while others feel abandoned. In an ideal world we should be able to choose but, of course, this is often not possible. Women with earlier miscarriages often find themselves together in a ward and many say how helpful they find this, to be able to share their experiences, learn from each other and realize they are not alone.

There is no 'right place' for miscarrying women in hospital; it is up to the individual hospital to create a place where a woman's needs for privacy, respect and understanding can be met. This does not have to be a ward only for miscarriage patients, but women are most likely to get the best care when they are admitted to a ward where they are expected, where all women who miscarry go, where the staff are both prepared for them and understand why they are there, where procedures are understood or information about them at hand, where the issues that miscarriage poses have been thought about and where staff work in a supportive environment with the opportunity to share issues that they may find difficult. If staff feel comfortable with miscarriage they are more likely to talk to women about what has happened and understand their feelings, to give information and do all the practical things, like make follow-up appointments and cancel antenatal and scan appointments.

The Need for Physical and Psychological Care

It is in the provision of health care that the split between the emotional and the physical reality of miscarriage becomes destructively apparent. When you are miscarrying you need to be physically looked after; miscarriage is usually unpleasant and it can be traumatic. Many women comment on the excellent nursing and medical care they receive which contribute to a feeling of being well cared for. But good physical care is not enough. A miscarriage is an emotional as well as a physical event and it is the recognition of this fact that is essential in ensuring good care. Women need to be cared for by people who are willing to take on the emotional significance that miscarriage can have, who accept how a woman feels and don't jolly her along or deny what has happened, who allow her and give her permission to talk about her experience if she wants to, so that she can discover how she feels about it and allow the grieving process to begin.

In the survey the aspects of hospital care described as being most helpful were staff who were understanding and caring, who made time to be with you to talk and to listen. It demands an openness from staff and a willingness to enter into another person's world and share their experience, not to know how they feel but to feel with them. One woman described how helpful it was that the staff shared her sadness and cried with her, another how she valued the nurse's sharing of her own experience of miscarriage. Lena also had a sense of the staff being with her.

The night sister, despite being very busy, sat with me and brought tea for me and herself, her words were comforting and I appreciated her company. When I was due to leave the day sister came in to see me and spent a long time talking to me and to my husband, when he arrived. She gave me information about the MA and talked a lot about how I must be feeling. I really felt she understood, although she had never had a miscarriage herself. I still remember our conversation clearly and am eternally grateful to her for helping me to understand what had happened and how I was likely to react.

Frances appreciated the care she got in hospital when she miscarried at eleven weeks.

I didn't see a lot of people but those I did were very concerned and sorry that a baby had been lost. They made me feel comfortable and acknowledged what was happening. When I left they gave me a booklet with lots of information.

The lack of this type of care is overwhelmingly condemned. Many women complain that the staff either ignore them or the reason that they are there, and are unable to communicate with them and fail to understand the reason for their distress or their need to ask questions. One woman said that no one spoke to her about the miscarriage or its effects and she ended up wondering why she was in hospital. Ella found the staff ignored her once she had miscarried.

The staff were very chatty until I lost the baby, after which they just kept away. I just wished they'd say 'I'm sorry you lost your baby' and then carry on as normal. Nobody would give me any straight answers and I felt as if I was being fobbed off.

It is easy to feel abandoned, both by the baby you have lost and by those who are supposed to be there to care for you. Lucy was admitted to a side room on her own, which was the privacy she would have chosen. Her husband was with her.

We were then left on our own, for hours. My husband commented that we were being treated like failures. We wanted privacy but we were forgotten about. We didn't want constant fuss and attention, just acknowledgement and information.

If you are left alone to miscarry it can be a devastating experience. Deirdre found that the doctor who dealt with her viewed the miscarriage as a physical event.

A doctor came to see me when I was upset and asked if I was in pain. I replied that I wasn't, and he asked me if I was feeling unwell. Again I replied that I wasn't and he then asked why I was so upset. I said it was because I had lost my baby. He patted me on the arm and said 'never mind'.

Many women contrast the medical care they receive with the emotional care; it seems to echo the split between mind and body, on which so much of western medicine is based.

Medically they were excellent, non-medically they were awful. They were sympathetic in terms of 'this is a sick person in hospital' but they ignored the dimension of meaning altogether.

It does not have to be like this. In accepting and legitimizing a woman's experience, both nursing and medical staff can play an important role in helping a woman to understand and come to terms with her loss. When Diana miscarried she was treated as if nothing was wrong and felt she was pressured into feeling she was all right when she was not.

I felt satisfied at the time with the medical care but looking back I deserved much better. There's so much more they could have done that would have helped me to feel that it was all right to feel the way that I did. If you were treated differently when you're in hospital, and given a more sympathetic response, you'd feel it was OK to grieve.

In units where staff work together, where policy is discussed and standards of care, both physical and psychological, are laid down these problems are more likely to be overcome. If units are under-resourced and staff pressured it is of course harder to achieve this standard of care.

The Need for Information

Women have a tremendous need for information. In the

survey the giving of information was cited as second in importance only to the understanding shown by the staff. Most
women are very unprepared for a miscarriage. It is something
they know little about until it happens. Information is needed
throughout about what has happened, what is happening,
what might happen next and why it's happening. And women
want honest answers to their questions. It is the responsibility
of the health professionals to provide this, to help you understand what is going on and to prepare you for what might
happen next.

It is important to know the details of your own miscarriage.
If an ERPC is performed you should be told clearly what was
removed, and given the opportunity to see it if you choose.
The nature and results of any tests that are done should be
clearly communicated. Often women are aware that some
tests have been done but they do not know what or why.
Expectations are raised that tests will bring answers, when
only the most basic assessment of the tissue has taken place. In
later miscarriages when there is a post-mortem your permission should be sought and again the results made available,
usually at a follow-up appointment. All the relevant information should be communicated to your GP. Often it seems only
scant information is passed on to the GP who is then not able
to answer all the questions you may have.

It is also useful if there is general information available
about the nature of miscarriage. Many women value discussion about the possible physical and emotional consequences
of a miscarriage and information about trying again and the
help that is available in a subsequent pregnancy. Most women
are unable to take all this in at a time when they are upset or in
a state of shock. Some hospitals do routinely give women a
leaflet about miscarriage, giving basic information about
causes, likely physical and emotional reactions, and advice
about trying again.

They gave me a leaflet which was helpful because it
contained a lot of information and also it felt like a recognition of what was happening. It was being recognized as

91

something other than just a medical problem. It was a life event and it was marking that.

The Need for an Explanation

Every woman who miscarries asks 'Why did it happen to me?', 'Is there something wrong with my body?', 'What did I do wrong?', 'Will it happen again?' It is known that most women will eventually have a successful pregnancy without any intervention and that even if a problem is discovered, there is probably little that can be done about it. Consequently it is current medical practice only to begin investigations into the cause after a third miscarriage. This is particularly cruel for women who are eventually investigated only to discover that some form of preventable treatment could have been offered (see Chapter 10 for recurrent miscarriage).

So the current state of scientific knowledge and medical practice determines the answers to these questions: 'We don't know why it happened'; 'It is unlikely that anything you did caused the miscarriage'; 'It probably won't happen again, but it might.' They are not very satisfactory answers. All too often the woman is left with memories of a rather half-baked conversation about how perhaps 'decorating the living room was not very wise' which was not intended as a serious discussion and has no firm basis in fact, but succeeds in confirming myths and superstition without the doctor realizing it – what is said even in general conversation by an expert is very powerful.

We have high expectations that things that happen to us can be explained. It comes as a shock that no explanation will be forthcoming and offensive that nobody else thinks it worth bothering about – 'It's just one of those things, try again.' To fail to deal with the issue of causation is profoundly unhelpful to women. Caroline understood only too well how easy it is to blame yourself.

They should explain, so women understand completely. I know they can't always tell you why, but they must have some idea, just to let you know that it's not all your fault. If you think it's your fault, it doesn't just change how you get over it, but all the other pregnancies you're going to have. If you blame yourself then it's much easier to get the ball rolling that everything else is all your fault.

While recognizing that it is not feasible for most women to know precisely what caused their miscarriage, it should be possible from the woman's account of her experience and the medical evidence, to rule out some of the possible causes, and come to a 'likely explanation'. As one woman wrote:

I feel the professionals hide behind this veil of ignorance. To not do this [give information] seems an abuse of the power the medical profession has. It raises political issues about priorities for treatment within the NHS and the second-rate treatment women get for 'women's problems', often at the hands of men.

The issue of cause can become a source of conflict between a woman and her doctors. She needs desperately to know why it happened in order to begin to accept it and leave it behind. The doctor can't tell her, finds it hard to say he doesn't know, feels unable to meet her needs and a frustrating encounter ensues for both parties. The doctor ends up feeling the woman is unnecessarily demanding and needy and the woman that the doctor neither cares nor understands. Many doctors do seem rather spectacularly bad at dealing with this issue. Some try to get round it by taking the statistical approach ('One in four pregnancies fails') or by going into the odds of it happening again. Whilst it's helpful to know these things, it does as one woman said tend to 'make you feel like a statistic and it doesn't answer the question of why you were the one and not one of the other three'.

༂

Follow-up Care

This was Jean's experience of follow-up care after her second miscarriage.

> My GP was helpful and he answered all my questions with understanding and patience. A visit from the health visitor was helpful and reassuring that people cared and understood, as it came at a time I was feeling low. A visit from the midwife was potentially distressing; she arrived expecting me to be seven months pregnant with the last pregnancy – the hospital hadn't informed her of the miscarriage! The appointment with the consultant was disastrous and left me in a state of deep depression. He seemed to talk down to me, and answered my questions in a very different manner than he answered my husband's. He had no concept of how a woman feels. He could not understand that for me it was so important to have a reason why miscarriages had happened to me twice, rather than be told it was just one of those things – I was unlucky, go away and try again, dear. Then he failed to read the notes and told me I had at least one child to be grateful for.

A woman's needs after a miscarriage are quite clear. Detailed information about the miscarriage, about any tests that may or may not have been done and why, information about miscarriages in general, and reassurance about any physical problems following the miscarriage (which may necessitate a physical examination) are all essential. Advice about a future pregnancy, when to try again, preconception care, and the antenatal care that should be available are necessary. It is also helpful to be told by someone authoritative that it is not your fault, that it is a perfectly natural but distressing occurrence, that there is nothing wrong with your body (assuming there is not) and that after miscarrying many women feel sad and grieve. You need the opportunity to ask questions, express your feelings about the miscarriage, and to feel you have been understood.

You need this sort of help to be able to understand enough about your own experience to be able to begin to leave it behind and to feel sufficiently informed and reassured about a future pregnancy that you are as confident as possible about trying again, if you wish. While friends, family and support groups are invaluable in providing the opportunity to talk over your experiences (see Chapter 9), the help of a skilled health professional is necessary to meet these specific needs. Miscarriage is not a uniform entity and neither are the women who have them. There needs to be some degree of flexibility but it is the responsibility of the health service to provide the opportunity for this sort of follow-up.

In practice, there is often confusion about what is needed and a feeling that perhaps because answers cannot be given, there is little to offer. Combined with the pressure of scarce resources and the feeling that miscarriage really does not matter very much, a somewhat haphazard system of follow-up care has evolved. Most women, but by no means all, see a health professional after their miscarriage. Many hospitals do not routinely offer appointments until a woman has had three miscarriages but suggest that a woman sees her GP, unless she has miscarried late in pregnancy. The onus is with the woman to arrange the appointment.

GPs can offer invaluable continuity of care and it is to their GP that many women turn. Over three-quarters of the women in the survey saw their GP and two-thirds of them described the appointment as helpful. GPs are valued for their support, reassurance and encouragement, their understanding, their advice and for the opportunity for questions to be asked, again and again if necessary. GPs are also in a unique position to pick up on minor health problems that can occur after a miscarriage and if necessary, to refer on to a specialist. Working women will need a certificate from their GP for the extra time they need off work (see Chapter 13), which was the reason Linda initially contacted her doctor.

He gave me a lot of time and was very sympathetic. He talked about taking time to get over it and that it was something that might make me depressed. He said he thought it was important I rested and took things easy. Just things like that, but it was very helpful.

Linda returned to the surgery several times over the following weeks as she got very depressed.

The quality of care a GP provides depends on the quality of information he receives from the hospital, as well as his understanding of miscarriage and his ability to communicate with his patient. It is very frustrating for women to ask questions that cannot be answered because the information is not available to the GP although it does exist. Many GPs are also limited in their detailed knowledge of miscarriage. It is not uncommon for women who have had several miscarriages to feel they know more about it than their doctor.

A significant number of women find their GPs are busy, dismissive, ill-informed about miscarriage, unwilling or unable to answer their questions and fail to take either their physical or emotional needs seriously. This attitude was confirmed for these two women by comments like, 'What a silly girl, what did you have to go and do that for?' and 'I don't know what you expect me to do. Come back again when you're pregnant.'

Half of the women in the survey had a follow-up appointment at the hospital. Women were more likely to be followed up if they had miscarried late in pregnancy or had miscarried before. Junior hospital doctors were found by far the least helpful (under a third of appointments with them were considered helpful) and were the cause of considerable complaint. Consultants fared better, but not much (half the appointments with a consultant were considered helpful). It is often at these appointments that a woman's frustrations with her doctors surface. Lorraine had two miscarriages at thirteen weeks. Her experience is not unusual and will unfortunately sound familiar to many women.

After waiting for about two hours, amid graphic tales of other patients' gynae troubles, I finally met the doctor, not the consultant, who I never saw at all. By this time I was pretty wound up although I'd started out quite calm. The doctor was very detached (I'd never seen him before) and asked a few rather haphazard questions about the first miscarriage and this one. His general attitude was 'better luck next time', 'third time lucky' etc – 'I've got ladies who've had eight or nine miscarriages and are still trying', as though this was something to be proud of and a mere two was hardly worth noticing. When I asked if they'd done any tests he said no, they didn't until you were a recurrent miscarrier. He refused to say how many you had to have to qualify. But the path report said 'no obvious malformations'. I asked if they would do any tests or monitoring during a subsequent pregnancy/miscarriage – no. Where could I go that would? A teaching hospital might. I got the impression that this hospital had no one specially interested and perhaps not enough sophisticated equipment. I asked if another miscarried baby would be sent for analysis – no. He quoted the consultant once or twice to get out of answering my questions. 'The consultant doesn't do it that way', 'the consultant doesn't believe it's worth it'. I asked if he thought there was any likelihood of a vitamin deficiency/effect of lead etc. He laughed and said he didn't think I was suffering from lead poisoning. I think he had a typically blinkered view. I don't know, and he certainly didn't, what my vitamin status is or was or whether I had been exposed to high levels of heavy metals. By this time I was weeping, largely from frustration at his total lack of interest, empathy etc. So he asked how my husband was coping, definitely a text book question I felt – I wondered if he'd even have asked if I'd not broken down.

This sort of encounter is unnecessary and destructive, it is a waste of time for the doctor and a source of added misery for the woman. It would be better not to give follow-up appointments if this is all that can be offered.

Although these sad tales are all too common, there are many women who are very grateful for the time, patience and dedication of their doctors and who feel their doctors are doing all they can. They feel they are treated as reasonable, feeling, intelligent human beings and their questions are answered as best they can be. Gillian had been unwell for some time prior to her missed abortion and was worried about her health. It was her first miscarriage but the gynae registrar arranged to see her in six weeks.

> She was an extremely nice woman and seemed to understand that this had been a difficult time for me. When I saw her she was very good and reassuring, and in five minutes confirmed that my body was functioning properly again, which was what I needed.

Gillian had very specific worries she needed help with. For Paulette a physical check-up was insufficient.

> Worse than feeling so empty was the lack of any concrete attempt to explain things at the hospital. When I had the check-up nine weeks later, it was treated as just a routine examination. I know that many miscarriages are no cause for concern but to me it was a tragedy and I badly needed a professional to sit down and talk to me, explain what could go wrong and generally reassure me about the future.

The need to talk about it is very strong for many women and this is what hospital follow-up appointments rarely offer. They are rushed for time, focused on active intervention and hard information of which, for miscarriage patients, there is often relatively little. There are ways round these problems and some health authorities are developing innovative patterns of follow-up care. In one area community midwives offer a home visit to all women who miscarry and will see them in their next pregnancy – the continuity of care many campaign for. In one hospital a nurse from a gynaecology ward runs a follow-up support group to which all women who have miscarried are invited. Another hospital is considering creating a post for a senior nurse with counselling skills to offer a follow-up system for gynaecology patients, including women who miscarry. Not all women want to take up these offers and these arrangements should not prevent women who need more specific help from a doctor from getting it.

Follow-up care after a miscarriage is rather a blot on the medical copy book. Currently it is the source of considerable dissatisfaction for women. Some women undoubtedly do not see anybody and of those that do a significant number find the help offered does not meet their needs. Some women with financial means resort to private health care and pay for a consultation with a gynaecologist in an attempt to get their questions answered. Others change their GP or consultant, often with some difficulty, to try and find the support they need.

Improvements can be made. Written information about a woman's miscarriage could be made more readily available. A midwife or gynae nurse could have responsibility for running a follow-up clinic with appropriate medical back-up, freeing doctors to spend more time with those women who have serious medical problems. Follow-up care should not be abandoned because it appears not to work but a more creative approach to the problems should be found.

Good care can only be given if the emotional importance and the meaning of the loss for each woman are recognized and if staff work in a climate where they can offer this sort of care. Women need to be realistic in their expectations and health professionals need to reassess the skills and expertise they undoubtedly have to offer women who miscarry. Miscarriage has remained an individual and private problem. It will, perhaps, only be when women come together to raise these issues that there will be the impetus to make fundamental changes in attitudes and care.

Section three

AFTER THE MISCARRIAGE

Jean's story – part two

'**N**ext morning, after the op, I went home, still philosophical and relatively cheerful. The depression came the next day when I felt so lonely and suddenly let go of my emotions and cried my eyes out. The bleeding seemed to last for weeks, never giving me a chance to forget about the miscarriage, no one had told me how long to expect it to last. I had developed an infection and needed a course of antibiotics before things returned to normal. My GP was very helpful, caring and understanding and even visited me, unrequested, after my discharge from hospital.

'After two weeks I went back to work and put on a good cheerful face, which really was an act. Christmas came – a time for children – I felt so miserable. The depression got worse. When my period came, I was near to tears every day – the loss really hurt. The depression was cyclical and always worse at the time of my periods. I couldn't cope with my work and several times came close to handing in my notice. I couldn't face the idea of getting pregnant, not to build up my hopes only to meet despair again. Around this time I went along to the Miscarriage Association and found it reassuring to hear people expressing some of the feelings I felt. My husband was wonderful and supportive all this time, although he couldn't comprehend why I couldn't forget about the miscarriage and carry on as though it had never happened. He couldn't understand why, weeks later, I was still bursting into tears. I think it was a film on miscarriage that helped him understand what devastating effects miscarriage can have on women.

'The emotional aftermath of the second miscarriage was disastrous. I had accepted the first miscarriage as unlucky and something that happens to lots of people, but the second miscarriage I couldn't accept so easily. It seemed so unfair that this should happen to me again. I wondered if anything I had done or not done had caused it, had I got pregnant too soon after the first miscarriage, hjad I done too much in the garden in the days before I knew I was pregnant? I was depressed by the thought that I might never have a baby. At 35 I felt like the biological clock was ticking away on my reproductive life. Had I been younger I think I would have given up trying to get pregnant for a year, I felt it was taking over our lives and ruining them. At this time, I still wanted and needed to talk about my miscarriages, but my friends assumed either I wanted to forget about it, or they didn't know how to broach the subject. In contrast, I was unable to talk to my relatives about the miscarriages and would ensure the subject was avoided – I don't know why, unless it's because I knew they were upset by it all. I bottled up my feelings and lived with the dream of holding a normal baby and the nightmare of another failure.

'During this period of grieving I understood a lot about human emotions. I could understand why people felt like committing suicide, I had a family who cared but if I hadn't there would have been nothing to stop me. I looked longingly at babies in the street, and I could understand why women are sometimes driven to stealing babies. I also understood how women could accidentally get caught for shoplifting – I found myself unable to concentrate on irrelevant things, like shopping, and I had to make a conscious effort to ensure I'd paid for things before I left a shop. I must admit I was a horrid person during this period, bad-tempered, irritable, moody and miserable. My husband was wonderful at putting up with all this. My husband's philosophy was very much let's forget about it all, and get on with life – did he really forget about it all, or was it all a show of strength? Miscarriage puts a lot of strain on a relationship and I'm sure if the relationship is not strong it will crumble under the strain. Yet in many ways these emotional experiences of the past years have brought us much closer together.'

The distress and depression Jean experienced are very normal. The full impact of what had happened did not hit her until she got home and then followed a period of depression and grieving. Facing the ouside world of work and family was hard – she wanted and needed to share it with other people, but she found it hard to find people who appreciated the depth of what she felt. And when it happened again, it was so much worse. Her sense of her own worth diminished and she ended up feeling she was a horrible person. Her experience is common to many women. These issues will be explored in the following chapters.

✤ 7 ✤

The physical aftermath

The Physical After-effects

Physically most women say they recover from a miscarriage quite quickly but it does vary. If the miscarriage was physically traumatic, dragged out over a period of time, or if you were unwell beforehand, it may take you longer to recover. Many women say they feel very tired after the miscarriage; an ERPC under general anaesthetic may contribute to these feelings. Tiredness is also a way of your body saying slow down and take time to readjust. Your body has been adapting to the changes of pregnancy and now it has to return to its non-pregnant state.

The extent of the bleeding after an ERPC seems to vary. Many women say it lessens within a few days, while others continue to bleed for two to three weeks. Some experience cramping pains afterwards but these usually pass within a few days. If you did not have an ERPC, it is likely that the bleeding will reduce over time but it may continue in decreasing amounts for up to a month. If the bleeding gets heavier, or if you begin to lose large clots, or you experience pain or fever, you should consult your doctor. It may be that you have an infection which may need treatment with a course of anti-biotics. If your womb has not been cleared of all the tissue from the pregnancy a second ERPC may be necessary.

Many women who consult their doctor after the miscar-riage, say it is difficult to describe accurately the extent of the bleeding and then to get appropriate advice. When you are unsure about what constitutes 'normal bleeding' you have nothing to measure your own experience against and it is not something that doctors are particularly well-informed about either. Women who do bleed for some time after their miscarriage often feel they are not taken very seriously. If you are worried about the bleeding you should persist in getting help.

If a second evacuation is necessary it can be extremely depressing and make the miscarriage seem like it is never ending. You may feel very critical of your original medical treatment. Returning to hospital for another operation, however minor, reminds you of all you have been through and makes the whole experience more traumatic. However, if the bleeding is severe, it is obviously a relief to be getting the appropriate help.

> I was in agony with stomach pains and still bleeding. I was so frightened as I was passing so much blood, I didn't know what was happening. I went to the nearest hospital and was kept in and had another D and C.

Many women are surprised by the lack of any physical aftermath and find it quite disorienting. One woman said that after a week she did not even feel tired and she began to wonder if she had ever been pregnant. Your body seems to be colluding with the wider social attitudes that nothing of any significance has happened. Sarah felt very well after her miscarriage at nine weeks.

> I had no physical reactions. I'm very healthy and the miscarriage was very 'easy'. My body bounced back. I was a bit shaky after having been in hospital for five days. I wouldn't have wanted to go on a long hike but I felt well.

Penny's experience was not quite so straightforward. She miscarried at ten weeks.

> My stomach felt as if it had been used as a punching bag,

and that wore off after about three days. I continued bleeding, well, spotting really, for over two weeks afterwards. I didn't know whether this was to be expected or not – so when I developed abdominal pains and a mildly smelly discharge as well, I went to the doctor. I got pessaries and was told that, apart from a slight infection, I was constipated and given laxatives. Within a week or so this sorted itself out. I continued to sort of bleed until my period. After that, physically I've not had any trouble, in fact, in physical terms it was all quite low key really.

The stage of pregnancy at which you miscarry will influence how you feel afterwads. The later your miscarriage, the more similar your experience is to full-term birth. As well as all the hormonal changes, tiredness and sense of loss, you may feel very sore and have all the after-effects of a difficult labour to deal with.

⤲

When Your Milk Comes In

One of the most distressing things after a late miscarriage is that a few days after the baby has been born your milk will come in. Some women can leak milk from about three months into the pregnancy but it is only later that lactation will occur – the exact time varies with individual women. If you do lactate (it is more likely if you have been pregnant and breastfed before), you can produce milk for several days and it can take up to a couple of weeks before you stop feeling uncomfortable. It adds insult to injury – it is not only a cruel reminder of the lost baby but it can be physically uncomfortable, if not painful, as these women describe. Fiona miscarried at twenty-two weeks.

Then, after three days, my milk came in, something I hadn't been prepared for, nobody had told me. That seemed to be a knife twisting in the wound even more. It reminded me even more of my lost baby – nature is very cruel. Also it was very painful. I wasn't given anything to dry the milk up, just advised to let it drip naturally. My breasts were so full and tender it used to hurt most of the time, especially at night in bed.

Paula miscarried at twenty-one weeks, while on holiday. She was admitted to hospital and was discharged a day after having the ERPC.

The next day I returned to my holiday and a day later my breasts were full of milk; no one had mentioned this. I managed to get tablets from a local GP but they take forty-eight hours to work. So I travelled home in agony.

Amy miscarried at seventeen weeks.

I cried again after about three days when I woke up dripping with milk. I phoned up the midwife, I'd never met her – she'd just left her number earlier. She said she couldn't visit me officially now but was ever so kind on the phone and reassured me a lot.

Drugs are available which help to dry up your milk but they are not usually prescribed because they can have unpleasant side-effects and they are expensive. It takes time for the milk to dry up naturally and this can be a difficult time when you need a lot of support. Most women get little or no professional support at this stage compared to that available to women who give birth to a live baby. It can help if you express enough milk to be comfortable, but not too much, as that will stimulate your milk supply. Cold compresses can help reduce swelling and discomfort, and it helps to wear a well-supporting bra. Homeopathic remedies are also available.

༄

Feeling Low

Miscarriage is a very exhausting experience for many women. It is not uncommon to feel physically low afterwards. The physical and emotional strains of miscarriage for some women seem to lower their resistance to infection and as a result. many women go to their GP with minor ailments after they have miscarried. Joan miscarried at eight weeks.

> In the first few days, apart from being very tired and a bit sore, I had no real after-effects from the miscarriage. However, I developed a urinary infection two days later, and then two days later again, very bad gastro-enteritis. There seemed to be no end to the disasters that were happening.

Kim's experience was contrary to her expectations. She had had flu early on in the pregnancy and felt she had never fully recovered.

> The miscarriage brought a sense of hope that I would be able to regain my strength and feel energetic and alive and could start again. I didn't suddenly get well but for several months seemed to catch every cold and infection going.

Sandra found this too, as she wrote three months after her miscarriage at sixteen weeks.

> I don't find things getting any easier; I don't seem to be able to get physically fit, which leads into the vicious circle that I'm not well enough to conceive. Finally I came down with a recurrent throat infection which doesn't seem to clear up.

Frances described herself as spotty, tired and run down and

said it took three months before she began to feel better. She too had been unwell prior to the miscarriage. Like Zoe, many women just say they feel very low.

> I wasn't ill but I wasn't well either. I was very pale and very tired and had absolutely no energy. The Health Visitor called the doctor out because she was worried about me. I did pick up in the end, but it took a while.

Feeling vulnerable physically as well as emotionally can be very miserable, it is as if your physical health mirrors your emotions. The two are intertwined: if you felt better physically you would probably feel better emotionally and vice versa. It is important to attend to your physical well-being and to take time to regain your physical strength.

$$\curlywedge$$

Periods

You will probably find that your periods resume about a month after the miscarriage, but this does vary. Several women told me that their periods changed after their miscarriage – some for the better, their periods were lighter or more regular, some for the worse.

> My periods started exactly twenty-seven days later and have been regular ever since, but they are now extremely heavy, with blood clots, which I have never experienced before.

Martha found her body took several months to settle down after her miscarriage at eight weeks.

> My system took a lot longer to recover and my cycle was sixty days instead of thirty-two to thirty-five days, which I found upsetting as I didn't understand what was

happening inside me. My cycle has just come back to normal.

If you are worried it is best to discuss this with a sympathetic doctor.

A period can be particularly difficult after you have miscarried, as Tessa found. The bleeding is double-edged, serving to remind you of the miscarriage itself and yet also it is further proof that you are no longer pregnant.

Each time my period starts I get very depressed and talk about pregnancy and motherhood, and how I feel I'm running out of time. My husband must be fed up with it, although he's very patient. With each period I feel I'm reliving the loss of my baby.

Maggie was able to be more positive about it.

Physically I was soon over the miscarriage and my periods returned three weeks later. This cheered me up as I knew I could start 'trying again' which made me feel I was doing something.

᠅

Taking Care of Yourself

It is important to take good care of yourself after your miscarriage. Pregnancy, however short, involves your body in many changes and it takes time to readjust. It is important to do all the sensible things – rest, eat well, exercise and take life a bit easy for a while – to give your body a chance to fully recover. For some women recovery comes very quickly but many are surprised how long it takes before they feel fully physically fit again. It is important to give yourself time to recover emotionally as well.

✌ 8 ✌

'It's OK to grieve':
Your emotional reaction

Women often find that their emotional reaction to a miscarriage is far more devastating than the physical event. And, as with the physical process, the emotional aftermath will vary from woman to woman. This chapter explores the feelings women have experienced following their miscarriage; their reactions are diverse, yet there are underlying themes of sadness, depression and guilt.

✌

The Meaning of the Miscarriage

There are many different influences on the way you feel after a miscarriage. The nature of the miscarriage, the stage of pregnancy, your personal circumstances, your personality and emotional inheritance, and whether you are able to share your feelings with someone close to you, are just some of them. Your miscarriage may have been physically traumatic: you may feel angry about your medical treatment, perhaps you felt abandoned or controlled in a way you find hard to accept. And if the miscarriage has brought to the surface feelings or events from the past you will have to deal with these too.

The hopes and expectations the pregnancy held for you will be reflected in the way you feel about the miscarriage. In this way some miscarriages can be more significant than others, and they are harder to deal with. It may have been your first pregnancy and marked your transition into motherhood. You may be well into your thirties and feel, with the biological clock ticking away, that time is running out. You may have found it difficult to get pregnant. The pregnancy may have had a special meaning for you; perhaps this was going to be a baby for you to enjoy as life is less pressured than when you first had children. You may have hoped that this child would bring you together as a couple or a family. The emotional consequences of miscarriage cannot be understood in isolation from the rest of your life. Inevitably your response is rooted in your wider experience.

It may take time to work out exactly what the pregnancy did mean to you, especially if you were ambivalent about it. Some pregnancies are planned, others not, some are anticipated, others a great shock. You may have had mixed feelings about the pregnancy – you may not have wanted to be pregnant at all – which may make adjusting to the miscarriage difficult. If you miscarried early in pregnancy, it may only be in the weeks that follow that the full impact of both the pregnancy and the miscarriage affects you. With a later miscarriage the loss may be more immediately apparent.

꒰

Coming Home from Hospital

In the immediate aftermath you may feel very confused. A miscarriage is a crisis and once it is over the process of readjustment begins. If you have been in hospital it can be a wrench to leave, if you don't yet feel ready to go home, or you may feel that you can't get out of the place quickly enough. Once home, you have to pick up the threads of your life and face the impact of the miscarriage, and it can feel very strange. You have fundamentally changed but everything around you stays the same. Fiona's husband was at work when she returned home.

He had left beautiful flowers and a load of fruit on the table which lifted my spirits. But I felt alone and displaced. I did not want to get back to the daily household routine so went out for a lot of walks. This seemed to increase the bleeding and tire me out, but I didn't know what else to do.

Joan felt very alone, as if nobody else had been through the experience. Others may seem very callous in failing to recognize what has happened to you.

My husband took me out for lunch then dropped me off home and went and played rugby. He had no idea how I felt. I sat alone feeling very empty, very sore and felt as if no one in the world cared.

It is quite common to feel high – relief that the crisis is over. Jessica miscarried at sixteen weeks.

I left hospital on a high, I think as a reaction to the awful physical ordeal I had suffered. I was so pleased to get home; to see my dog and my family and hadn't had time to think about what my miscarriage would mean.

And then you may be overtaken with feelings of sadness and emptiness.

I've never cried so much in my whole life. I was walking about with an empty feeling where I should have been holding my baby.

It may take a while before your feelings surface. At the time of the miscarriage many women say they feel shocked and bewildered by the experience, they feel numb, 'like a zombie', and as if they are 'working on automatic pilot'. There can be a sense of detachment, as if everything is happening to somebody else.
  Distancing themselves from what is going on and maintaining a false sense of composure enables many women to

cope with the public performance, which the last stages of a miscarriage in hospital often are. Kerry found that her feelings of numbness and unreality lasted a while.

> My initial reaction to the miscarriage after three weeks of trauma and worry, was one of relief that it was all over, and we could try again. However my feelings over the next few weeks altered and I became emotionally very sensitive – my mind was in turmoil, coping with sadness, disappointment anger and a deep sense of loss and an intense desire to become pregnant again.

It took Deborah even longer. In her forties, she has teenage children and she miscarried at eleven weeks. Her pregnancy was unplanned and came as a shock. She wanted to continue with the pregnancy but her husband wanted her to have an abortion. She refused.

> Six weeks after losing the baby I had a reaction. I received a card from a friend telling me she was pregnant and how she was hoping for a little girl. I raged. I sobbed, I was angry, I was jealous, I felt evil with hatred. Even The Archers radio programme distressed me: Jennifer Aldridge deciding to have a baby – she's in her forties. I couldn't bear to hear it, her yukkie husband all over her. I just ached and ached at the bloody romantic nonsense.

Maralyn compares her different reactions to her miscarriages.

> My first miscarriage was such a shock to the system that I cried from the moment I really understood what was going to happen. This time the emotion has taken a long time to reach the surface. Firstly, I was dazed and a non-believer – it couldn't happen again! Then, gradually, anger and guilt – I must have done something terrible for it to happen twice. Then being frightened that I must be terminally ill – cancer of the ovaries! Now, on going back to work two weeks, the tears have just continued. People

at work cannot cope with this crying and I feel a nuisance and therefore depressed. I continually sob and my heart aches with such pain. No one knows what anguish I feel and how I feel such a failure.

༄

Your Need to Grieve

Grieving is the healthy response to any loss – the death of someone close or the loss of your job. There is often an initial phase of shock and denial, of carrying on as if it hasn't happened, followed by a phase of personal disorganization. It is common to feel out of control, vulnerable, unable to cope and do the things you would normally take in your stride. You may find that you feel very angry, your moods are extreme and change very quickly and you feel guilty. This then gives way to a phase of loss and loneliness, a phase of depression, before it is possible to re-establish yourself and move forward, perhaps in a different direction from before.

 Grief after a miscarriage is complicated. You grieve for the lost baby, for the lost pregnancy and for lost motherhood. Because it is not generally perceived as an important loss, the ensuing grief is widely misunderstood. What is unique to the loss of miscarriage is that you know very little about who you are grieving for: the baby was a part of you, it is as if you are grieving the loss of a part of your self. The loss is private and hard for others to share. Added to which, few people may have known of your pregnancy.

I wanted to mourn the baby's death but it had never seemed real as a person, only real as an event that would affect our lives, and I had to adjust to the fact that those changes wouldn't happen now.

Often it is not recognized that it is legitimate to grieve after a miscarriage, particularly an early one. The lack of public acknowledgement and social definition can make you feel that your grief is unacceptable. Faced with these pressures it becomes hard to understand and express your feelings.

> I am still in the stage of realizing I was pleased to be pregnant and somehow it didn't seem acceptable to make a lot of fuss about the miscarriage. I didn't feel I could go overboard about it. I felt under pressure from myself not to mind too much.

For many women the realization that it is acceptable to grieve after their miscarriage becomes a turning point. Diana's father had died some years before. She compared the feelings she had after her miscarriage with the way she felt after his death.

> I began to cope much better and to be able to accept what had happened when I felt it was OK to mourn. Before then I had the feeling from other people that it's not such a big deal. Perhaps it's because they don't know how to deal with it and don't talk about it. So I ended up thinking it was just me moping around, and you don't get over it that way. When I started to grieve I felt OK about it and that I could get it out of my system. I know about grief. My father died and I grieved for about a year for him.

It is often through reading or talking with others that we begin to make sense of what is happening to ourselves.

> While reading I did begin to realize that I was experiencing the perfectly normal state of grief, and once I realized that I began to feel better. No one had ever just said that I was in grief and that mourning my loss was acceptable, understandable and necessary. I thought I was having some sort of breakdown – not at all!

It is easy to feel that grief for a miscarriage is a lesser grief, that it is not due the time and importance of a more acceptable grief. This becomes very obvious when there is the death of someone close to you around the time of the miscarriage, and the miscarriage is pushed into the background. Your own grief is overshadowed.

> It's a horrible, lonely, experience. My sister's baby died the same month and she got all the family sympathy because we all knew the baby – it was real to all of us. My baby was real to me and my partner.

It is often hard to take the time you need to grieve. There is pressure to get back to normal quickly, to pretend it never happened and to resume your usual responsibilities.

> Everyone expected me to be over it within a week and to be my old self again, but my baby had died, how could I laugh and joke? I wanted to talk, they changed the subject, fearing they hurt me.

> It tends to be 'swept under the carpet' after a time as if these babies didn't exist.

There may be pressures from those around you to meet their demands.

> My husband seemed to be becoming depressed so I did what everyone expected of me – pulled myself together and didn't talk about the experience any more. Perhaps that's why I need to now, a month afterwards. Everyone said I'd done well getting back into things.

The mismatch between the expectations others have of you and your own timing often means that when you are at your most depressed and most in need of support, help is least available. It took Jenny a couple of weeks to feel the full impact of her miscarriage at twelve weeks.

> By this time people had stopped being 'sympathetic', having found I'd apparently taken it so well. I don't think

they expected me to be depressed at this time, so I didn't get the support when I needed it most. The subject was avoided or forgotten.

Expressing Your Grief

Grieving is difficult for some women. You may not be used to expressing feelings freely and are perhaps more susceptible to the pressures to feel that miscarriage does not matter that much. It is easy in these circumstances to brush feelings aside, to ignore them, and suppress them. For some women to grieve is a more conscious process and they need time and space to allow feelings to come to the surface. Loraine did this in a very deliberate way after her miscarriage. Not everyone would want to take this active approach but it was helpful to her.

We spent a lot of time positively deciding to grieve about the baby by admitting it was a baby and not bothering what other people thought. We wanted to put it behind us but I didn't want to be the victim of burying things that come to the surface ten or fifteen years later. We were both prepared to cry about it, both prepared to get upset about it and both prepared to say to other people that we'd lost a baby rather than I'd had a miscarriage.

It can be very difficult to let go of your feelings perhaps because you fear what you may uncover, but bottling them up can be very painful.

Seven weeks after the loss of the baby the tears have yet to fall. Will the pain be less intense next week? Right now the pain seems almost tangible. I know I would feel better if I could cry, but the tears won't come.

Celia needed help to express her grief. She had not faced the feelings the miscarriage had aroused for her. She thought she was coping well emotionally, but physically she felt awful after her second miscarriage at nine weeks. She still felt pregnant and she was exhausted. She went to see her GP, who was very understanding.

> The doctor could find nothing wrong. My five minute appointment lasted twenty-five minutes. He asked me about my miscarriages and my feelings about them, about my mother's miscarriage and how I felt about that, and I broke down in tears. When I apologized for this 'soppiness' he explained that this was what I needed to do – to grieve for my lost babies, especially the last one who, because it didn't develop very far, I felt unable to recognize as a 'real' baby. I was glad it was a dark evening as I walked all the way home with tears streaming down my face, but the doctor was right. Within a week I felt much better and able to cope with life again. I did have to go through all the telling it over and over to anyone who would listen, but I had now acknowledged the baby's existence, rather than denying it.

Being given permission to grieve was the help that Celia needed.

ᔓ

Not All Women Grieve

Not everyone grieves after a miscarriage – if you don't see it as a loss of some kind, there will be nothing to grieve about. You may have understood it as an illness or a physical mishap which is soon to be rectified. Sue bled for seven weeks before miscarrying at seventeen weeks. She had never felt right about the pregnancy, feeling unwell all the way through, and so she had never felt 'properly pregnant' as she had done in her previous, successful pregnancy. She had never felt there was a baby there and when she had a missed abortion, she was told it was probably due to a blighted ovum. Her emotional experience paralleled the physical reality.

It was relief rather than grief. I don't think I have ever grieved for it. I wasn't ever aware that I was carrying a baby. I never got upset about it at all. I shed no tears and normally I cry quite easily. I felt sorry for myself because my husband had not rushed home from work to be by my bedside in casualty. I wanted to be looked after better, that was all. I came home and felt fit and full of energy, in fact, I felt quite high.

Pauline had not realized she was pregnant when she miscarried at six weeks. She was shocked, but not upset, when her GP suggested she had miscarried. She was not married and did not want to be tied down with a family. Sarah who miscarried at nine weeks had a clear understanding of why she had miscarried. She had not begun to think about her pregnancy in terms of a baby – that would come later. She already had a child and felt optimistic that she would have another.

I was very upset for about an hour at the time of the scan result. And then I felt sad and disappointed, and a bit upset, which lessened over the next couple of weeks. I wasn't going to fight against what my body was doing. If my body was going to expel the pregnancy, I wasn't going to will it not to, or get angry for it doing it, or feel it was my fault. I think of it as an illness, rather than the loss of a baby, and not a very bad illness at that. It was a physical thing that happened to me, and a very natural thing.

Pauline did not know she was pregnant. Sue and Sarah had little emotional investment in their pregnancy. The extent to which you have invested in your pregnancy seems to be central in influencing your subsequent feelings. If you have not begun to get attached to the baby then it is unlikely that the miscarriage will be an overwhelmingly distressing event. If, on the other hand you have, it is almost certain that you will experience the miscarriage as a loss with all the feelings that may arouse.

૨૭

Depression

Depression is a natural response to loss and part of the grieving process. Many women describe how at some point after their miscarriage they went through a phase of feeling very low, tired, lethargic, with no energy and interest in life at all. They felt worthless and without confidence. It can be a very bleak time when you feel helpless and hopeless. If you get depressed after the miscarriage this may affect your physical health. Changes in appetite and sleeping habits are common symptoms of depression: some women say they want to sleep all the time or they find it hard to sleep, and that they either eat too much or too little. Pat described herself as depressed, down and very tired all the time.

> I wasn't unwell, just tired and I ate too much afterwards. I came out of hospital at my normal weight but eighteen months later I'm still trying to lose the weight I put on. It was comfort-eating – I stuffed chocolates. And I didn't sleep well because I was having terrible dreams.

A recent study in Oxford demonstrated that almost half the women interviewed a month after their miscarriage were clinically depressed. This is four times the number you would expect to be depressed in a random group of women.[2] Another study in Sheffield showed that a high proportion of women did get depressed at some point in the six months following the miscarriage but that the depression may not become evident immediately; the lack of depression in the first two weeks was no indication of whether depression would occur.[3] Both studies clearly show that depression is very common after a miscarriage. Some women feel depressed for a few days only, others for weeks or months. Some women suffer more acutely and may require a great deal of support and professional help (see Chapter 11). Gina describes how she felt after her second miscarriage.

I felt a complete lack of enthusiasm for anything in life. I felt I had no purpose in life, and my life was not 'worthwhile' or of any good to anybody. I saw my life in the long term and lost sight of small, everyday events. I looked for a grand scheme to devote my life to in place of the vocation of being a mother. I felt anger and jealousy. Sometimes I could turn the anger to my advantage and say to myself, 'I'm not going to let life get me down – why should I be so miserable?' I felt inferior to people who are parents, I overcame this by developing a feeling of superiority because I had suffered and they were merely 'spoilt children' who had had life easy and didn't know how difficult life could be. Gradually I became more philosophical.

Frances was very distressed by her miscarriage at eleven weeks. Looking back she finds her behaviour quite strange. Her pregnancy had not been confirmed until she miscarried although she had been unwell for some weeks and had worried that she was ill.

I shut myself away: I closed the curtains at the front of the house; I didn't answer the phone; I was too frightened to venture out of the house; I left the front of the house in darkness. I couldn't face the outside world. I lived in the back of the house with James [her one-year-old son]. I can honestly say I think I was quite mad for about a week. I stayed behind locked doors for four days. I couldn't let my husband know. If he phoned and I didn't answer, I'd just say we were asleep or up the garden. But by 5.30 pm the lights went on – I just couldn't admit to being so stupid. I got dragged out of it by the normal routine, things had to be done. When I stopped being upset about it, I just felt very low.

Gemma also thought she was going mad when she found herself crying in the garden in the middle of the night. Cherry was worried about herself when, shortly after the miscarriage, she got out of the bath and found she had wrapped up a towel in the shape of a baby and was rocking it. Although it is very frightening, it is not unusual to do things without fully realizing what you are doing, when you are very distressed.

It may seem endless at the time but depression usually passes of its own accord. But it may take some time. When you are depressed your ability to solve problems is reduced and if you withdraw from normal activities you are also withdrawing from things that might make you feel better. It helps if you can break this cycle. Frances had her one-year-old son to look after and was dragged out of her depression by the daily routine. Other women find it helpful to write down how they are feeling as a way of unburdening themselves or monitoring their own thoughts and feelings.

Feeling Unable to Cope

This is how some of the women I talked to described their reactions to their miscarriage:

I find being at work very hard, unable to really concentrate.

I became frightened that my husband would die and that there would be no one. He didn't understand that.

I couldn't let my partner out of my sight, not even to the newsagents. I was so sure I would lose him too.

I hate being alone in the evenings. I now feel vulnerable and not in control.

My judgement was askew and my confidence almost nil.

I could cry at anything, without warning I would burst into tears. I lost all my confidence. I even found it difficult to drive. I just couldn't cope with anything.

When I was with people I wanted to be on my own and when I was on my own I wanted to be with people.

I was very unpleasant to be with because I was so miserable.

I was still incapable of coping with big crowds of people and a queue in a shop would send me into a real state. I felt as if I was gradually losing my grip on reality.

Particular parts of the day may be worse than others. Sue said she found evenings hardest, especially bedtime, as she was tired and more vulnerable to outbursts of crying. Pat found night-time the worst.

I used to have all these dreams of this baby coming out of my stomach. When you're in bed you tend to think about things a bit more because it's quiet. I used to get more upset at night. In the day I'd be very busy – I'd perhaps think about something and cry for five minutes and then get on.

᪥

Guilt

Many women worry that they are to blame for their miscarriage. Was it caused by something I did or did not do? Could I have prevented it? It is highly unlikely that the miscarriage is 'your fault'. The lack of a clear medical explanation means that many women have to reach their own understanding of why it happened, based on what has been said to them by medical staff, discussions with other women (particularly those who have also experienced a miscarriage) and written information, and this is an important part of the recovery process.

Women who have a clear understanding of what has happened to them and a probable explanation for why it happened, are less likely to feel guilty. It was fairly clear that Sue's miscarriage was as a result of a blighted ovum. She felt that there was little she could have done about this and that it probably would not happen again. The absence of any clear explanation and the need to search for a reason make it very easy for women to take the responsibility upon themselves and search their own lives for the cause of the miscarriage. Elaine felt a general sense of guilt.

> For about a year after the miscarriage I didn't try for a child. During that time I used to think about it a lot, in a very negative way. And I would think about it as a failure on my part, which I know is totally wrong, and I don't blame myself for anything that happened, but underneath it all I still feel guilty that I have failed in some way.

Jenny took the responsibility on herself.

> I felt like I had murdered my baby. After all no one else had anything to do with it dying, it was me. I still don't know what I did wrong.

Teresa blamed her enjoyment of the New Year festivities.

> When I thought about it afterwards I conceived over New Year, when I was drinking heavily and smoking too much and generally having a good time. You think, well it's obviously all my fault. I shouldn't have such an unhealthy lifestyle. You do think you've done something terribly wrong and don't deserve to be pregnant. I felt guilty and blamed myself.

Pat had not wanted to be pregnant. She was using the mini-pill and was also breastfeeding. She already had two children and while she wanted a third at some point she did not feel ready. She decided against a termination and began to adjust to the pregnancy and was getting quite excited about it.

Then to lose it makes it worse, makes you feel really guilty because to begin with we'd said we didn't want it. I can remember saying that the best thing that could happen would be if I lost it. Then when it happened the guilt you feel is tremendous. I felt like I was being punished for not wanting it initially.

Lisa directed the blame away from herself. She already had a child from a previous relationship.

I blamed my partner. I argued with him saying it was all his fault because I could have children. I think now that was really hurtful. People used to say to me I should get a man who could do it properly.

It is easy to feel a generalized sense of responsibility and to look for things in your life that would have made a difference. Val found herself doing this.

My husband and I were in some difficulties. I had been involved with someone else for some time and felt trapped by my marriage, unable to leave because of my daughter, wanting to maintain my other relationship as it was so important to me and yet make the most of what I had with my husband, and create as good a family life as I could. The decision to have another child was almost an act of faith that all this was possible. I contracted a bad virus infection early on in the pregnancy which probably caused the miscarriage. If I hadn't been so emotionally vulnerable, I may not have been so susceptible to the infection. I felt guilty that I had not looked after myself properly and neither had anybody else.

There may be some truth in this but it is very easy to be unnecessarily hard on yourself, to criticize and almost punish yourself for your failure. Margaret felt very responsible for her two miscarriages, which combined with infertility problems, had come to dominate her life.

My husband had put away the few things we had for the baby, like the cot which my sister had given us, but I had to keep looking at it and getting out all the tiny baby clothes my mum and I had knitted over the years and touching them. I was hurting myself on purpose I suppose, as a punishment for failing again.

As well as feeling guilty some women have a strong sense of having let other people down.

I feel guilty that my daughter will not have a sister or brother. I feel I have failed her and also my mother-in-law who loves children and was an only child herself.

My mother tried to help but I felt I had let her down most of all. I may never be able to give her the grandchild she so much wanted and I didn't want to make her suffer any more by letting her know how badly I felt.

Feelings of guilt, blame and responsibility are very common and quite understandable, but you cannot change what has happened. It is important to be able to leave those feelings in the past where they belong and not to carry them into the future.

ᢌ

The Time-scale of Grief

Many women describe how their grief peaks and then fades, their feelings about the miscarriage become less intense, the times when they are upset less frequent. For some women this happens earlier than for others. There is no set time-scale. Immediately after her miscarriage Veronica used to cry every night.

Then I'd find I hadn't cried for a few days. Like any grief, I realize since I lost my dad, it passes slowly. I used to get through one day. My husband was very understanding. He knew I'd get through.

As you begin to move forward you will probably have good days and bad days. Six weeks after her miscarriage, Shirley found she still was getting upset.

I still have very weepy moments (like just finding out my sister-in-law is pregnant). I also have incredibly black moods – most uncharacteristic of me. They may last for a few hours or all day.

Jan was in tears most of the weekend after her miscarriage, then she felt low and glum until three months later, when she was pregnant again. Four months after her miscarriage Pat was still getting very upset. It was only when another five months had passed that she felt her grief had diminished and life was looking up again. Diana described how she felt at the time of her miscarriage.

It was difficult for a few weeks after. I was calm most of the time but the slightest upset and I burst into tears. I couldn't handle anything additional. To begin with I got upset every couple of weeks, now [ten months' later] I get upset every six weeks or so and I'm much more controlled.

Grief has to take its course. You cannot force yourself through it or make it go away and it is important to do things in your own time. It may surprise you how long your feelings of sadness persist. Hilary describes the phases she went through.

Initially I was terribly upset, crying all the time. Then we went on holiday to France for two weeks and that was very healing. Then I felt much better. But I was upset on and off until he should have been born. That was a turning point.

Diana was very aware of the date her baby was due.

> The very day I was due we had visitors and I thought well perhaps that's just as well I don't have to stop and think about it. It was a couple of days later when the visitors had gone and things had quietened down in the house that I did talk to my husband about it. I didn't want to make a big thing out of it. But I did feel very low. It hasn't been as bad as that since.

Grief after a miscarriage can pass quite quickly or it can linger. Most of the women I met felt they grieved the loss of their baby, although the extent of their grief varied. It becomes easier for some women once they are pregnant again. Getting pregnant can be a protection from the sadness the due date might bring. Others do not feel free to get pregnant until the baby they miscarried would have been born. Time helps but it is through sharing and expressing your feelings and making sense of what has happened that the grief eventually passes.

Sharing the miscarriage

Sharing the experience is, for many women, the way forward, a turning point in their grief. It does not take away the pain but it may be eased if you feel understood and know you are not alone. Many women say how they need people to be with them, to understand their feelings, their vulnerability and confusion, to share their sadness, to care and acknowledge that something important has happened. The response of other people can be crucial in helping you through the difficult time after the miscarriage. This chapter looks at the difficulties you may encounter in sharing the miscarriage with your partner, family and friends, and the alternative sources of support available.

~

The Power of Others to Help or Hinder

While in many ways it does not matter what other people think about something so personal, particularly those less close to you, lack of understanding can make a miscarriage a very alienating experience and add to the sense of isolation you may feel. It is much harder if the people around you don't understand, pretend the miscarriage has not happened or treat it as if it is nothing to get upset about when you are feeling very sad. Beth, who had two miscarriages, one at eight and one at eleven weeks, found other people's comments particularly upsetting.

> When I told one of my friends her first comment was 'Was it planned?' Of course we really wanted our baby, it had become part of our lives, we talked to it, made plans including it etc. One old aunt's comment was 'You young girls, we never had this in our day!' As if it were my fault. I think you feel guilty enough without comments like that. A lot of friends said at least we'd got one healthy baby and we could try again, but you don't think like that – we just wanted the baby we'd lost. I don't really think our families could understand me grieving, 'It's better losing it now than when it's bigger, that must be awful.' My sister told me of someone having a stillbirth and said that must be worse. But to me I didn't see it like that.

Beth felt that no one had looked forward to the birth of her baby and therefore no one cared when it died. People may not know you are pregnant or assume because you miscarried early 'it doesn't matter' and 'wasn't a real baby'. Zoe, who miscarried at fourteen weeks, also found other people's reactions hurtful and felt that they did not understand about miscarriage.

> When I came home my husband, mother and friends just didn't know what to say, so pretended that nothing had happened. I now know that they were all very upset and friends left quickly as they had all had babies recently with no problems. I felt a complete outsider – everyone stopped talking about babies when I approached and I was hurt that no one ever mentioned the event. If that had been a normal bereavement people would at least have expressed sympathy. I was given the feeling that I wasn't supposed to be upset but should just get on with life as it was before I was pregnant – being grateful for my little daughter.

By acknowledging what has happened and recognising the meaning it has for you, the confirmation others give can be very supportive. Although living several thousand miles away, Diana's family recognised the importance of the miscarriage.

> My mother, my grandmother, my sister and my brother and his wife all wrote to me. My grandmother sent me some money and said I was to buy something for myself, which is what she always does.

Linda's friends were very supportive.

> They came to see me, talked to me, lots of people. I got lots of flowers which meant an awful lot. I don't know why, but it did. People offered to babysit so we could go out.

Like many other women Linda valued the practical support her friends gave – one woman said what she needed most after her miscarriage was a housekeeper and a childminder for a couple of weeks. Practical help and understanding can make a bad experience manageable. The comments, attitudes and actions of those around you are very powerful in confirming or legitimating your experience, in helping or in hindering you.

ॐ

Your Needs

Some women say they need to talk and talk about what has happened to them and consequently feel they are being very demanding on those they are close to. Talking about the miscarriage makes it a shared event rather than a purely private and personal one. Some women feel that they were never pregnant when afterwards they have nothing to show for it. Julia felt she talked over the same ground again and again, without getting anywhere. She felt conscious of not overwhelming or boring her friends and husband. Pat talked about it to her husband every night.

> I used to go over it in great detail; we went down, sat in that corridor, when I had the D and C they did this . . . I went over the whole event again and again. My husband was very supportive and put up with it, but he did get fed up with it after a few weeks and he wasn't really listening. But I needed to go over it again and again and again to get it out of my system.

Pat wanted other people to remember her baby long after most had forgotten. She wanted others to acknowledge her feelings. Heather had two miscarriages, one at eleven and another at fifteen weeks. She found talking made her babies more real and helped her to remember her loss.

> I found I wanted to talk about them a lot, as if by doing this they were still with me, and it did help. Now I can talk and think a lot, and have a special feeling that is mine, and it doesn't upset me that family and friends don't show this as much.

But it isn't just talking that is important. Often there is nothing you or anyone else can say. Miscarriage is usually distressing and it is important to be able to express your emotions, to release the pain and sadness you may be feeling. You need someone to understand and be with you, to know what you feel, not necessarily to feel the same but to feel it with you, someone who will allow you to express your feelings, to cry and to be sad, if that is how you feel, and not jolly you along and pretend everything is normal. Karen got this sort of support from her husband.

> He just held me in his arms and I cried and cried. He never rushed me or told me to snap out of it when I got depressed. He let me take things at my own pace for which I am eternally grateful.

Veronica's partner was with her at the time of her miscarriage.

> He just sat and held my hand all that time. He was with me
> from 10 till 5 pm when the baby was born. He never went
> out of the room once. He wouldn't leave me, he was
> terrific. If we ever split up I would never forget what he
> did for me then. I think that helped tremendously.

Talking and expressing your feelings about something as
sensitive as a miscarriage is easier for some women than
others. You may feel very confused and unsure, bottling up
your feelings because there is nobody to share them with or
because you are frightened of the consequences if you let go.
Joanna feared what might happen if she wrote freely of her
three miscarriages.

> If I was to write down everything it would be a flood.
> Would I be in control at the end of it? . . . I have sat here
> thinking about what I have just written for half an hour. It
> sounds daft to the 'old' me. The 'new' me feels like a timid
> shadow and worse after the last year's experiences.

Susanna had not shared her feeling with anyone.

> I cannot discuss the emotional side with anyone. I do not
> know how I feel and I do not know what to do about it, so
> I shelve all my feelings away. People I meet say how jolly I
> am and how well I cope but really I don't think I have
> come to terms with anything.

If you are not used to accepting help from others but someone
who normally manages well on your own, you can end up
pretending to yourself, as well as to everybody else, that you
are coping, and so shut yourself off from the help that might
be available.

࿖

Sharing the Experience with Your Partner

Many women turn to their partners for the support they need when they miscarry. It may only be you and your partner who feel the loss of your baby and who can help each other through the bad times. Linda found her husband particularly helpful when she got very upset a couple of weeks after her miscarriage.

> He was very good and he did spend a lot of time talking to me and listening to me, helping me sort things out, really listening, because he made lots of suggestions. He was actually taking in what I'd said because he'd say 'I was thinking about what you said yesterday and do you think maybe it's because you feel this . . . ' He was really good at that.

Susan had had three miscarriages and needed her husband's support and encouragement to try again. Without his belief in her that she would eventually have a successful pregnancy she would have found it hard to keep going.

> In my case it was of tremendous importance that my husband remained at all times positive and optimistic about the problem and determined to win. Unlike my gynaecologist, who I felt could leave us 'in limbo' for endless months, my husband always ensured that we were doing something about the problem – getting information about possible treatments, being tested by other doctors for possible defects, etc. He always promised me that we would have a superb child, no matter what, even if we had to adopt. This was a great comfort.

Kaye felt she was letting her husband down and needed his reassurance after her second miscarriage.

I said to him why don't you leave me and go and find someone who can give you a child? I thought I was stopping him from having a normal life. He's ever so kind and deserves a lot better. We talked about it later and he was very hurt by that. He said he'd married me and not anyone else. He reassured me that it was me that he wanted and if we couldn't have children we'd have a good life, just the two of us.

Many women say their partner is supportive but not the most supportive person to them. Over three-quarters of the women in the survey said their partner was helpful but under a third named him as one of those most helpful. It may come as a shock to find your partner is unable to understand your feelings or meet your emotional needs as fully as you would have wished or expected. Even if you do not expect him to be supportive, it can be hurtful when you feel vulnerable and needy. Jane wanted her partner to hug her and tell her it would be all right but she knew he found this difficult. Sue's husband did not come to see her in hospital until the day after the miscarriage. On reflection she felt it might have been worse if he had been there.

We just wouldn't have known what to say to each other. I think I coped better on my own, but I wanted more from him than he could give. He didn't really respond to me. We talked a lot about it and shared it on an academic level, rather than on a feeling level. He's not a good communicator.

Women who say their partners are unhelpful say that they are uncomfortable with expressing strong emotions, that they do not show their feelings and they appear to fail to understand the significance of the miscarriage. Pauline did not expect much help from her husband.

My husband was in the same place as me when I miscarried but he wasn't 'with' me. He hadn't been very helpful, perhaps he doesn't know how. He's not the kind of chap to talk it through or get emotional. He's not a great communicator and when something like this happens he clams up.

Anne needed to cry and talk about her experience, but her husband could not or would not and needed to 'shut it out of his mind'. Carla felt she was 'getting on her husband's nerves' and she never found out what his true feelings were. Joan said her husband was very concerned for her at the time of the miscarriage, but afterwards he thought everything was all right. He could not understand why she kept on crying. It may be difficult to get across the depth and complexity of what you feel, especially if you continue to feel upset for some time after the miscarriage.

The Experience for Your Partner

The miscarriage may have been a very upsetting experience for your partner: the physical aspects can be very alarming and he may have seen you in pain and distress and felt helpless to alleviate it. Debbie's husband said he felt he could be supportive but that seemed so inadequate and there was little else he could do. The hospital may be a very frightening place. He may be unsure what procedures involve and what will be done to you. He may fear he will lose you. Jan's partner was very worried when she did not come back from theatre at the time he had been told to expect her.

> He was very frightened because I'd lost a lot of blood. I was delayed going down to theatre and he just thought I'd been down there an incredibly long time and that something had happened to me.

If you are very upset and emotionally distressed or very dependent and demanding, it can be overwhelming for your partner. Frances said she expected her husband to 'anticipate her needs

139

in advance' which, looking back, she knows was totally unreasonable. Mary felt she took it all out on her husband, 'I vented my depression and anxiety on him but fortunately he took it and he understood.' Loraine was aware that her husband was totally confused and worried by her behaviour over the few weeks after her miscarriage. She wished someone had warned him. If you have never experienced grief before, watching someone close to you display the extremes of emotion which grief entails can be quite alarming.

Men have the conflicting responsibilities to both their partner and the unborn child. It seems it is common that concern about their partner takes precedence when attachment to the unborn baby is less strong.

> He had been more concerned about the effect on me than about losing the baby itself. Perhaps he hadn't been able to picture the baby so much as me with feeling sick and getting a small bump and sore breasts.

Some women find their partner's apparent lack of concern about the loss of the baby upsetting. Ginny's husband regarded the miscarriage as a 'set-back' which the birth of their son made up for and Paula's as a 'hold up' to the completion of their family, rather than a loss in itself. For some couples this difference makes it hard to share the experience. Alternatively your partner may view the miscarriage as a sort of illness. Elaine had two miscarriages and although her partner did get upset about it, his feelings were very different from hers.

> He was very upset, but not in the same way. To this day he doesn't understand how emotional I feel about it. To him it was more like having an operation. I was an invalid and I had something to get over. He didn't feel any emotional link to the unborn child. He didn't feel they were his. They were something that was in progress. I don't think he felt it as a bereavement at all.

It is common for men to feel disappointed rather than to grieve when their partner miscarries. A man has not experienced the sense of connection with the unborn child that a woman may have felt and he is less likely to have the intense feelings of sadness that some women feel. At the time this may be hard to understand and it may make it difficult to understand how your partner is feeling.

> The baby wasn't real to him, so the distress wasn't the same for my husband as it was for me. I was very angry with him, accusing him of not caring about the baby we had lost.

> I felt he was being unsympathetic at times and found it difficult that he wasn't as emotionally upset as me. It made me feel very insecure.

Men Have Feelings Too

While men are less likely to have invested as much in the pregnancy this is obviously not true for all men. Some will have been anticipating the birth of a child with great pleasure, they will have become attached to the unborn child and so they will feel an enormous sense of loss. It was Alice's second marriage but her husband's first; she already had a son.

> He was very upset. He was very sad at leaving me in hospital. He said he stopped off at the fish and chip shop on the way home and could have cried his eyes out. I think it affected him more than me, being his first.

Wendy's husband had seen their baby on a scan the day before she miscarried.

> We were told it was a viable, healthy pregnancy. As a result he, too, was devastated this time and was very tender towards me.

When you are upset yourself it is easy to forget about other people's needs and to ignore their feelings. Caroline felt she was so bound up with what was happening to her that she could not see her husband's pain. Kaye wanted her husband to be strong for her.

> He needed support when I couldn't give it. I'd always depended on my husband. After I lost the baby I looked round and he was crying. That was the worst thing of the whole lot, to see him, whom I've always seen as the strong support in my life, crying. I couldn't understand why he cried when I needed him most. I was so wrapped up in myself and the miscarriage, it took me a while to realise – he's going through what I'm going through.

Men are often less skilled at expressing their feelings or they do it differently than women. It is easy to think your partner does not care and to feel angry and frustrated with him, when in fact he is not showing what he feels. Penny and her husband rowed because he would not talk about the miscarriage. It was only then that he showed how hurt he had been. Gail initially thought her husband did not care so much but she realised later that he did. He was silent and kept his feelings to himself but his stress allergy got worse. Pat only realised how upset her husband had been when, a few months after the miscarriage, he spoke about his feelings at a support group they were attending.

> I couldn't believe what I was hearing. I didn't know the half of what he was feeling. He did get upset about it but he was trying to be strong for me because I got upset. I wanted him to be upset and show that he cared because I thought he didn't.

Some men feel they have to be strong and do not express their feelings. If you have been very distressed and dependent on your partner, it leave little space for him. Nina's husband could not begin to cry about it until she was more able to cope. Jill's husband was depressed for a while once she was fit and well again. It may only be when you are feeling better that his feelings emerge.

So whilst for most women their partner is a source of support the miscarriage is also likely to put the relationship under some strain. It is often difficult to meet each other's needs. Those closest to you are not necessarily the best people to help you. A lot of women need to turn to other people, as well, to get the support and understanding they need.

⌇

Mothers and Mothers-in-law

Some women will turn to their families for the support they need. Over a tenth of the women in the survey said their mother was one of the three most helpful people. It may seem natural to want to share the miscarriage with your mother. The birth of a child is a big event in a mother/daughter relationship, a time of change and, sometimes, a time of getting closer again. You may feel vulnerable and more child-like yourself, in need of a good mother. Tricia said her mother listened, talked and let her cry, and gave her time to come to terms with her grief. Judith thought her mother felt as bad as she did and was grateful for her support.

It can be disappointing if you do not get the response you feel you need or expected from your mother. Several women told me that the miscarriage was a turning point in their relationships with their parents, of realising they had to be independent or of facing up to change. After her miscarriage Jenny went to stay with her parents but she couldn't stand it and came home to her husband. Margot felt her mother was her biggest disappointment.

She has had three miscarriages and six children! She seemed so matter-of-fact and, at time, thoughtless. She is normally so loving and caring, it hurt that she didn't seem to understand. It's not that you want attention the whole time, but a hug or asking how you feel, goes a long way.

Miscarriage is not always an easy subject to talk about with your mother, especially if you have not been open about such things in the past. Lil said her mother just did not know what to say so they did not talk about it. Kath was unable to talk to her mother because her attitude was 'never mind, there'll be another' and she wanted the baby she had lost, not another one. The miscarriage may be painful to your mother. It may arouse feelings about her own experiences which she wishes to leave behind, especially if she lost a baby herself. Caroline found her mother's distress difficult to deal with.

> My mother kept crying all the time. It was as if she had lost the baby. Her crying upset me. I wasn't upset when I phoned her but by the time I'd finished I was in a right state. Who had I been having the baby for?

She may find your distress painful and feel helpless to do anything about it. It is of course also a loss for your mother too. Pat thought her mother was as upset as she was herself. Her mother said to her at one point, 'You know I've lost this baby too.'

Some women find their mother actively unhelpful. You may feel very let down if you expect help which she cannot provide and this may arouse feelings from the past about not getting what you wanted and needed from her, or about unresolved difficulties between you. Just under a tenth of women in they survey said their mother was one of the three least helpful people to them. Linda expected little from her mother but still found she was angry with her reaction.

> My mother was dreadful. I was feeling so depressed. She's very 'life is unfair' and you have to get on with it. She never once said 'oh, I'm sorry' or 'this must be very hard for you'.

You mother may not deal with emotional issues very well or have little understanding of what miscarriage is about, or what it has meant to you, and your parents may have strong feelings about the pregnancy which influence their reaction. Lisa was eighteen and unmarried. Her family came to visit her.

> Their visit greatly upset me. Certainly nobody could say they were sorry, as nobody was. My mother's view was that 'it was all for the best'; my older sister was relieved because she had been annoyed that I had got pregnant before her.

There may be other people in your family with whom you are particularly close or people in your family with whom you are regularly in contact who seem very insensitive. These women found relationships with their mothers-in-law particularly difficult.

> My mother-in-law uttered the classic statement on hearing that Pete was having blood and sperm tests, '. . . but why? There is nothing wrong with him. It's not his fault.' I don't think he has ever felt quite the same way towards her since then.

> My mother-in-law said I had brought bad luck to her son and I was cursed both the times.

> On return home my mother-in-law had all the answers. It was my fault for lifting my son, not relaxing, doing the home pregnancy test, etc.

These ignorant comments are particularly hurtful because they place blame firmly on the woman's shoulders and they may be hard to ignore.

א

Friends

Friends can do all the things women find helpful after a miscarriage; they can understand, care, be with you, listen, talk and help out. Some women (over a fifth of the women in the survey) find friends more helpful then anyone else, and it is with them that they primarily share the miscarriage. It may be easier to talk to women friends; you may find them more sympathetic, particularly if they have experienced a miscarriage or a loss themselves. Pauline got little support from her husband but she wanted to talk to someone she was close to.

> I think the best people I've spoken to have been best friends of mine, women who can relate to what has happened. I've got a couple of women friends who've had miscarriages since I've had mine. I think they understand a lot more than men.

Friends can be as unhelpful as anyone else. In the survey just under a fifth said that friends were among the least helpful people. Judith was very disappointed that one of her close friends did not make time for her to talk about her miscarriage. On reflection she realised it may have been too difficult, arousing feelings about the abortions she had had. Many women, like Linda, find that they need support over a longer period of time than their friends realise.

> There was a rush of support for the first two weeks which is probably why I was fine, and then it tailed off and things got back to normal. It was almost euphoria. All this attention, and suddenly I felt on my own, with no baby, and I had to go back to work as if nothing had happened. It all just felt impossible.

꒰

Support Groups

The only people who mentioned it without my mentioning it were people who'd had miscarriages. I appreciated them. Some women feel that it is hard for people who have not experienced a miscarriage to understand what they are going through. Of course not all women who have miscarried are sensitive to others' needs but there is something about the general lack of awareness about miscarriages that makes those who may have had similar experiences especially important.

> By the end of the week I had discovered how pointless it can be trying to talk about miscarriage to people who have no experience of one, or of any other bereavement. I started to dread the question 'How are you?' and it seemed easier to say 'fine' or 'better' than to explain how I really felt, as it made other people uncomfortable.

It is because women and their partners find it helpful to talk with others who have been through a similar experience that miscarriage support groups have been set up. The Miscarriage Association is a voluntary organisation with support groups and telephone contacts, run by women who have experienced a miscarriage themselves. The National Childbirth Trust also has some support groups. Most have regular, informal meetings as well as contacts you can talk to over the phone. It is an opportunity to talk without feeling you are imposing or going on and on. The Miscarriage Association publishes a regular newsletter and information leaflets. Most groups have a small library of books that you can borrow.

Contacting a support group is not what everyone needs but if you feel you would like more information or would like to talk to someone who has had a miscarriage you may find it helpful. Plucking up the courage to phone someone you have never met before may be difficult, but many find the support they get invaluable, especially during the immediate after-math.

> My GP gave me the address of the Miscarriage Association whom I wrote to immediately, pouring out all my troubles. Their newsletter became a lifeline and I knew I wasn't alone and that there were others far worse off than myself. I also realised that my feelings of grief were perfectly natural and that I should be allowed to grieve as a natural healing process.

Others take longer to feel they need to approach someone outside their immediate circle.

> It wasn't until about three months after the miscarriage that I contacted the Miscarriage Association. I was still feeling depressed and by then everyone around me had forgotten all about it. I felt alone and needed people who understood to talk to.

Some women, when they become pregnant again, value support from others who appreciate their anxiety, and know that it can be an extremely worrying time. After meeting other women with similar experiences one woman said she was relieved that she was not going mad, that others felt the same, and another that she was not some kind of freak for feeling as badly as she did.

சு

Seeking Help from Professionals

Sometimes it is easier to talk and share your feelings with a more objective outsider, perhaps a health visitor, midwife, GP or a counsellor. It often does not matter what professional background the person is from, it is the quality of their under-standing and the time they can give you that are important.

Pauline talked at length with her health visitor.

> Talking with her brought it all out in the open and shifted a whole load off my shoulders. Once you've done that with someone you feel a whole load better. You don't have to carry it round with you any more. She sat and listened, which is what I wanted.

Lucy's health visitor visited her weekly for a while then reduced the frequency of the visits when she realised Lucy was coming to terms with her experience. But Lucy and Pauline were lucky, it is not routine for health visitors to visit women who miscarry although some will let the women know they can be contacted. They could play an important role in providing those women who want it, with the opportunity to talk about their miscarriage. In a few areas community midwives offer a similar opportunity. Both health visitors and community midwives tend to follow-up women who miscarry later in pregnancy and, unfortunately, the importance of this sort of support for those who lose a baby early in pregnancy is often unrecognised.

If your health visitor and GP have not been very helpful or are too busy and do not seem to understand about miscarriage, but you feel you need help that your friends and family cannot provide, it is hard to know where to turn. Hilary approached a homeopath, at a friend's suggestion, because she could not cope with the milk she was producing after her miscarriage at twenty-two weeks. He proved to be far more helpful to her than she ever imagined.

> I felt dreadful, physically, and was depressed and crying all the time. I ended up seeing him for about a year. He was tremendously helpful. Talking to him enabled me to take on the emotional strength of it all and to express and explore the feelings I had and feel that was OK.

Amelia had seen a therapist before and when she found herself unable to cope after her miscarriage she went to see him again.

He was wonderful – in one session allowing me to understand the grieving process and not to try to hide away
from it.

Lorna was helped to express her grief by her therapist.

The therapy I was doing enabled me to really express this
grief, so that although the pain will always be with me in a
sense, I don't blame myself any more, and don't feel I have
to be 'brave' and hold on to my feelings or hide them.
There is so little space in our society for a healthy expression of grief. I have been lucky to have had this kind of
support, a much more active kind than the usual plati-
tudes served up by people who really wish grieving people
would go away.

These women found the help they needed from a variety of
sources. If you want further help it is worth approaching your
GP or health visitor. If they are unable to offer help themselves they may be able to refer you to someone else. Some GP
practices have counsellors and social workers attached to the
surgery. Clinical psychologists usually offer a counselling
service and your GP would have to refer you. Services vary
enormously in different localities but in some areas there may
be a drop-in centre where you can see a counsellor without
prior referral. There will also be counsellors and therapists
working privately whom you can contact yourself. These
opportunities are normally only open to women who can pay.
(See page 276 for suggestions of where to go for further help.)

WHEN IT'S MORE DIFFICULT

When it happens again . . . and again . . . and again: Repeated miscarriage

I started to get crampy feelings in the pit of my stomach, like in period pains. The possibility of miscarrying suddenly flashed through my mind. I had believed it couldn't possibly happen to me again. This was such a different pregnancy. My world turned upside down again and I was totally unprepared for it.

Kim assumed her first miscarriage was just bad luck. A second miscarriage can be more of a shock than the first or it can be an anticipated event. Some women lose confidence and assume they will miscarry their next pregnancy. Others experience intense anger as opposed to sadness because it has happened to them again. A third can become quite routine. One way of protecting yourself from the pain of another potential loss is to expect failure, another way is to distance yourself from the reality of the pregnancy. One woman said that after several pregnancies she no longer related to the fetus as a baby.

For women who have had several miscarriages there may be one that stands out as particularly traumatic, either because of the nature of the miscarriage or because of the meaning of that particular pregnancy and the hopes that were pinned on it. The grief of recurrent miscarriage can accumulate to erupt after a particularly distressing event. Cathy had five early miscarriages; her sixth pregnancy was successful following immunotherapy.

The first miscarriage was just a shock, then when it happened again it just seemed unfair. When the third happened I expected nothing else and the fourth was like going to the dentist it was so familiar. The fifth was devastating as I had seen it on a scan at seven weeks, a little forming baby with clear limb buds and a heartbeat, so to see it dead two weeks later on a scan was dreadful. We both went through an extended grieving process which was a very difficult time as we were arguing about the next step.

In this chapter the issues that are raised by repeated miscarriage, whether it be two or five or more, will be considered – the personal impact, the issues of cause and treatment and the steps women can take to help themselves.

ج

The Impact of Repeated Miscarriage

It is rare to have five miscarriages before a successful pregnancy, but having two or three is not so unusual. Some women have a pattern of miscarriages interspersed with a successful pregnancy. Even if, after one miscarriage, you recover quite quickly and remain optimistic, it is harder to be so unaffected by a second or third. Your confidence is undermined and it comes to play a dominant part in your life – trying to get pregnant, worrying about staying pregnant, miscarrying, feeling miserable afterwards and wondering if you can face it all again. Miscarriage can become a way of life, as it was for Cathy.

I feel as if I lost five years of my life – 1988 is the first year I haven't been pregnant since we got married in 1981. I was either trying, knew I was, or recovering and, consequently, my activities were restricted.

Cathy wrote this about the impact her miscarriages had had on her:

I'm now a stone lighter than I was when I was first pregnant. Any illness or upset and I lose weight rapidly. My menstrual cycle has become more regular and I became very aware of the process of the cycle, much more in tune with my body. In between pregnant states I improved my diet, took more exercise and, despite it all, I think I'm fitter and healthier now. Emotionally I completely lost my self confidence. I was unable to make decisions or choices, just wanted to be on my own, cried in shops etc, felt aggressive towards pregnant women and parents who complained about their children. I had anxiety and panic attacks. Why me? Why is my body letting me down?

The consequences of miscarriage affect other areas of your life. Some women feel they are preoccupied and unavailable to their partner and children, unable to be with them as they would wish. It can have a profound effect on your relationship with your partner. He may be reluctant to try again and feel he is just being used. Other women feel their work suffers from their lack of energy and interest and so it can be a time of reassessing life and making new priorities. As a result some women make important changes: giving up a job or going part-time at work, spending more time with their partner, family and friends or moving house. It can be impossible to make any longer-term plans in case you are pregnant. Mary said:

It affects my whole life. Future plans have to bear in mind the thought that I might be pregnant, in which case I would have to curtail my activities. And now that I have a child I have to consider his welfare and the strain on my husband if I should be in hospital. No outside agency seems to be able to offer any practical help in this situation.

త

The Cause of Repeated Miscarriage

After two miscarriages many women fear that there is something fundamentally wrong with them. Most women can accept that one miscarriage is 'nature's way', possibly two, but after three that answer seems far less convincing. The need to know the reason for the miscarriages and the demands that something should be done about it become even stronger. If these issues are not dealt with it becomes impossible to embark on another pregnancy with any confidence. But there is no general agreement on the cause or treatment of recurrent miscarriage and this has profound implications for women who repeatedly miscarry. Women are subject to conflicting advice and the treatment offered (if any) seems to vary with the clinician.

While it is generally accepted that there are specific conditions that cause miscarriage, for example an incompetent cervix and certain uterine abnormalities, there are different approaches to the problem. Some obstetricians support the idea that most women who have two or three consecutive miscarriages do not have something wrong with them that will cause them to miscarry every pregnancy, but that their miscarriages are caused by random factors.[1] It is just as likely they are miscarrying due to abnormalities in conception as women who miscarry only once. In other words it is bad luck. This is the background to the traditional 'try again' medical response and the reason why tests and investigations are rarely undertaken before three consecutive miscarriages. It is assumed everything will be all right next time.

It is this view that leads women to feel their experience is belittled. Seeing recurrent miscarriage as bad luck, and not as a valid problem that needs to be understood and dealt with, is yet another example of focusing on the physical nature of the experience at the expense of the emotional, and of minimising the impact that miscarriage can have on a woman's life. This is echoed in the way that some women find that each miscarriage is treated as 'one off' – the cumulative physical and emotional effect is ignored. Similarly, if you have a successful pregnancy, however many miscarriages you have had, it is assumed there is no problem. There is a reluctance to view a second or third miscarriage as part of a woman's reproductive history, and to link it with any problems she may have had in any successful pregnancy. Women themselves make connections between their experiences of different pregnancies to make sense of what has happened to them.

Alternatively there are those obstetricians who support the idea that there are underlying factors, probably a variety of them, which predispose some women to miscarry. This approach is supported by recent research that indicates that once you have had one miscarriage you are more likely to have another and that therefore there must be factors influencing this.[2] The immunological research is based on this premise. It is suggested that some women reject the growing embryo because their body reacts to it as foreign tissue. It is thought that most women produce antibodies to prevent this process but that if you do not you will miscarry. This research is in its relatively early states and immunological incompatibility is not generally yet accepted as a proven cause of miscarriage. Much more research is needed before it will be possible to say clearly what these factors are, whom they affect and what might be done about them.

In practice it is likely that, for some women, recurrent miscarriage is just 'bad luck' while for others there is a persisting causative factor that makes it more likely. But at an individual level, information that would contribute to an understanding of the possible cause of a miscarriage is often not available. An accurate recording of the process of the previous miscarriages and the precise nature of the loss is often not made, either because it was not thought important to record such detail or because the woman could not supply the information. Tests that could give additional information are not done because they are expensive and time consuming, and usually do not reveal very much. However most obstetricians would strongly recommended that after three recurrent miscarriages (some would say after two) a womb X-ray (hysterosalpingogram) is done to check for any uterine abnormalities and that blood samples are taken from both partners for chromosome analysis.

ॐ

Treatment

Without knowing the cause of a miscarriage it is difficult to give the right treatment. Medical treatments have come in and out of fashion based on rather shaky foundations. They are to a certain extent experimental although they do have fairly high success rates. It is thought that the interest and support and the knowledge that something is being done, may be the key to their success. Many, it would seem, have been offered in response to women's strong demand for treatment, even when the scientific proof for the effectiveness of the treatment is dubious.

Undoubtedly some women do need and are extremely grateful for the treatment they are offered. Women with an incompetent cervix, for example, will only carry a pregnancy to term with the insertion of a cervical stitch. However the diagnosis of this is not always straightforward and probably more women have a stitch inserted than actually need one. The physical intervention ends up serving a psychological purpose for the doctor to do something and for the woman of something being done. It provides the reassurance for the woman to feel confident that the next pregnancy will be successful. The physical intervention may be unnecessary in itself.

Hormone treatment is an even better example of a physical treatment being given to meet a psychological need. There is no evidence that, for the majority of women, hormone treatment is effective in preventing miscarriage and, in the past, when DES was prescribed, it had damaging consequences. Yet many doctors continue to prescribe it. Carol was very aware of these dilemmas:

> I do not know if the folic acid supplement or progesterone injections really were necessary or that I might have had a successful pregnancy without them. What I am certain of is that knowing that something was being done, and having a fairly supportive GP and fortnightly hospital appointments made me believe that I was being taken care of and gave me the psychological support I needed.

After four miscarriages Janet's consultant reluctantly prescribed hormone treatment. She felt she had more faith in the treatment than he had, because her mother, after two miscarriages, was prescribed it in her following two pregnancies which resulted in her and her sister. Janet's pregnancy was successful and understandably she valued the treatment highly and to deny it would be cruel. It is clear that many women value the treatment they are given and choose to have it even when there is no clear scientific basis for thinking it will work.

Perhaps it does not matter whether the reasons are psychological or physical, if women find treatment helpful, but it does raise issues about psychological support. There is evidence to suggest that appropriate support of this kind is as helpful to some women as any physical intervention.[3] If it is what is important then it would be more appropriate to offer it in the first place than to confuse the issue with apparently unnecessary physical treatment. It is another way of undermining women's confidence in their own bodies and of not meeting the needs that they have.

๛

The Need for Support and Medical help

Psychological support will mean different things to different women. For some there may be underlying emotional conflicts and difficulties of overwhelming practical events, over which they have no control, which create stress and tension to add to the burden of recurrent miscarriage, and which it may be helpful to try and resolve if at all possible. There is some evidence to suggest stress may contribute to miscarriage. But recurrent miscarriages are stressful in themselves and, for many women, whose confidence has been severely shaken, a more straightforward, 'sticking with you through it all' sort of help is what is important. Kathleen got this from her consultant.

> I got myself referred to a sympathetic consultant, who agreed to oversee my entire pregnancy – were I to get pregnant again. He was as good as his word – he allayed all our fears and anxieties through what proved to be a very difficult pregnancy and saw me personally on each of my antenatal visits. I am sure he contributed greatly to the success of my last two pregnancies. I found that having a member of the medical profession that I could actually talk to, ask questions of and not be made to feel inferior, and whom I could see on a regular basis, made all the difference.

Woman vary in the amount of help they want from doctors and the degree of medical intervention they feel comfortable with. Those who find a doctor they can trust, who will explain, reassure, understand and still be there if you have to do it all again, are very appreciative. Having faith in their doctor is very important to some women but equally as important is that someone significant has faith in you and believes that as far as is realistically possible you will achieve a successful pregnancy. Cathy valued the support from her GP and consultant, particularly through the maze of medical treatments.

> The consultant was very helpful – she did every test, X-ray and examination possible, to eliminate every known condition, from diabetes through anaemia to syphilis. She saw me every three to four months and immediately when

I thought I was pregnant again. Our GP was very good –
he never once offered me tranquillisers or sleeping pills,
and very patiently explained every test result or potential
condition.

Undergoing tests it not easy but some women find that tests
keep them going. Again the fact that something is being done
is reassuring and there is the hope that there may be a solution.
But the tests themselves may be uncomfortable and
unpleasant. If nothing is found it may be very comforting that
there is nothing seriously wrong, but it can also be very dispir-
iting and only postpones the decision whether to try again. If
tests are undertaken it often seems quite arbitrary which ones
are done. The same woman approaching two different consultants is likely to be tested for different things. Miscarriage is
not something of great interest to many obstetricians and
gynaecologists and levels of expertise vary.

It is easy to feel that doctors are being evasive, difficult or
deliberately unhelpful, that they are withholding information
and opportunities for investigation or treatment when they
say they will not or cannot do anything. But in fact it is probable, in many cases, that this is good advice but may well be
poorly communicated. Follow-up appointments (see page 94)
are often badly handled and many women are left feeling
extremely frustrated, rather than informed, about their individual case and reassured about their prospects of a successful
pregnancy in the future. The counselling that many women
and their partners need is rarely available during rushed
hospital appointments.

It is hard to accept that nothing is being done. Jenny
describes how she feels about her GP and the dilemmas over
seeking further help. She had two miscarriages both at thirteen weeks and has no children.

My GP has been very helpful though not perhaps as
constructive as I could have hoped. He's been very
supportive, in a matter of fact way, explaining the likelihood of a successful pregnancy next time and why he

doesn't think further investigations are necessary at this stage, but totally willing to refer me anywhere I want to go. I don't agree that proper tests are a waste of time after any miscarriage. Reason told me that this is the official line and I'd probably come up against the same arguments and a lot of hassle if I did look for referral elsewhere at this stage, before another pregnancy.

Embarking on the next pregnancy can seem like a jail sentence while you wait for it to go wrong, before you reach the magic number of three when someone might take you seriously and do something about it. For the relatively few women for whom treatment is essential this is a particularly cruel strategy. Karen had three miscarriages; her fourth pregnancy was monitored. It was only when that too failed that she was referred to a recurrent miscarriage clinic for immunotherapy.

I was referred to St Mary's for tests and treatment with the result that I now have two beautiful daughters. Since they were treating women with upwards of two miscarriages, I wonder whether it was necessary for me to suffer two more before being offered the treatment.

꒳

Taking the Initiative

All follow-up has been as a result of my own pushing and insistence. It has been an uphill struggle.

Ellen, even though she had had three miscarriages, felt she had to fight for every bit of help she got. She already had a child and it is usually assumed that this is evidence that there is nothing serious wrong with you. Many women find they have to take the responsibility for finding out about miscarriage and the medical help that may be available - the nearest miscarriage clinic or consultant who is interested in miscarriage, or information about the latest research. Cathy felt she read everything ever written about miscarriage, from medical journals and text books to women's magazines. Like other women who miscarry she was in the position of seeking out detailed medical information to ensure she got the help she felt she needed from her doctors.

> We found out about the immunotherapy from reading the *Lancet* (with a dictionary and a doctor friend) and then had to make lots of phone calls to find out if and how we could get on to the treatment.

Cathy was referred for immunotherapy and her sixth pregnancy was successful.

Women vary in how much help they want from medical experts but repeated miscarriage is an extremely depressing and debilitating business and it can be easier to cope with if you have a doctor you can trust, who is willing to discuss the details of your individual case and undertake any intervention that is appropriate, or explain why it is important not to do anything. It can be very important to feel you have a doctor on your side.

Some women are sufficiently dissatisfied with their medical care to wish to change their doctor. You are quite within your rights to insist on being seen by the consultant rather than a series of registrars, and also to ask for a second opinion. Apart from medical etiquette, there is no reason why your GP cannot refer you to a different consultant. You can also change your GP through application to your local Family Health Services Authority (address in the phone book), but GPs at present do have the right to refuse to take on patients and in practice this may be more difficult if their lists are full.

It is important to keep the value of medical help in proportion. A different doctor may be less attached to one particular theory about miscarriage or better informed about recent research or a more skilled communicator, but he or she will still be working within the limitations of current knowledge and practice. Equally as important for the vast majority of women is to keep on trying. Unless there are established medical reasons for the miscarriage there is good cause for optimism in the next pregnancy, although understandably you may worry that the cause has not been established. Sarah, who had three miscarriages followed by a successful pregnancy and another two before her second child was born, wrote this:

> Please emphasise to other women – never, never give up hope, and make sure you go to the best hospital and insist on being treated by the best consultant.

It is important to be realistic in your expectations of medical help and treatment. Offering effective help for women who repeatedly miscarry cannot be done without understanding why those miscarriages occur and, even if the cause is understood, there may be no effective treatment to offer. But a woman should not be fobbed off with treatments known to offer little or abandoned to try again with optimistic statements about the statistical chance of success next time, and with little attention to her individual predicament. Many couples would value highly the opportunity to talk through the emotional consequences of their experiences with a skilled and informed counsellor. It would help if information about centres of excellence was more freely available and there was more open access to doctors who are experts in the field. All too often, it seems, women are not referred to places where they could be helped.

In the long term, the answer is further research; in the short term, the answer is for the importance and misery of repeated miscarriages to be recognised and within the limitations of present knowledge to attempt to understand why individual women repeatedly miscarry. It is only then that effective advice can be given about trying again and appropriate treatment be considered. Women will then be in a stronger position to choose whether they wish to embark on another pregnancy or not. Some women may well choose not to spend their life agonising over getting pregnant and miscarrying.

✀ 11 ✀

Added misery

There is a range of factors which make miscarriage more difficult to cope with; some miscarriages are clearly more distressing experiences than others; some women will be more vulnerable than others and this is not necessarily defined by the stage at which the baby is lost. There may also be other difficulties in your life which make the miscarriage difficult to cope with. There is no clear-cut boundary as to when a miscarriage is problematic or not; there is a range of experience. In this chapter we will look at some of the issues that can add to the misery of a miscarriage.

✀

Difficulty Getting Pregnant Again

We live in an age when we expect to control our fertility. Contraception is freely available and abortion is an option if we need it. We have been educated to plan our families, we assume we can choose when to get pregnant and have children when we want them. One miscarriage followed a few months later by a successful pregnancy is a hiccough along the path to mother-hood. Repeated miscarriages or problems in conceiving, or a combination of the two, make any notion of fertility being within our control seem like a bad joke. It becomes very clear that we are better at preventing pregnancies than promoting them.

If it takes you time to conceive, any unhappiness caused by a miscarriage may be prolonged and fuelled by worries and frustrations about your difficulty in getting pregnant – the longer it takes the harder it is to brush the miscarriage aside. At the time of her miscarriage at twelve weeks, Jane was upset but also relieved that the bleeding she had been experiencing for some weeks, was over. Twelve months later and still not pregnant her feelings resurfaced.

> I got in a right state. I was crying all the time, going into work and bursting into tears and one day at work I just walked out and left my till. It all came out then because I was not pregnant and I allowed myself to think about it all when one of the girls at work was pregnant and kept going on about it.

Jane took some time off work. She was depressed for a couple of months and found it hard to explain her feelings to other people, particularly her colleagues, so long after the miscarriage. Some months later she was pregnant again and she was able to look to the future. But Jane and others like her, have to face the limitations of the control they have over their own lives.

Miscarriage acquires a painful intensity for women who know they have problems in conceiving and who miscarry a long-awaited pregnancy, knowing that it may be their only chance to have a child. The possibility of childlessness, with all the difficult personal issues that raises, is never easy to face.

Amelia has been unable to get pregnant since she miscarried. She recently discovered that pelvic inflammatory disease may have affected her fertility.

> Eventually I became very detached from everything, my husband, my family, and my marriage. It was a form of self-defence. If I'm not with my husband then I can't get pregnant, or perhaps it's a way of ensuring that I can't be disappointed, month after month. I know I was totally out of order and I've lived with the guilt for an awful long

time, but I had an affair, left my husband, and lived a year swinging between depression, drink, sex and 'loose living'. It was the news that my sister-in-law was accidentally pregnant that cracked me up. I loved my brother very much but I was so jealous and confused. I drank more, because more aggressive and even attempted suicide.

Amelia did manage to sort things out with her husband and they are trying again.

$$\backsim$$

Abortion

If you have had an abortion it is almost inevitable that when you miscarry you will find yourself remembering the earlier termination. The contrasts and similarities of the two experiences are so interconnected that only a few women seem able to keep them separate. The circumstances of the abortion and the extent to which you have or have not resolved your feelings will influence your reaction when you miscarry. But a miscarriage often stirs up feelings about an abortion which can become an additional burden. Rebecca was able to sort out her feelings.

I initially felt that I was being punished. Then I sorted that out and I have not felt that again. I have never had any regrets, or thought 'if only' about terminating the pregnancy. It was the right thing to do at the time and I would do the same again.

Hazel did not regret having the termination either, as she felt her life would have been very different if she had gone through with that pregnancy, but it did influence her feelings about the miscarriage.

I felt as if I'd let my husband down and this made me feel

guilty. He was very understanding and supportive. He'd known about the termination before we got married.

You may not have dwelt on the abortion until you miscarried. However right the termination may have seemed at the time a miscarriage can make it harder to deal with. Becky felt guilty.

I hate thinking of terminations now. I didn't fully realise what I was doing at twenty, but I couldn't have been a good mother then, I was too unstable.

Most of the women in the survey who had had an abortion before they miscarried said they felt guilty and that they were being punished, which may be a reflection perhaps of how unacceptable abortion still is. For some women the guilt was transitory but for others it was more problematic. Jenny and Hazel describe their feelings:

At the time of the termination it was the right thing to do. Years later, I was convinced I was being made to suffer for my earlier mistake. The guilt was terrible.

I think the abortion is the reason for the miscarriages. God's punishment. I got over it quick at the time. I was just turned seventeen. Two weeks later I was out at discos. But I think about it more as I've got older and it all came back when I had the miscarriage.

The feelings of guilt that the abortion caused a subsequent miscarriage are almost always unfounded. For relatively few women a late abortion done in the early seventies or before, may have damaged their cervix which may cause them to miscarry in the second trimester of their pregnancy, unless they receive the correct treatment. Even so, it is rarely certain that this caused the problem. Madaleine had an incompetent cervix.

I felt not so much guilty, as the clear connection between

the two events. My miscarriage at sixteen weeks was considered to be because of an incompetent cervix as a result of the abortions. I have come to terms with my unhappy past and I have forgiven myself, as I was very young and under a lot of emotional pressure at the time.

Madaleine was able to forgive herself, but some women are unnecessarily hard on themselves. One woman wrote that she did not think she deserved any help. Heather said:

My terminated baby was by my husband but we were far too young to cope with a baby and were still at school. I felt this was our punishment. I have never told my doctor or the hospital about my termination. I feel ashamed in case they think I didn't love the baby, but there isn't a week goes by when I don't think how old it would be and wonder what it would be like.

Clearly these women felt that their past was catching up with them. They felt guilty and punished which was an additional burden to them on top of the loss of the miscarriage itself.

✌

Severe Depression

While depression is a natural response to loss and it is part of the grieving process, some of us are more vulnerable to getting very depressed. Your previous experiences and psychological make-up may make it more difficult for you to deal with the miscarriage, and you may be affected by how traumatising it was. Judith had had a difficult time. She had miscarried and then, four months later, haemorrhaged. It was unclear whether this was a second miscarriage or not but it was a physically unpleasant and confusing experience. She felt out of control and became very depressed, without realising it herself.

I had enormous problems but refused to admit to myself that I could not cope. To start with my concentration was very poor. I was only getting two hours sleep a night because I was reliving everything that had happened in the last six months, but most especially the hospital admission and events leading up to it. I also cried most of the time but did not know why I was crying. On many occasions I went to my GP, and eventually he prescribed a small dose of anti-depressants, since mild tranquillisers had not improved my sleeping pattern. I felt sorry for those who I worked with who knew straight away if I was having an off day, when I felt unable to speak unless it was essential and felt very withdrawn. I lost a stone in weight and felt very lethargic. In retrospect the news of two miscarriages played on my mind and things went from bad to worse. I really tried to do my job and even though I was crying most days and did not know why, I would still not accept something was wrong with me. I remember thinking of walking under a bus because I felt so bad, but my GP still did not recognise how ill I was, and neither did anyone else who knew me.

She struggled on for six weeks until after a morning at work trying to read one letter and failing to remember what it said, she accepted something was wrong. She saw a different GP who recognised her depression, prescribed stronger anti-depressants and referred her to a psychiatrist.

The psychiatrist called to see me at home and said I had a reactive depression to miscarriages and arranged outpatient appointments on a monthly basis [which lasted nine months altogether], and also arranged for a psychiatric community nurse to call and see me once a week for three months. I think it helped to talk to someone 'objective' . During this time I had panic attacks and felt unable to go out of the house, although I don't know why. While I was off work [for three months] my crying episodes became less frequent. I muddled through the year somehow.

Christmas was the worst time, probably because there should have been three of us and there were only two. We did not go out very much because of my depression and the fact that work, when I returned, took all my energy, and I went to bed at 8 o'clock every night for a few months.

Judith feels she does not know what the crying episodes were all about. They stopped ten months after they started. The next month Judith was discharged from the psychiatrist. Two months later she stopped taking the anti-depressants. She now feels she is coping all right but still has times of feeling sad and empty.

Gail had three miscarriages after the birth of her first child. Each occurred at about three months into the pregnancy. She also had various gynaecological problems which caused her a lot of worry and uncertainty, and raised questions about her future fertility. She described how she felt when she got home from hospital.

> I had this terrible depression. I felt like a zombie. In retro-spect it was just like the post-baby blues. I sat in bed feeling ill, alone and totally despairing. I felt helpless and a loss of control. I didn't feel guilty but I did feel frightened.

She found it hard when her depression did not pass.

> What I had not anticipated but found occurring was a great apathy and loss of motivation. My self-expectations remained high and my 'standards' didn't alter but without realising it I was drifting into a clinical depression. I failed to become pregnant again. Each period (and pre-menstrual days) grew harder to bear; it was as if I was having another miscarriage every month. I became angry at my daughter and I cried at lot. Eventually I went and asked the doctor for help.

Her GP did not treat her problems seriously. She then had

three panic attacks, the first of which she thought was a heart attack. Eventually a friend suggested she saw a behavioural therapist.

> I have seen my therapist on several occasions and he has provided me with the means of coping with the depression and loss. He listened with a practised ear and didn't pooh-pooh what was happening to me. He taught me behavioural strategies for coping with the panic attacks and depression, and through guided mourning, allowed me to express some of my feelings about my lost babies.

She feels now that the immediate crisis is over, that she is ready for more long-term therapeutic help so that she can begin to make sense of what has happened to her. Maggie's depression was less severe. She had found the miscarriage at ten weeks very distressing.

> I wasn't convinced the D and C was necessary and thought I had killed the baby. I cried for days. I didn't want to get out of bed, I didn't want to go to work. I didn't care about myself, I didn't want to get dressed. I didn't want to clean up the house properly and, normally, that's important. I did manage to get back to work in a couple of weeks. I needed more support and to be helped through the grieving process. In the end I was on a course and the senior tutor noticed that I wasn't mixing with the others and that I was very withdrawn. I realised that I couldn't go on feeling like that and I needed to do something. I went to see a counsellor. I cried the hardest with the counsellor but basically I began to realise that it was OK to grieve and it was OK to move on. I began to realise that I had been very hard on myself and was being too critical, and I realised there was my husband to think about, too – it was very hard for him and I wanted to give him more.

Gradually Maggie found she was able to do more.
A miscarriage can arouse feelings to do with important

issues in your past which are not resolved. It is as if ghosts from the past are reawakened. Linda's father had died when she was young and her sister had recently lost a baby through cot death. She had two children and miscarried her third pregnancy at eleven weeks. Two weeks after the miscarriage she became very depressed.

> I was crying all the time. I was waking early, really early, 5 o'clock in the morning and I was waking up as if I'd heard a sudden noise. I'd wake up with a start and just start crying, and just feel that I couldn't face the day and just that the world had come to an end.

Linda approached her GP who was very sympathetic and offered anti-depressants or to refer her to a counsellor. Linda opted for the latter.

> I saw my counsellor weekly for about three months. Going to the counsellor gave me a chance to talk about how I felt, also, what felt important, was being able to go and have a really good cry and not feel that I had to pull myself together for somebody. That I could go and be a hopeless wreck and that was OK. It meant that the rest of the time I could cope with it because I'd got this outlet, whereas I'd been spending all my time thinking pull yourself together, and not managing to do it at all. I think I just needed to feel it and go through it.
>
> I used to spend a lot of time crying and talking about other things. In fact I didn't talk that much about the miscarriage itself. The conclusion I came to in the end was that the miscarriage had actually precipitated all my fears about death and the deaths that had happened around me and the feelings I had for being responsible for them. I felt responsible for the miscarriage. In the end I grieved so much I grieved it right out my system, but it took much longer than I had expected.

Sometimes it is a while after the miscarriage, when the immediate trauma is over, that you become aware that there are unresolved issues which are getting in the way of your life. It is then when you are not in crisis that it is possible to do something about them.

> The main reason I started to see my counsellor was when I started to try and get pregnant again. I have some problem with conceiving, in fact conceived my daughter on treatment with Clomid, and found that the whole issue of having babies and the fears that went along with it, were interfering with my life, so I felt that some therapy might help. I have since found that a lot of the problems I have now are connected with unresolved grief following the miscarriages. Therapy is helping me to look at the various losses in my life and how I have coped with them in the past, not just the miscarriages. I am also becoming more able to look at the whole issue of becoming pregnant again and face the fears. The fears for me are not just the fear of more miscarriages, but what for me, is much more frightening, postnatal depression.

Miscarriage can also highlight problems that existed beforehand but which were possible to cope with until the additional strain of the miscarriage. It can tip the balance. Greta had a difficult relationship with her partner. They had been having problems for several years and she hoped that a baby would make things better. She had had several late miscarriages and after the last one was severely depressed.

> When I came out of hospital, I couldn't go to work. I couldn't face people. I couldn't go out shopping or back to work for nearly a year. I cried so much I didn't realise I had so many tears. It was really hard for me. I knew Ken [her partner] was drinking a lot and I was worried about him. I felt really ill. My mum and dad and his mum and dad tried to help, but I just wanted to be left alone. His mum used to do my shopping. I only saw people if they came to me, I used to stay in the flat all day. I had a dog and I used to play

with the dog, just to make a mess, and then clear it up. I used to do housework like there was no tomorrow – washing, ironing, cleaning. I was forever changing the cupboards around. I used to love reading but it was hard to concentrate. One day I was sitting indoors and I was feeling so low and fed up, I cried my heart out. Then I got up and put my coat on and went up to the park. I don't know what made me do it. It was about eight months after the miscarriage. It was such a relief.

She eventually split up from her partner and established an independent life for herself, but it was two years after her last miscarriage before she felt she was back on her feet.

All these women were coping with their lives before they miscarried. Afterwards they plummeted into a trough of depression and they were unable to cope. For some women miscarriage re-awakens the experience of past loss, it touches deeper psychological issues about control and femininity, and it brings unresolved issues to the fore. It may bring to the surface things you had not previously thought about or been aware of. You may feel abandoned and alone trapped in your own experience. It may be the last straw for some women, upsetting a precarious balance of difficult circumstances, so that they no longer feel they can cope. The lack of recognition of the degree of their distress and the difficulty they had in getting appropriate help is striking. If you do feel severely depressed it is important to get professional help to see you through the crisis and to help you make sense of your experience. (See page 150 about seeking professional help, and page 276 for suggestions of where to go for further help.)

FAMILY, FRIENDS AND THE WIDER WORLD

♫ 12 ♫

Relationships with others

Like any crisis, a miscarriage can heighten your feelings and make you feel closer or more distant from the people around you. It is a very private experience which can be difficult to share and it can set you apart from others. But it is also a time when you need other people and make demands on them, which may or may not be met. In the longer term a miscarriage can provoke a time of personal change, so it is likely that the miscarriage and its consequences will affect your relationships with other people. The more you have been affected by the miscarriage the greater the impact on the rest of your life will be. This chapter looks in particular at the impact a miscarriage or miscarriages can have on your relationships with your partner and with other women who are pregnant.

♫

The Relationship with Your Partner

Many women say the miscarriage affects their relationship with their partner, for better or for worse. The miscarriage may be the first major crisis or loss you have experienced together, it maybe a time of finding out about each other and learning how to cope together, learning about each other's deficiencies as well as strengths. It can bring you together, only for differences to emerge later, or vice versa.

For some couples the impact is relatively short term, the crisis is over quickly or it is manageable. For others there are more far reaching implications. Other problems that you have to contend with, and the resources at your disposal, will affect your ability to cope and it is generally easier to cope with one miscarriage than with two or three, when the effect accumulates and it can feel like it is taking over your life and symbolises the failure of your relationship.

When You're in It Together

It has strengthened our marriage because my husband shared my whole experience, grieved deeply, cried with me, loved me through it, when other people made light of it, which hurt.

Many couples value highly the comfort they find in each other. To be with someone who cares for you and understands is probably all most people ask for. It can only strengthen a relationship to be able to help each other at such times. Leila said it brought her and her husband closer together.

We both cried, had similar feelings of despair, anger and guilt. For the first week to ten days after the event, we did not want to see anybody except our GP or midwife. It proved to me that my husband is undoubtedly my best friend.

If it is the first major crisis you have shared it will be heartening to discover that you can rely on each other. Sarah was reassured that she could share something as unpleasant as a miscarriage with her husband without problems or friction or it dragging them further apart.

Sharing something important together can strengthen a relationship. It is often easy to lead quite separate lives and the miscarriage may bring you together. Jill felt that she and her husband had shared something together, or nearly together. She said, 'It was the first time in ten years of marriage that we cried together.' Tracey valued the strength of her relationship with her partner.

> I certainly feel 'we're in this together' and I tell him all my fears and worries and the things I have noticed about my body changes. The miscarriages were preceded by temperature charts and sperm counts. I am grateful that our relationship can withstand this clinical approach and that we shall be so grateful if/when we do have a baby, that we will never moan about the disadvantages.

Some couples feel they come together to protect each other against the outside world. Jenny said it made her and her husband want to 'stick together and shut out the world'. Helen described how she and her husband 'joined forces to win the battle with great determination'. She said it made them both long for a child desperately and therefore have the same common objective.

The miscarriage may put things in proportion, it may clarify what is really important in your life. One woman said she and her husband stopped arguing for a long time after the miscarriage, as other things seemed so trivial. You may find you begin to look at things differently and want to make changes in your life. Sylvie and her husband felt closer and decided to make an effort to spend more time together.

It can be a turning point in a relationship. Couples say that they have grown through the experience, that sharing something difficult confirms adulthood. Sheila and her husband felt they grew up and came together to cope. She said her husband was very upset for her and protective of her. Jan also said her miscarriage had a positive effect on her relationship with her partner.

> It made us a bit more mature, going through something bad together. We were going to have a child and then not going to have a child. It's not something we'd done with

anybody else and whatever happened we couldn't take that away.

The Strain on Your Relationship

It is not unusual for a miscarriage to create difficulties within a relationship and for tensions to run high. It may have been hard to share the experience with your partner. He may have been unable to give the help and support you needed, and you may feel let down and alone. If you feel that he does not understand what you have been through, that your feelings are being ignored and you are under pressure to get over it quickly, a rift can develop between you.

> I felt a gulf as my husband did not seem as grief stricken. He didn't seem to understand how deeply depressed and upset I was, or he tried to withhold his emotions so as not to upset me, but it just seemed that we could not share in our feelings. I felt I was making a fuss about nothing, as I had my miscarriages early on, and although I felt as if I had been pregnant for years, my husband really hadn't acknowledged that I was pregnant in the first place.

Because a miscarriage is emotionally and physically exhausting, you may have little energy left for anything else and issues that have been problematic between you may come to the fore, or you may find it difficult to cope with other problems that arise. Problems that you were previously able to cope with become unmanageable.

> I found, after both miscarriages, that any areas of tension or difficulty between us became far more marked. They had to be sorted out. I think a miscarriage, like any crisis, brings other things to a head.

Julia found the differences with her partner hard to cope with.

Our relationship has taken an absolute battering. My husband was less than keen to be a father and was doing it for me. The strain has been very great, though we have had professional help.

If the miscarriage has affected you profoundly, has revealed to you problems that you had thought you had left behind or has made you very anxious or depressed, this will inevitably place a strain on your relationship with your partner. Cathy had five miscarriages between eight and twelve weeks.

I became very aggressive and tense. The relationship with my husband was shaken severely by my state of mind – looking back I think I was dealing with leftover feelings from the break-up of my first marriage – after I realised what I was really going through we could help each other resolve it and our relationship got stronger and stronger. We can now joke over funny incidents, my odd behaviour etc. Our roles changed dramatically when the next pregnancy carried on to term – so now we are balanced again.

Gillian said her husband was very understanding to begin with, when she cried a lot, but that he was less able to cope with her depression months later. If you are depressed you may seem very preoccupied and self-absorbed, unable to do the things you normally would and for reasons it is hard for someone else to understand. It can be a very wearing experience for those around you. Rebecca got very depressed after her miscarriage.

We nearly broke up because I became very depressed. This didn't go away after the birth of two children but got worse. It put a terrible strain on us, which is sometimes still evident. We have never really talked about it yet.

The miscarriage may have left you feeling vulnerable and in need of being looked after yourself. Faye became much more dependent on her partner which upset the balance in their relationship.

> It changed our roles completely. I became the one in need of a shoulder. I didn't want any physical contact of any kind. We didn't know one another any more. We lost sight of what we had which produced our pregnancy.

Sexual Relationships

Sex may be an additional strain after a miscarriage. If you feel that your body has been medically invaded by the ERPC, or other procedures, it may take time for memories of that to fade and with later miscarriages you may feel very sore and uncomfortable afterwards, as you would after full-term birth. You may equate sex with babies and if the miscarriage has been difficult for you and your partner, and you are finding it hard to be sensitive to each other's needs, you will probably find it hard to respond to each other sexually. You may not feel very close or like making love. Lisa said her body felt too much like a coffin for a baby than a receptacle for love.

It may take time to feel like making love again afterwards. Some women say they feel ready in a couple of weeks, for others it takes a few months. The usual medical advice is to wait a couple of weeks to make sure that your cervix has closed and the bleeding has stopped, to minimise any risk of infection. It is important to allow yourself enough time and not to rush yourself. Lucy was worried she would never feel like making love again.

> I had difficulties on each occasion that we tried to make love. I felt guilty that I was trying to enjoy myself soon after losing the baby, but knew that if I didn't start making love again I'd put it off until it became a serious hang-up, so I forced myself to gradually respond again.

It may not be easy and may become an additional strain on

your relationship, not because you argue about it but because you have temporarily lost that source of closeness, affection and comfort. Helen said she felt closer to her husband after the miscarriage.

> But the sexual side fails, which causes anxiety. Both being depressed, angry and bitter is bound to cause a reaction and things that wouldn't normally matter, matter so much more.

It is likely that feelings about other things will be reflected in your sexual relationship. If you feel very sad and depressed, you are unlikely to want to reach out sexually. You may feel hurt and resentful at the lack of help from your partner. You may feel that your body has let you down badly and that you want to ignore it. Fiona said she was not interested in sex but worried that that made it harder for her partner. Pat said she could hardly let her husband touch her, let alone make love.

Sex may seem to have only one purpose and a purpose you do not feel very confident about. Sex to get pregnant can be very stressful, so it loses the pleasure of 'making love'. Fran said it took her two months to start making love again and the only reason she did was to get pregnant. Isobel said that she was so aware of the critical times of the month that it made her anxious and reduced any spontaneity that making love might have. For Teresa sex to have a baby took on a whole different meaning.

> It's less of a pleasure and more of a job, and I think I don't want to conceive doing this.

Lesley felt that her relationship became insecure from the time she miscarried until her daughter was born.

> This was probably due to my overwhelming desire to become pregnant again. Once I was pregnant I was very protective towards my baby. I think my husband could not

fully understand what I was thinking/worrying about all the time. I also think he felt left out.

She is not alone. Many women describe how they become obsessed with getting pregnant and then with carrying a child to term. Once you are pregnant again, rejecting sex as a possible threat to the future of the pregnancy is also very common. Some doctors do advise against sex for some women, but for the vast majority, there is no medical reason to do so. With the desperate need for sex and then the withdrawal from it once pregnancy is achieved, some men can feel they are just being used. Susanah summed it up:

> It was a terrific strain on our marriage. He became ill due to stress, but nothing altered the fact that we loved and needed each other.

Resolving Problems

For many couples the difficulties do pass and often lead directly to an improvement in their relationship. If you and your partner have not been able to be much help to each other, you may be able to learn from what has gone wrong. Gillian felt she and her husband both learned from their first bad experience, and built on it.

> We didn't get through it together – we got through it separately. We weren't close at the time but we were afterwards, and in the next pregnancies he was very supportive, close and concerned.

Jessica said she and her partner nearly separated.

> He didn't want me to suffer any more by getting pregnant again – in fact he didn't really want another child at all. I desperately wanted another baby. However, we were able to talk things through, and I did go on to have another healthy son.

Airing the differences between you can be one step towards resolving them, but it may take time. Talking about it is often difficult. Paula and her husband were in opposition to each other.

> My husband found it hard to talk about it – he felt if he mentioned it, I got upset. It got to the stage he could not stand me any longer, so he spent all his spare time at work or down the pub. It took many months to sort ourselves out, we nearly split up.

For some couples their relationship is damaged severely by their experiences. Sheila had been in hospital before her baby was born at twenty-five weeks. She contracted a serious infection which was hard to clear and was in hospital for some time after the birth. She was very distressed about her loss and had been very ill. The strain was enormous and she felt her marriage was disintegrating.

> It got so bad. I went through a phase when I just wanted to get divorced. I'd been in hospital for some time. I couldn't show my husband affection, if he was in the house I told him to get out, if he was out I couldn't cope with being on my own. I took my husband to the support group – he was reluctant and we ended up having a flaming row about it. Then we talked about thinking the other one needed help and decided to go to marriage guidance. I went on my own, then he went, and then we went together. The counsellor was like a referee. She pulled us up, kept us to the point and encouraged us to do things better. He explained how he felt – it made me realise it wasn't just his fault, and him, that he had got to try. It was me as well. I understood that deep down he does care and that he's supporting me in his own way. I understood that we had to rebuild the relationship. We had to start from scratch. I understood that he is concerned and that he's been upset, but that he's been strong for me and a support for me. Eventually we got back to normal again.

Sheila and her husband contacted marriage guidance (now re-named Relate) although it was not easy for them to seek help. If you feel you would benefit from such help, you can find the number in the phone book or your GP may be able to refer you both to a counsellor or psychologist. You could also contact a private counsellor or therapist (see pages 150 and 276).

Many couples would benefit from being warned in advance of the possible consequences of a miscarriage. Kathleen found her husband's response very unhelpful. If they had been adequately prepared for how she might feel afterwards, she would probably have had no need to consult a therapist.

My husband tried to cheer me up after a couple of days, and the strain began to show with me crying, and being furious with him for anything. It could have affected us considerably but I saw a therapist who explained the grieving process, and once I explained this at home, my husband allowed me to cry and was very understanding. We were both ignorant of what we were going through.

Splitting Up

When a relationship is in difficulties the additional strain that distressing miscarriages impose can be enough to cause the rift to widen and the relationship to break. Sylvie had three late miscarriages, she had no children. After the last miscarriage she was severely depressed. Looking back she sees how she had got locked into a bad relationship which the miscarriages seemed to perpetuate.

He turned to drink. As each miscarriage went on, he turned more and more to drink. In the end I was getting the brunt of his drinking, in my opinion – he was beating me up and I just couldn't take it. We had a really bad row and he virtually locked me in. I had to get the police and they got me out with my cases. We separated. If I'd thought about it after the second miscarriage I shouldn't have tried again but I thought, if I try again it's going to bring us that much closer. But it didn't – it made things ten times worse. Each miscarriage his drinking habits got worse till he was out seven nights a week and coming home drunk. His coming home drunk made my nerves very bad and I wondered if that caused the miscarriage. It's taken me years to work all this out.

Hazel blames herself for the breakdown of a relationship with a man she loved very much. She feels her inability to handle her grief made her 'wicked'.

I tried to put my guilt on him – we argued about the miscarriage and I threw it in his face that it was his fault. It got wicked, and it was my doing. I had an affair out of spite. I just wanted to break away and the only way I knew how was to hurt him.

Hazel still regrets the breakdown of her relationship with the only man she has ever really loved. Sylvie, after a couple of years, has rebuilt an independent life for herself and is embarking on a new relationship which she feels very positive about.

$$\sim$$

Relationships with Friends and Family

It is not only within the intimate relationship with your partner that the miscarriage has repercussions but also among your wider social circle of friends and relations. A miscarriage can bring an unexpected bonus because sharing the experience can open up a relationship. When Teresa talked about her miscarriage, her sister started telling her of problems she had experienced in her pregnancies and they became much closer. Likewise, Natasha discovered a friend had also miscarried and in sharing their experiences they become closer. But if you are exhausted, and absorbed in your own troubles, you may have little time and energy left for other people. Your friends may feel neglected and rejected or you may feel that other people will not understand and so, like Kirsty, keep the miscarriage to yourself.

> When people asked if I had children, I wanted to say that I had lost one, but often I couldn't because I thought that most people would not appreciate my torment over a twelve-week fetus. But I felt disappointed with myself – I knew I was becoming a bore.

Other people will have to adjust to the change in your life. They may find it difficult because you do not seem to fit in any more, and you make them feel awkward. Claire found one of her friends, who was pregnant, overly sensitive.

> I felt quite irritated by some people's reactions, probably quite unfairly. It's difficult to get it right. A friend was pregnant and she felt very uncomfortable about it. I just felt annoyed with her – I didn't want her baby.

Sharon was very upset by her brother-in-law's hostile reaction.

> My husband's brother and his wife, who were expecting a baby around the time our first was due, avoided us for months. We tried to meet them but they didn't want to know. I found that very difficult to cope with – even though I realise they were in a difficult situation.

It can even create problems with close friends. Joanne and her friend conceived about the same time.

> When I miscarried and she didn't it put a great strain on our relationship. She felt bad about her continuing preg-nancy and I felt bad about her guilt![1]

As well as the strong feelings that were engendered they would no longer be able to share their pregnancies, their babies would not play together, and they would not be able to share things as they had planned. Pregnancy and motherhood give you a certain social position, which, when you miscarry, is lost. You are barred from all that goes with it – the activities and people to share them with; you are excluded from the pregnancy and baby club.

୬

Feelings about Pregnant Women and Babies

It is not unusual, after a miscarriage, to find that you are very sensitive to women who are pregnant or have young babies. They may remind you of your own loss and failure and arouse feelings of envy and jealousy. Christina said she felt as though the world was full of pregnant women and, for a while, took the sight of any pregnant woman as a personal insult. Another woman said she hated everyone with a baby and hated anyone who was pregnant even more. Pat said she would spot large women a mile off and would then be obsessed with working out if they were fat or pregnant. Kerry found that she noticed pregnant women everywhere when she hadn't before and that she got upset at work when someone was pregnant or brought in their new baby.

Not all women feel like this, some women clearly separate their own pregnancies from others. But even if your response is not as strong as these women's, it can affect you quite profoundly. There is no escape, except to isolate yourself from other people. If you already have young children you will be living in a world full of pregnant women and young babies – at the school gate, at playgroup or toddler group.

Relationships with Pregnant Women

It can be particularly difficult if someone close to you is pregnant.

> My sister-in-law gave birth to a beautiful baby boy. Again, I knew it was something I'd have to cope with, but I was surprised to find how depressed I felt, torn by conflicting emotions. Holding him and seeing the happiness he's brought to the whole family reminded me of what might have been for us. My husband feels the same but no one else seems to have remembered, or to think that we may be upset – perhaps it is selfish to expect that.

The unthinking response of others can reinforce your own sensitivity. Someone else's pregnancy, especially if it is someone with whom you feel a degree of rivalry, can arouse deeply jealous and competitive feelings, which you may feel guilty about.

> Then the next bombshell dropped – my younger sister rang to say she was pregnant. I felt like someone had stuck a knife in me and was slowly and maliciously twisting it. She was nine weeks pregnant – one week further than I had been when I lost mine. I got through the phone call without being nasty, but dreaded having to speak to her again and knew I'd be seeing her in three weeks' time at a cousin's wedding. At the wedding all the relatives crowded round wanting to know about her baby. No one even glanced across at me to see how I was taking it, and I slipped out of the room and cried for an hour.

For Gail it was very painful. She had a daughter but subsequently suffered three early miscarriages. The birth of her twin brother's child served to rub salt in her own wounds.

> My sister-in-law, Jenny, was pregnant at the same time as me, when I had the second miscarriage. The baby was

born just after the third miscarriage. I found this exceedingly difficult. When my brother said on the phone 'Jenny's tired', I thought, 'poor bloody Jenny, she's had a baby'. When he said 'the baby's grown', it brought home the fact that my baby was never going to grow and was, in fact, dead.

The combination of your own sensitivities after the miscarriage and others' reactions to you, can present an additional hurdle to overcome. Troubled by the strength of your own feelings and hurt by others' reactions to you, you may feel cut off from people you have previously relied on. A miscarriage can be a divisive experience, separating you from other women and from people who do not understand what you are going through or cannot handle the changes the miscarriage brings.

ᵔ 13 ᵔ

The world of work

The impact a miscarriage has on your working life is largely unrecognized. How you feel about returning to work will depend on the sort of work you do, whether you enjoy it or not, and the relationships you have with your colleagues. For some it is a welcome return to normality, but it can be another hurdle to overcome in the aftermath of the miscarriage. It is often at work that the disruption created, when a pregnancy takes years rather than months to achieve, causes problems. In this chapter the short-term difficulties in returning to work, and the longer-term effect miscarriage may have on your feelings about your job, are discussed.

ᵔ

Telling Your Colleagues

Returning to work can be very stressful. You will have to face people with whom you are not necessarily very close but who will know of your absence and for whom some explanation may be necessary. If your colleagues do not know of your miscarriage you will have to decide whether to tell them the reason for your absence or not. These two women decided to tell their colleagues of their miscarriages at eleven and ten weeks respectively:

Returning to work was daunting since only two people knew I was pregnant, but, when asked why I was away, I found it helped to tell the truth, and people were very understanding.

I think the worst moment was returning to work. Not many people knew I had been pregnant but I decided it was easier to tell them about the miscarriage, than to explain why I had been off work for three weeks with a pack of lies. It took two or three days for people to want to come and talk to me: no one was sure how to cope, and they didn't want to upset me, but eventually people did start to talk and say how sorry they were and then admitted that their wife had had a miscarriage, or their daughter, or even one or two themselves.

They both felt able to be straightforward about it and bene-fited from the understanding this brought in return. For some women it may be easier not to say why you have been away. Carla did not want to tell people about her miscarriage at ten weeks.

I came home on Wednesday afternoon and felt like nothing on earth mentally, but decided that getting back in the swing – forget about it – was probably the best thing. So I went back to work on the Monday. Only a very few people at work knew I was pregnant, or about the miscarriage, but I didn't want anybody to know, so I pretended I'd had flu!

If people knew about the pregnancy they have to be told. Jan was glad she had only told a few people so she didn't have to tell people endlessly about the miscarriage. In contrast Teresa had told 'everyone' that she was pregnant. When she returned to work after her miscarriage at sixteen weeks, she then had to explain what had happened.

The first person I saw on my return to work asked me to

turn round so she could see my bump – there was a lot of that. Despite working in a hospital and expecting word to have got round, it hadn't.

If you haven't told people, you may have to explain both the pregnancy and the miscarriage, if you want them to understand how you feel. If you have told people, you may have to explain what has happened to people you would rather not discuss it with.

⤲

Returning to Work

You will be returning to work a different person in some respects. Plans may have been made for maternity leave or for you to leave work and your colleagues will have to adjust their expectations of you. You may also feel vulnerable and fragile and need your colleagues to be sympathetic and understanding. Rose is an accountant; she miscarried at sixteen weeks.

> I returned to work after four weeks' absence, feeling fitter and optimistic about the future. Most people didn't mention what had happened, but I could talk to those who did without bursting into tears.

Alice worked as a nurse in a day centre for the elderly. One of the women she worked with was a close friend, and her colleagues were very sensitive to her needs and she was very grateful to them.

> They acknowledged my grief and allowed me to talk when I wanted to, and to opt out and cry when I needed to. And they didn't push me to talk about it if I didn't want to. Nobody tried to change the subject and I wasn't treated with kid gloves. I feel that the positive help from my

colleagues and the fact that I could do things in my own time and didn't have to hide from anybody, helped me enormously in getting over it all.

If your colleagues are not so sensitive, returning to work when you still feel vulnerable, can be something of an ordeal. When Lucy, a secretary, was upset at work, her supervisor told her that the organisation was not a nursing home and that she should leave her personal life at home. Mary's employer said her difficulty in coping was making problems for her colleagues and asked her to do something about it – she worked as a social worker. Jane worked as a credit control clerk.

> It was difficult because I felt so unwell, but I didn't want to be at home. But at work I had to deal with difficult people on the phone and I kept bursting into tears very easily. My supervisor was very aggressive and unsympathetic and told me to pull myself together when I burst into tears.

If your work is physically or emotionally demanding, you may not feel able to resume your full responsibilities straight away. Helen felt she soon recovered physically from her miscarriage but she did not feel ready to return to work for about ten days, and then she was able to take things slowly for a while. She worked with children and felt she would have made some bad decisions if she had rushed back earlier, because she was so bound up in the miscarriage. Vicky was still feeling fragile and vulnerable when she returned to work a week after her miscarriage at nine weeks.

> Although I was physically ready to return to work, I was extremely emotional – liable to burst into tears etc. Teaching is not a job where you can slip off to the ladies when feeling weepy – you've usually got thirty pairs of eyes looking at you. I broke down a couple of times which was extremely embarrassing to the children, colleagues and me, and not my normal behaviour.

When Linda returned to teaching two weeks after her miscarriage at eleven weeks, she found she kept bursting into tears in front of her class. Returning to work made the miscarriage a reality for her, confirmed that the pregnancy was over and life should be normal. She took more time off and eventually returned to work seven weeks after her miscarriage.

శ్ర

When to Return

The time needed away from work after a miscarriage varies. It depends on the sort of work you do, how you feel about it and the relationship you have with your colleagues and employer. It is easier to take time off in some jobs than others. Also, as some miscarriages are more emotionally and physically draining than others, some women will be ready to return to work before others. Only you know when you really feel ready to return to your job, but it is often hard to take the time you need.

Many women feel they return to work before they are ready. Two-thirds of the women in the survey had returned to work within a fortnight but over a third of these women felt they had returned too soon. As the process and significance of miscarriage is frequently misunderstood, so the need for time to recover and readjust is unrecognised and the pressures to 'get back to normal' may be very strong. It is hard to resist these pressures and take the time you need for yourself.

You may feel under pressure to return to work, worried about losing out financially or that you will lose your job if you are away too long. You should be covered by the normal sick leave arrangements. You may worry that your work is piling up in your absence and that your colleagues expect you to return soon. Jenny, a partner in a firm of solicitors, was very aware of this after her second miscarriage at eleven weeks.

I felt both emotionally and physically unwell for weeks

afterwards. However my partners [who were all male] put pressure on me to return to work before I felt ready to do so. Only a few days after I came out of hospital, one of the partners telephoned me to tell me to sort out various problems at my office, and in the same conversation told me that his wife was pregnant with their third child!

She returned to work three weeks after her miscarriage but felt it was far too soon.

Most women are encouraged to return to work fairly quickly by the hospital doctor or their GP. Just under half the women in the survey said the advice they were given about when to return to work was right for them. They were either advised to return when they felt ready or a set time was suggested. A quarter said they were given the wrong advice – they were advised to return to work too soon – and a quarter were given no advice at all. Advice to return to work fairly promptly can make you feel that you are under even more pressure to forget the miscarriage and pretend it has not happened. Many women say they needed several weeks before they really felt ready to resume work. Katrina, a lab assistant who miscarried at sixteen weeks, took a month off work and felt that was about right.

A nurse and a hospital doctor both suggested I return to work a couple of days after the D & C, a week after, at the most, providing I was OK emotionally. It depressed me terribly; to go back to work and carry on normally seemed awful to me. I needed time to re-adjust. I kept crying and didn't want to embarrass myself in public.

The later your miscarriage the more time you may feel you need to take off, and the survey showed that this was often the case. It may also be that it is more acceptable to take time off if you miscarry later and were more visibly pregnant. Even if you feel physically well and the miscarriage was not traumatic, it can help to take some time for yourself, as a way of marking what has happened, of giving it some significance and giving yourself time to adjust. Claire miscarried at seven weeks. It was her second miscarriage. She felt that, in the long run, she benefited from the time she took off.

> I took two weeks off. It seemed a nice excuse. I felt well, and my son was at the minder's, so I had some time to myself, and it seemed quite a bonus.

It is easy to underestimate the time you need. Diana didn't realise quite how vulnerable she was when she returned to work.

> I needed a week off physically. I was very tired and I got pains in my stomach if I over-exerted. I couldn't see any reason for not returning after a week and I thought I should get back to normal. But a week after I was back I got a virus infection, I had severe pains in my stomach and had to go home. I just broke down in tears at my desk – I thought it's one thing after another, life just can't be this complicated. Emotionally I just couldn't handle it, my resistance was down and I had to take time off work to get over it.

Sometimes it is difficult to stay at home and take the time you need to recover. If you are used to working full-time and your life is organised around your work, staying at home when you're not 'ill', in the conventional sense, may be quite difficult and lonely, as Jan found. She is a nurse and had been advised to take a couple of weeks off work after her miscarriage at nine weeks.

> I had started to mope around at home. I've got no life at home so I wanted to go back sooner.

ᘒ

Work Helps

Like Jan you may find that you want to return to work. As one woman said, 'returning to work was my salvation'. It can take you out of yourself and it can help you to feel more competent. Amy is a systems analyst. She miscarried at seventeen weeks.

> I went back to work after three weeks and from then began to feel much better. The job made me feel worthwhile, as I had felt my self-confidence badly affected.

Anne teaches typing at evening class. She miscarried at eleven weeks.

> I went back to work on the Monday evening, four days after the miscarriage. I was still feeling weepy and felt I ought to tell my class why, just in case I broke down. They were sympathetic – mainly women – and as I love my work, it did take me outside of myself and my self-pity.

Sophie works part-time as an adult education tutor. She miscarried at eight weeks.

> I went back to work nearly a fortnight after losing the baby and everyone was really sweet and very patient. It helped to be able to take my mind off my problems for a few hours a day, although I cried my heart out each day when I got back to the flat.

༆

Finding Work Difficult

If you get severely depressed after your miscarriage this is bound to affect your ability to do your job. If you do need a lot of time off work the understanding of your employers may wear a little thin. Tessa, who worked as a secretary, had several months off work, but found it hard when she went back. Her boss was very understanding and arranged for her to work part-time until she was better able to cope and, she was very grateful to him. Although Jane's immediate boss was very unhelpful, her employers at her bank were, in the end, considerate. A year after her miscarriage at twelve weeks her feelings about the miscarriage came to the surface.

> I got into such a state at work – it was the anniversary of the miscarriage. I walked out one day and left my till unattended and unaccounted for. My boss demanded an explanation, so I wrote a four page letter saying I was upset, because it was a year since I had lost my baby and difficult for me at work, and I couldn't cope. He kept asking me why I was crying. I said to my GP I didn't know why I was crying. He said I was depressed but my boss didn't understand that. My GP suggested I contact the personnel department because I wasn't being treated properly at work. I ended up seeing the personnel manager who put me in touch with an assistant in personnel who'd also had a miscarriage. The bank's doctor said I'd suffered a bereavement and it was all perfectly normal. In the end, because the manager was so difficult, a transfer was arranged to another branch.

჋

Longer-term Implications

In preparing to have a child you will probably have made plans about your job which, when you miscarry, have to be amended. Pregnancy may have been a way out of a job you disliked and so with the miscarriage, your escape route will have been closed, if only temporarily. If you enjoy your work it may seem unimportant in comparison to having a baby, which now seems a much harder goal to attain. Rose found it very hard to pick up the threads.

> One of the hardest things was readjusting our plans for the future. My pregnancy was very much wanted and I'd been looking forward to giving up work in September and taking up a new career as a full-time mother. Now, having a responsible position, I needed to regain commitment at work, since I would be staying a lot longer than expected.

Janet who works as a court reporter found she had little energy for her work after her second miscarriage at twelve weeks.

> I have a total inclination to try for a family again soon – totally putting aside other thoughts. I find no interest in my career any more. It is undergoing technological changes and I couldn't be bothered, because I hope I won't be in it for much longer. Males in my profession don't understand that I don't want to get involved where I did before. I often think some of the females don't either. It's largely a single person's career and those without children.

The future may seem unpredictable and it can be difficult to make career plans. You may feel unable to apply for a new job as you hope you will be pregnant again soon. Even if you plan to continue working, it is probably not the time to be making major changes and you can feel frustrated and thwarted. One woman wrote that she felt as if her career was ruined as there was no hope of promotion in case she tried for another baby. Carla worked in a managerial job. She felt devastated by her miscarriage at nine weeks and decided that she needed to make fairly major changes in her life. Eighteen months after her miscarriage she wrote:

> I also left my job as I couldn't cope. I have been working freelance in order to be able to work part-time and control things a little better. I am not psychologically 100 per cent yet, but am very nearly normal, and I have a job interview for a good job at the end of the month.

Caroline couldn't face returning to her office job which she didn't enjoy very much. She was shortly to move house and chose to invest her energy in that.

> I sent a letter saying I wouldn't be going back. I left because there were other women there who were pregnant. I didn't have to work and I didn't want to so I didn't.

These women were able to make choices about what to do, whether to work or not; they had skills that were flexible and they were financially able to opt for part-time work or give up work altogether even if they made compromises they would not have chosen. A lot of women are not so fortunate – they have financial pressures, limited opportunities and they are dependent on the goodwill of their employer. For these women the issues about returning to work will be more immediately pressing.

๖ 14 ๖

'Mummy, where did that baby go?': Children's understanding of and response to miscarriage

It's all right for you – you've got one already.

It is commonly assumed that if you already have children, the miscarriage doesn't matter so much. Not only may this be untrue but it also ignores the fact that having a miscarriage may be more complicated for women who are already mothers. Children have to be thought about and looked after, arrangements have to be made and questions answered. Extraordinarily little consideration has been given to the impact on children.

Most children cannot be completely insulated from the experience. If your life is disrupted it is likely so spill over into their lives in some way. The degree of disruption or trauma to which a child is exposed will vary but a miscarriage often involves separation from you and it also demonstrates your vulnerability. Perhaps for the first time your child sees you unwell, upset and unavailable. Family routine may change, if only temporarily.

Different families will deal with the crisis in different ways: in how open they are about the miscarriage and the extent they feel children should be involved or protected from information and experiences they are too young to understand. And children will differ in their reactions. Age and emotional maturity will influence how much your child understands, but some children are much more inquisitive and aware than others.

But what do children know, what are they told, what do they

understand and what effect does it have? In this chapter we will look at how parents handle a miscarriage with their children, and the ways in which children respond.

〜

When There's No Need for Them to Know

For many children there will be no need for them to know of the miscarriage. If you have not told your child of your pregnancy and there has been little discussion of the coming baby, it is clearly possible for you to explain the miscarriage in terms of an illness. In the survey just over two-fifths of the mothers said their children knew nothing of their pregnancy or miscarriage; mostly the children were under four and the miscarriages occurred earlier in the pregnancy.

The younger your child the more likely he will experience you as being poorly and getting better. Sarah miscarried her second pregnancy at ten weeks. Her two-year-old son, James, was well looked after by Sarah's mother and was told that mummy wasn't well. He visited his mother in hospital and was not worried by leaving his mother there. He never saw Sarah upset or in tears and when she came home as far as James was concerned his mother was perfectly normal.

You may have good reasons why you do not want your children to know of your pregnancy and miscarriage and you may go to some lengths to ensure they are not involved in any way. A few weeks before her early miscarriage, Anthea had slipped in the kitchen and broken her wrist. She had fainted and her seven-year-old son had been distraught, disappearing into his bedroom, sobbing. She later discovered that he had thought she was dead. When it became clear she was going to miscarry she was determined that the children should not be given any further reason to worry and that Christmas would not be disrupted. When she needed to lie down, Anthea sat the children down in front of the video telling them she was going to rest because she didn't feel well. She did not have to go to hospital and 'got over it' until Christmas and the school holidays had passed. The day the children went back to school, she returned home to an empty house and broke down in tears.

Clearly there are women who are not greatly affected by a miscarriage or who manage to keep their feelings to themselves and their children are untouched or relatively untouched, by the experience. But it is extremely difficult to conceal everything. While James is probably unaware of his mother's miscarriage, he nevertheless had to cope with her sudden disappearance into hospital and three nights on his own at granny's. Anthea managed to conceal events and her distress from her children but it is possible that the children may have noticed something was awry and may have wondered what. If you feel low and sad after the miscarriage, your children will probably notice.

꒰꒱

When Children Know Something Is Wrong

Other women say that while their children did not know specifically that they had miscarried, they certainly knew something was wrong. A fifth of the mothers in the survey indicated this; half of those who said their children were too young to understand then went on to describe how their child had reacted in some way. Jane's fifteen-month-old son was upset by the panic in the middle of the night. Liz's three-year-old couldn't understand why she kept crying and kept coming over and cuddling her.

If you have had several miscarriages your child may well experience you as being unavailable and preoccupied for several months. Gail had three early miscarriages over fourteen months. She did not tell her two-year-old daughter about the miscarriages but she described her as being upset and unsettled.

During that period there was relatively little time when I

was 'normal'. I was either in the early stages of pregnancy, miscarrying or ill. I couldn't give my daughter the attention she needed because I was so bound up in myself. I used to fall asleep on the sofa when I was looking after her.

They will often be aware of events that have taken place because they may have overheard adult conversations and have picked up more than you intended. They may have seen you upset and had to cope with your sudden disappearance to hospital, possibly in an ambulance. Hurried arrangements may have to be made and someone they are not used to may mind them.

Gillian had already had two miscarriages and thought her three-year-old son did not know of her pregnancy.

We decided not to tell him, which was probably a mistake. His cuddly toy became his pretend sister and, painfully, still is. Mummy's 'going to stay with a friend' for ERPC and subsequent tears have all been accepted.

༃

Deciding to Tell a Child

It is easy to understand why you may be reluctant to tell a child about something as difficult to explain as a miscarriage. It is hard to know what to say and, as one women put it, 'There's no point in bothering children with unnecessary facts and burdening them with information they can't handle.' You might also avoid the tricky questions, but the risk you take is that your child may be quite confused and possibly disturbed by understanding that something is going on and not knowing what. Often the truth is far less frightening or bewildering than a child's fantasy. In protecting children from experiences that are important and arouse strong feelings, we also deny them the opportunity to experience a wide range of emotions.

Kate initially decided to tell her four-year-old son about her pregnancy because he thought she was ill and was worried.

> We told him that there was a tiny baby growing in my tummy and that they didn't always carry on growing and that was why I had to rest. My mother came to help. My son reacted well and seemed happier after we had explained the situation. When I was taken to hospital miscarrying, my mother, who is very close to my son, told him gently that the baby had stopped growing and I needed an operation.

Your own distress may make it difficult to tell your child. Jane describes the difficulty she had in telling her seven-year-old son, when she miscarried at fourteen weeks. He was particularly looking forward to having a baby brother or sister.

> I was so upset that I couldn't bear to tell him. So my husband collected him from school and told him. He immediately burst into tears. When he came home he hugged me and told me he was sorry that there wasn't going to be a baby. He was also quite upset that I was going into hospital.

If your child did not know about your pregnancy you may have been prompted to tell him by the miscarriage, feeling an explanation is necessary. Diana was planning to tell her daughters, aged seven and two, of her pregnancy when she had the results of her amniocentesis, but she never got that far.

> I felt that it was right that my daughters should know and I told them that I was having a baby but that it hadn't developed properly, that it had never been a real baby and that I had to go into hospital to have what was left removed. My eldest daughter worried about me going into hospital but didn't seem to feel the loss of the baby, as she hadn't known I was going to have one. Later on she was quite upset by my friend's miscarriage, a baby that she had been anticipating. Sometimes I think I did wrong by not telling

her. She ought to feel that this baby was part of our family. I don't know what the little one makes of it.

If you have shared the news of the expected baby with your children before the miscarriage happens, you can treat the miscarriage in a similar way. Half the women in the survey said their children knew of both the pregnancy and then the miscarriage. The older the child and the later the miscarriage, the more likely he or she was to know. Most of the under two-year-olds did not know, while most of the children of over three did.

It may have been necessary for you to give an explanation for your changed behaviour, your tiredness, sickness and need to rest. Or you may have wanted to share your excitement and pleasure and included the children in making plans for the new arrival. It will have become an expected event. Pat was completely open with her son.

> We did include him in everything. He was just three, but he's sensitive and quite old for his age and you couldn't fob him off. He knew there was something happening, so we told him.

But the decision may have been made for you. Your child's knowledge of the pregnancy and the circumstances of the miscarriage make some explanation necessary. Martha's son, Dan, who was nearly three, was woken up in the middle of the night by his mother crying when she miscarried at fifteen weeks. He came and found her in the bathroom.

> His father told him that the baby had come out of mummy's tummy and that I was upset because we'd wanted the baby so much. I have no doubt that the right thing for us and for him was to tell him honestly and openly what had happened. I did worry that we were burdening him with too much at such a tender age, but in the circumstances we couldn't really do otherwise. His persistent chatter and questions would have made it

almost impossible to deny or pretend it hadn't happened.

Jennifer had little choice either.

> I was in the toilet when I noted the show. My daughter, who was five at the time, was in the toilet with me, so she knew something was wrong. We tried to play the distress down as much as possible, but my daughter told everyone I was bleeding and was upset. When things got really bad, I told them that I had no baby in my tummy any more and that there would be no baby. My daughter was confused but took it well, or so I thought. My son, who was eight at the time, took it really badly. He cried and screamed, and it broke my heart.

Linda felt she was too open with her children, aged six and four. While she didn't want to hide what was going on she felt they witnessed too much.

> It was happening all over the weekend and the children were here and my husband was decorating. I was lying on the sofa in a state. The children were in and out of the bathroom ali the time anyway. I was up in the loo and there was blood and everything, and the children saw and heard far too much. I felt quite angry with my husband about it. I felt totally lost in the whole experience and totally frightened and bewildered, I really didn't know what I was doing and I wasn't thinking about them at all. Afterwards I felt dreadful that I hadn't made an effort to get them out of the house to play with friends or told my husband to do it. They were quite bothered by it.

༕

Explaining the Miscarriage

In telling their children about the miscarriage parents say that 'the baby died', 'the baby wasn't strong enough to live', 'the baby was poorly', 'the baby hadn't grown properly', 'the baby didn't want to live any more', and simply 'that the baby's not in mummy's tummy any more'. Telling a child about a miscarriage may well mean talking about death and if you yourself conceptualise it as a death then this is the understanding you will convey to your children. Children are less exposed to death these days and you may feel you want to protect them from thinking too much about it. It is these dilemmas that create difficulties in knowing what to say to a child.

If you have a faith you have a system of beliefs to guide you in your explanation. Christian parents can say that the baby has gone to be with Jesus, or has gone to heaven, or that God is looking after it. If you do not really believe this yourself your children may sense this. When she miscarried at sixteen weeks, Maralyn told her three-year-old that the baby had died.

> Once or twice he asked, where's that baby gone? I tried to explain about dying and things but it was very difficult. We talked about Jesus. We said the same sort of thing to him when my Nan died, as we did for the baby.

Children will often make the religious dimension real for themselves by relating it to practical events in their own lives. After her second miscarriage at 13 weeks, Deborah said:

> As Christians we told them that the babies are with Jesus. My granny died six months after the second miscarriage and my eldest daughter asked if granny played with the babies now.

Another three-year-old was worried that Jesus wouldn't have enough nappies.

It may be your child's first encounter with death or they may be able to relate it to a previous experience of a relative or a pet dying. Julie describes telling her three-year-old daughter.

> My words to her were that the baby had died and gone to heaven. She said 'like Tiggy', I said 'Yes, just like Tiggy' (our cat who had died the previous autumn and was buried in our orchard). She didn't ask what happened to the body. She had words of comfort for me at the time, and said she was sad that she wouldn't be getting a brother or sister.

Death is a difficult concept for children to understand. Many researchers claim that children do not initially grasp the finality and irreversibility of death, that although three-year-olds know about death, they cannot distinguish between a temporary and a permanent absence, and that the concept of death is something that develops over time.[1] Those studying children's understanding of death have split the concept into several parts, encompassing ideas about where the dead are, what they can do, what they look like, finality, causation and mortality.[2] They suggest that children grasp different elements as they mature and their comments and questions will often reflect these different dimensions. Current research demonstrates that eight- and nine-year-olds are likely to have a reasonably full understanding of death, but so will many five-year-olds (60 per cent in recent research) and that many children under five will have an awareness of death.[3]

Some children persistently ask questions about where the baby has gone and when it is going to come back. The questioning can be quite taxing. Try explaining the difference between a period and a miscarriage, said the mother of a five-year-old girl: the questioning may go on for several months as the child continues to try to make sense of what he or she has been told and needs to go over the same ground again and again. One woman recalls her three-year-old's repetitive questions.

He had many questions about what had happened to the

baby - where it had gone, was it in bits, was it still in my tummy? He was trying desperately to make some sense of death and its finality. He asked the same questions over and over. I can clearly remember him asking me several months after the miscarriage, totally out of the blue, while we were driving along in the car, 'Mum, what exactly happened to that baby?'

Others seem to display a very strong need to make things all right, to almost deny the reality of the loss, constantly saying that the family will get another baby soon. One-four-year old, when his sister finally arrived, talked about the time his sister had come out of his mother's tummy before. He had turned it all into the same process, which came right for them in the end. Other children deny the reality of the miscarriage alto-gether. One woman described her three-year-old periodically asking when the baby was going to come and telling other people they were going to have a baby, despite the clear expla-nations she thought she had given her.

However some young children seem to accept the explana-tion given them and don't need to question. Some children talk about it very little either because they do not need to or, perhaps, because they feel their questions will not be answered.

A miscarriage is, of course, a particularly hard form of loss for young children to understand. Although they may have known they were going to have a brother or sister in a few months, they won't have know for very long. It is something that is going to happen in the future and young children do not have a clear grasp of time. They will never have actually met this baby. They do not know its name or what it looked like or anything about it, except that it was a probability in mummy's tummy. It was going to happen and now it is not. Older children will be able to cope with the time dimension more easily and they are more likely to have a clearer under-standing of what was going to happen. They may have been anticipating a brother or sister to play with.

Some women have found that one of the ways of making it

easier for their children is to make the baby real for them by naming the baby and using the baby's name when talking about it, and sharing photographs with the child, if there are any. It may be appropriate for some children to be involved in a funeral if you have one. Jane describes how she handled the loss of her twins with her three-year-old daughter.

> She didn't fully understand but she saw our photos, and knew the babies were her sisters and they had gone to heaven. She knew why I was sad and understood when she saw me upset. She now speaks their names openly.

This may be less appropriate for earlier miscarriages. However one five-year-old took things into his own hands. His mother, who had lost twins at seventeen weeks some months previously, and had recently miscarried at ten weeks, describes his behaviour.

> Yesterday, as he was getting out of the bath, he suddenly said, 'You know the babies you had that died, what were their names?' I replied that they didn't have names. 'I want to call them Sarah, Anna and Peter,' he said, 'Sarah and Anna, the twins, and Peter the other one.' I started to say that we didn't even know if they were boys or girls but thought better of it – he had wanted sisters and had been very upset when they died. They were real to him, and they were real to me, so they should have names. He disarms me with his openness and directness.

Mary, who miscarried a complete fetus at fifteen weeks, at home, describes how she wished she had shown her three-year-old son the baby.

> I do wish we had shown him the baby. It just didn't occur to me at the time. I think that it would have made it easier for him to grasp – the baby was so tiny and very beautiful. I don't think he would have found it strange. He had seen and been very curious about dead mice in the garden,

dead insects and a dead frog he had found. I think he would have seen it as part of the same business, and it would have made more sense.

Children seem to vary enormously in the extent of their questioning and understanding. Even quite young children demonstrate an awareness and some understanding of the miscarriage and its implications. They will struggle to make sense of what they see and are told within the limits of their understanding. It is difficult to know how much they understand of what they have seen and been told. Not knowing what they know makes it harder to help them.

༜

Children's Reactions

Some children show little reaction and seem hardly affected by their mother's miscarriage. As far as they are concerned nothing out of the ordinary is happening and although their mother is unwell and away for a few days, they aren't unduly worried by this. Claire told her three-year-old son of her pregnancy. She miscarried early and felt he was not particularly upset.

> He was annoyed he didn't have a baby, especially as his friend who he's looked after with, had two. It was a bit like she had two toys and he didn't have any. He didn't ask about it and he wasn't upset by my being in hospital, I'd left him before. He came and visited and bounced all over the bed.

Emily was fifteen months old. Her mother describes what she thinks it was like for her:

> When it all happened there was lots of blood. I rushed upstairs to change my pants and then lay on the floor, with

the phone, waiting for my mother-in-law to come. Emily shuffled round the floor playing and waving at me. Then Granny came to see her, which she liked. Mummy went off in a big white van and she stood with Granny and waved to me. My mother-in-law is very good with her and explained things. She didn't see me for two days and was perfectly happy with her dad and her granny. The only reaction was in the hospital when they came to pick me up. My husband put her on my lap and she cried and immediately wanted to go back to him. By the time we got home that was all forgotten.

However not all children take it so much in their stride.

He [a three-year-old] saw me bleeding a lot, for a few days, and knew I was anxious. He watched me disappear, yet again, in the middle of the night, in an ambulance, and was very insecure for several days. On my return he was tantrummy for several weeks and still hates me to leave his sight.

My daughter decided she didn't want to be four and became rather babyish and cuddly. She asked about the baby all the time.

It upset my four-year-old daughter a great deal. It affected her sleeping and she kept saying things like, 'We'll have another baby one day, won't we, Mummy – if it doesn't die?'

He [a four-year-old] was naughty and difficult and was obviously seeking attention and comfort. I cuddled him a great deal and he told me that he didn't mind his Nana looking after him when I was pregnant, but now I had lost the baby, he wanted me to look after him, and not his Nana.

It is very normal that young children react to the separation from you while you are in hospital, however short your absence, particularly if you cannot prepare your child and your parting is rushed. Many mothers find on their return home that their child behaves coolly towards them, if only for a brief period, and then is very clingy, easily upset and tearful and anxious about being left with anyone. For most children this soon passes once they are reassured that family life has returned to normal.

The longer the separation the harder it may be for the child. Sheila had been very ill and was in hospital for three months in all, over the time of her late miscarriage. It was a sad and anxious time for her and her family. She describes the effect it had on her twenty-month-old son.

> He was staying with my mother-in-law whilst I was in the hospital. When I first came out he didn't feel like my son. He was really naughty, biting, pulling hair, terrible tantrums, wouldn't eat anything, wouldn't play with anyone. But he was OK with his grandmother. If anyone visited he'd be really difficult. I still wasn't well at this time, with the encouragement of the support group I came to realise that he didn't understand what had happened at all. So I explained to him what had happened to the baby and he got a lot better. But he wanted his grandma, and that really hurt me. I don't know how much he understands but we're happier now I've talked to him. Occasionally we get out the baby's book and I show him the photos.

He was clearly very troubled by the separation from his mother and angry with her; it then took them a long time to re-establish an easy relationship, for him to settle and begin to trust her again. If you are experiencing similar difficulties it may be helpful to approach your GP or health visitor. If they cannot help they may be able to refer you to someone who can.

The impact on a child may well spill over into other parts of his life and you may not always be fully aware of the effect on him. Some children may choose to express their feelings outside the family home. Laura hadn't realised the impact her recurrent miscarriages were having on her six-year-old daughter.

> She showed more affection, was a bit weepy and a bit inquisitive but that was all, we thought, until we had a parents' evening at school and her teacher surprised us by saying she had lost her enthusiasm and appeared with-drawn.

One woman described the behaviour of her three-year-old son after her second miscarriage at fifteen weeks. He had been very aware of the pregnancy and the circumstances of the miscarriage. His parents were finding it very hard to help each other and they felt he was very sensitive to their distress.

> The upset he was experiencing manifested itself in many ways: at his nursery school he went through a stage of moving toys and equipment around, deliberately putting things in the wrong place. He seemed to be creating the chaos he must have felt for himself. Whilst not disrupting others, he did little that was constructive in terms of play or activities, unlike his normal self. He did black paintings and drawings that he told his nursery teacher, were of dead babies. It was with his nursery teacher that he chose to share these feelings, by telling her about his drawings and talking a little about Mummy and Daddy being upset, and Mummy not being very well. It seemed important that he had someone other than us to share it with.

Your child may well be reacting to the changes in you: if you are distressed after the miscarriage your child is far more likely to be affected. Some children will be more sensitive to this than others. Linda describes the different reactions of her two sons, aged four and six.

I was in a state, particularly when I got very depressed. My eldest son really suffered from that, I know he did. They told me at school he wasn't himself and asked me if I knew any reason why he might be like this. They didn't know at school [about the miscarriage] and he was obviously bad enough for them to comment on it. They said he was miserable and short-tempered and just not very happy. But I wasn't spending much time with him really, I was here but I wasn't engaged with him properly. My younger son was fine. He copes with people being upset by cuddling them, kissing them, telling them to feel better and running round doing things for them, and you can see that's very helpful for him. Whereas my eldest son just doesn't respond that way at all. He needs engaging with and I couldn't do that at all.

Another woman described how she shared her distress following her miscarriage at sixteen weeks with her three-year-old son. She was also clear that any upset her son showed was a reflection of her own distress and not his own reaction to the miscarriage.

> He was upset for me. If I was upset he was upset. He'd sit on my knee and get me a hanky and everything. He got upset because I was upset, not because he was upset by what had happened. He didn't understand enough. He wanted to know why I was in hospital but on the whole he didn't ask complicated questions.

For some children the miscarriage clearly arouses anxieties about their mother's health and well-being. If a child knows his mother has been very unwell and has also begun to understand more about death, it is perhaps quite understandable that he may worry about losing his mother too. This concern may manifest itself when a woman becomes pregnant again and a child is reminded of the difficulties of the previous pregnancy. One woman described her nine-year-old daughter's reaction.

> She wished that she had never known about the preg-nancy. She didn't want me to ever become pregnant again because of the risk to my health. She asked if we could adopt a baby instead.

Some children may have feelings about the loss of the baby just as you do. Just over a tenth of the children in the survey were reported as either disappointed or upset that there wasn't going to be a baby. Those who have a clear understanding of their mother's pregnancy, anticipate the arrival of a brother or sister, or appreciate the importance of the pregnancy, are more likely to feel the loss. They will have formed some attachment which will have been broken by the miscarriage; this is more likely when the miscarriage is later in pregnancy. Although one woman described her three-year-old as being very disappointed, it is generally older children who react in this way.

> He [four-year-old whose mother had miscarried at twelve weeks] burst into tears and was very upset when we told him that the baby had died. He had been quite keen on having a baby in the family and I felt his tears were genuine. His sadness soon passed.

> They [seven- and nine-year-olds whose mother miscarried for the second time at twelve weeks] were both profoundly saddened. I encouraged them to talk about it to me but as one of them said 'It's just too sad to talk about.' They were both very loving and caring, and soon bounced back to their usual happy selves.

Younger children will not necessarily understand the meaning of the loss of the baby. They may be more aware that their friends have a baby and they don't. There may even be some relief in not having to cope with the intrusion of a brother or sister. One three-year-old described his mixed feelings about the pregnancy and miscarriage when he told his father that he felt 'both sad and glad' that the baby had died. Older children may have very clear expectations of a baby brother or sister which have now been dashed; a particular pregnancy may have a special meaning, just as it does for the parents.

  The issues of guilt and blame can be as apparent for children as for their parents. One mother felt her three-year-old blamed her for the miscarriage; in her next pregnancy her daughter kept saying to her, 'Please don't let Jesus take this baby away.' Just as many women feel a deep sense of guilt that they may have caused the miscarriage in some way, some children also take on this responsibility, a cause of great concern for the parents. One woman describes her three-year-old son's behaviour after her second miscarriage at fifteen weeks.

Sam obviously worried that he had done something to harm the baby, saying at one point that the baby had died because he had bounced on my tummy. It was the second miscarriage he had experienced me going through and we were cautious this time and had undoubtedly told him to be careful with me. We tried very hard to reassure him that it was not his fault.

༄

The Implications for Parents

It is more than likely that your child will have sensed that something is going on and, as a parent, you will have to deal with the miscarriage with him. If you have been upset your child is more likely to respond to this. This does not mean you should not be upset or show your feelings but your children will probably notice. Younger children will be upset by the separation from you. You cannot avoid this but you can try to understand and allow them to express their feelings about it when you return.

Older children will find being apart from you easier but may be more upset by the loss of the baby and with their greater grasp of the meaning of death may find the miscarriage itself more upsetting. In this sense they are more vulnerable. In the survey over three quarters of the six- to nine-year-olds were reported as showing some signs of being upset, compared with only a quarter of the two- to five-year-olds. Adults often underestimate a child's ability to understand loss and bereavement. It is important to make time to talk with your child about what has happened, to give the information he needs and to answer his questions honestly, although this may be painful for you if you are feeling sad yourself. Younger children delight in asking persistent questions as they try to make sense of new experiences. They will be grasping the mechanics of the situation rather than taking on the emotional meaning.

The longer-term effects on children are not known. The mothers of all the children in this chapter who had been upset told me they returned to normal relatively quickly.

> Now he's older and none the worse for the experience and may even have benefited from it. He is sensitive to others' emotions and, despite his ups and downs, is reasonably mature.

Tina was worried about the effect her repeated miscarriages would have on her son.

> My son is now six-and-a-half. If he thinks back to the first four years of his life, he'll probably remember his mum used to cry a lot. But he used to give me lots of hugs and I used to try not to burden him with my grief.

You may not have wanted it to be like this for your child but there is nothing you could do to stop a miscarriage and you cannot change your feelings. Learning about difficult times and strong feelings is all part of growing up. Sharing a mother's experience of a miscarriage may help a child to understand about loss and death and the feelings that go with it, assisting him in his emotional development.

There are a few cases reported of adults whose problems later in life are linked back to their experience of their mothers miscarrying. This is not something that is often considered and is probably very unusual. But it is perhaps wise to give some thought to the longer-term implications. How will a girl who can remember her mother miscarrying feel about pregnancy when she is pregnant herself? What about families where the child who comes after a miscarriage is never felt to be the right one? Some women who have felt the baby they miscarried was a part of their family have said they intend to tell their subsequent children of the brother or sister they might have had in order to complete their family picture.

꒰꒱

The Children You Already Have

Even now [one year after the miscarriage] he says, if there's a baby on the telly, 'that baby it died, didn't it Mummy, what we were having?' Sometimes that gets to me.

We were watching a television programme about pregnancy. My four-year-old said, 'That's what you can't do, isn't it Mummy?'

While the children you have may remind you of your failure when you least want it, and they can be demanding, if only in their need to be looked after, they are also a source of pleasure and distraction. Things have to be done and often there's nobody else to do it, which means there's less time to wallow. As the mother of a four-year-old said:

I must admit that already having a child waiting for me at home when I came out of hospital made the miscarriage easier to deal with. I was just too busy to stop and think about what had happened.

Another woman described how caring for her fifteen-month-old dragged her back into her normal routine and out of her lethargy and depression, which she saw as very positive.

It may though be very difficult to get back to normal. You may feel very preoccupied, unable to reach out to meet others' needs and consequently feel guilty at the lack of time and attention you are able to give your children and the lack of interest you feel in them. You may feel you are letting them down. A situation can escalate and for some women this can be very frightening. Joyce described how on her return from hospital her one-year-old annoyed her intensely. She just didn't want to be bothered with his incessant demands. She found she was intolerant of what she knew was very normal behaviour for a child of his age.

> About three weeks after the miscarriage I felt particularly low. We were going out and I was trying to get Mark ready. He wouldn't put his arm out to put his coat on. So I pushed him so he fell over and hurt his head – I felt awful.

It seemed a peculiar irony to Joyce that she was unable to enjoy the child she already had.

But to many women their children are a great source of comfort and are especially caring, loving, supportive and almost protective of them at the time of the miscarriage. And it can be a very positive experience for your child to be able to help you.

> On one occasion, when he [a three-year-old] saw me crying, he hugged me and told me not to worry, as we'd get another one soon.

> She [a fifteen-month-old] gave me the greatest strength after the miscarriage.

> They [ten- and six-years-old] both cried and cuddled me.

> My son [a five-year-old] was the only person to help me.

> I was desperate to see him [a one-year-old] the following morning. I just wanted to cuddle somebody small.

> Throughout all this, my five-year-old son has been loving, helpful and caring. I really don't know what I would do without him. I have to be strong for him

> She [a five-year-old] was sympathetic and loving and tried to cheer me up.

She [a two-year-old] was very sensitive to me when I was upset, and if I looked like I was going to cry, she came and cuddled me. She was a great source of comfort to me.

Not only are they a great source of comfort, but the children you have become very precious to you. A reminder perhaps of what has been lost but also a greatly valued source of pleasure and joy.

I have become much closer to my son since the miscarriage and, I suppose, I value and cherish him more.

I became very aware of appreciating every detail of her babyhood, in case I had no experience of babyhood again.

They became more precious to me and I realised that I did have them and maybe if you realise how important things that you have are, then that's not a bad thing.

Section six
THE WAY FORWARD

✌ 15 ✌

'It's never the same again':
The next pregnancy

Rightly or wrongly I feel the way forward is to become pregnant again and thus give me a sense of direction that nothing else seems able to do.

The longing to have a baby after a miscarriage can be very intense. It is not necessarily a need to replace what has been lost but that the desire to have a child is kindled by the loss. If you do not have children that miscarriage can seem like a threat to your femininity because the pressures to have children in our society are very strong – it is what is expected of us. Your ability to be a 'proper woman', to conceive, carry and mother a child are questioned. If you already have children the desire can be just as strong. The children you have are just not enough.

The consequences of miscarriage can be far reaching. It isn't just a matter of mourning the lost baby, but of also coping with the attacks on your identity as a woman. It may cast a shadow over all future pregnancies and it may only diminish when childbearing comes to an end. Although the desire for another child can come to dominate your whole life, the prospect of actually getting pregnant, and of being pregnant again, is another matter.

How you feel about trying again for another pregnancy will, to a large extent, depend on how much your confidence has been shaken. The number and stage of your previous miscar-

229

Miscarriage

riages and the extent of the emotional and physical trauma you experienced, will influence this. If the miscarriage was difficult, if it has raised other problems in your life and if the sadness has been hard to cope with, it may be that you will not feel able to try for another baby for some time, until the aftermath of the miscarriage is behind you and you can look forward rather than back. Being able to plan for the next baby, and feeling ready to try again, can be a turning point in the recovery process, even if it does seem another hurdle to overcome.

༚

When to Try Again

Women are often given very confusing and conflicting advice about how long to wait before getting pregnant after a miscarriage – 'after one normal period', 'give it three months', 'wait six months'. The advice is given more as a response to the question, rather than because there is genuine advice to give. The only research that exists concludes that women who conceived within three months of miscarrying early in pregnancy were just as likely to have a successful pregnancy as those who waited longer.[1]

In practice different intervals are appropriate for different women. Miscarriage is a diverse experience and some women will find their miscarriage more overwhelming physically and emotionally than others and will take longer to recover. The stage of your miscarriage may influence how long it takes your body to get back to normal. Ultimately you have to decide for yourself. The best advice is probably when you feel ready and not to rush but to give yourself time. Some women feel happy about trying again fairly quickly and are confident the pregnancy will be a success.

I have been extremely lucky – two months later I was again pregnant at the first attempt and all is going well so far. I can now look at the miscarriage as a great tragedy but a bearable one.

For others it is not so straightforward. It is not unusual to feel bound up in the miscarriage for several months afterwards, unable to look forward. The prospect of another pregnancy may seem daunting. Bryony felt clear she was not ready to embark on another pregnancy.

> When the possibility seems quite real, waiting for a period, I feel real fear at the months of anxiety it would bring.

It may of course be hard to know when you do feel ready and often it only becomes clear in retrospect. For some women it is when they feel able to take on the risks involved in another pregnancy, and when they can face the possibility that, although it probably will not go wrong again, it may. After two miscarriages which were close together, Elaine decided to give herself a break from pregnancy for a while. She had recently moved house.

> I didn't say I never want to have a child. I did say I don't want to have a child now. I threw myself furiously into both doing up the house and looking for a job in this area. I seriously thought about taking up a full-time, hard work, career-type job, had one been available.

It took her a year to feel she could face trying again. Jo also felt she had to put the miscarriage firmly behind her first.

> It took me about five months to accept the miscarriage. Then, I could believe that it had happened and feel that it wasn't the end of the world, that it wasn't the most terrible thing that had ever happened to me – it was getting it into a sense of proportion. Other things in my life were changing. I was planning to go abroad, getting a new job and finding other things to look forward to. I was finding positive things about not being pregnant.

Many women find that the impact of the miscarriage does not begin to fade until they are pregnant again, or their next child has been born, or until their childbearing years are over and the threat of miscarriage recedes. For them it is not a matter of getting over it, but of getting on with it, of coping with the anxiety.

ॐ

The Waiting Time

Waiting to try again can be very difficult – an anxious and frustrating time: you feel in limbo, focusing on the past or in the future but unable to live in the present, biding time, unable to make long-term plans and unsure what to do. Using contraception when deep down what you want is to become pregnant seems to echo these feelings.

One thing you can do is prepare yourself for your next pregnancy by adopting a more healthy diet and lifestyle. This may mean changing to a more wholefood and nutritious diet, reducing, if not cutting out, alcohol and cigarettes, avoiding unprescribed drugs (even asprin), trying to reduce the stress in your life and taking regular exercise. That is not to say that these things in themselves cause miscarriage, but that it is helpful to be in the best possible physical and emotional state before you conceive again. Some experts recommend six months preparation before you try for another baby and a very thorough physical examination, but others believe that this is excessive.

Many women say how helpful it is, in this interim period, to have something specific to do which also involves their partner. It is important for him to be fit and healthy before you conceive, too. (See page 274 for the address of Foresight, the association concerned with promoting pre-conceptual care.)

When It Takes Time to Conceive

The feelings of failure that miscarriage can arouse intensify if you are not able to conceive once you are ready.

> For the next few months I became more and more despondent as I failed to become pregnant again. Eventually I became pregnant a month after the miscarried . . . I hesitate to say . . . baby . . . would have been born. It was almost as if having started, the pregnancy had to proceed for the right number of months.[2]

Worries about being able to conceive can overtake the feelings of loss; it is easy to get your worries out of proportion and to feel you will never have a baby. Margot was worried when, four-and-a-half months after her miscarriage, she still was not pregnant.

> The ache for the child I lost and the one I want isn't getting any better, in fact it's probably getting worse. My periods are still somewhat strange. Each time my period starts I get very depressed and talk about pregnancy and motherhood and how I feel I'm running out of time. With each period I feel I'm reliving the loss of my baby.

༺

Deciding Not to Try Again

For some women, the decisions about trying again in the aftermath of the miscarriage take on a different proportion. Pat's miscarriage raised many dilemmas for her about having another child. The pregnancy she miscarried was unplanned and as she already had two children, she considered a termination, but then decided against it. When she miscarried she felt a tremendous sense of loss and wanted desperately to replace her lost baby.

Initially we thought replace it, get pregnant again soon. I though I'd got to be pregnant again before it was due. But after three months I just didn't feel ready, either physically or emotionally. Losing that one in some ways makes me want one less. I think I'd be very anxious, and the pregnancy would take over my whole life. I'm working now and enjoying it, and I don't think I could if I was pregnant – I'd be giving up my other life. Yet, if I don't have another one I'll always regret it – it's like saying we never wanted the one we lost.

Repeated miscarriage brings a lot of stress to both the woman and her family. The prospect of putting everyone through it again can seem unwise. If you already have a child, it is perhaps an easier decision to make. Veronica was unsure about embarking on another pregnancy.

I don't know whether I can face trying again. I've got a job, but it's not that. I don't know I could put up with losing another one or causing all the upset to my husband and son. I'm 35 and I don't want to have tests. I would dearly love to have another one, I get broody occasionally but I'm not sloppy about it most of the time.

Jill had several late miscarriages and had definitely decided not to try again. She already had a daughter.

We have given up trying again because of the pressure it puts on us as a family. Also, from my own point of view, these poor little babies who don't make it and die, they are beings who cannot be treated as expendable commodities.

After four early miscarriages, Maggie and her husband considered applying to adopt but eventually decided against it.

It was a harrowing time of questioning and self-analysis. Eventually we came to the conclusion that, although in no doubt we could love an adopted baby, we were not prepared to stop trying for our own baby and considered the stresses and strains of possible further miscarriages an unsuitable climate in which to bring up a child. So we made the momentous decision that, if we were not able to have a child of our own, we would remain childless – a decision which left us both emotionally drained.

Maggie's fifth pregnancy was successful. Paula and her husband after several late miscarriages, with no reason found and no prospect of successful treatment in any future pregnancy, decided not to try again.

I have only just begun to accept what has happened to us and I live from day to day. Some days are good and some days are bad. I can't forget my babies. They are always in my thoughts but hopefully we will reach our aims. We have only just started the long procedure for adoption and have been invited to our local social services meeting to discuss about adoption, and to see if we do still definitely want to go ahead. We know that adoption takes a very long time, but we can wait. All we want is to be a family. We will have to wait and see what life brings.

For some women a miscarriage will pose serious decisions about having more children, for others it will mark the end of their reproductive career and some couples will embark on the long and difficult road of adoption. Sometimes a miscarriage is not just a hitch on the road to the family you planned.

꙳

The Next Pregnancy

Each pregnancy is unique in circumstances and meaning. Some women feel very different about their next pregnancy. Frances's previous pregnancy had ended in a missed abortion and she had felt very unwell throughout. This one was different.

I didn't worry. I just knew it would be all right. I've had a few visits to the doctor and this pregnancy has progressed very nicely, all on its own. I wanted the least medical intervention possible and I'm planning a home delivery if all goes well.

The contrast was also marked for Sue. She had also felt very unwell for some time before she eventually miscarried.

It's a much better time to be pregnant – I feel better physically. I feel much more in control and resourceful. I feel very good about it. I'm making plans and generally preparing myself, which I didn't at all for the last pregnancy.

A change in your circumstances may help you to feel more positive about the next pregnancy. After several miscarriages, Sylvie's relationship with her partner broke down. She felt secure and loved in her new relationship and she felt much more confident about being pregnant.

He makes me feel very different about being pregnant. I feel very secure and very relaxed. He knows all about it and we talk about what happened. He says it won't happen again because he'll always be there for me, and I won't ever get aggravation off him. I feel like it's the right time now, and I've never felt like that before.

Feeling Anxious

The legacy of miscarriage lingers on into the next pregnancy for many women. When you are haunted by the possibility of it all going wrong again, it can become a very difficult time. Gillian was twenty-four weeks into her next pregnancy when she wrote to me describing her feelings.

I have very mixed feelings – joy at being pregnant again so

soon, coupled with deep anxiety about whether this baby will be healthy. The hardest part was counting the weeks until the 'magic' date of twelve weeks was reached. I think I'm much less confident and more anxious about the pregnancy than I ever would have been had I not lost the previous baby. It's not very easy to take all the signs and symptoms of pregnancy calmly, without worrying too much about complications. I'm also very superstitious and can't bear to make too many preparations for this baby. Still, the way ahead has to be one of hope; I don't think I'd have been any more settled had we decided to defer another pregnancy, or indeed to remain childless.

It introduces the notion that things can go wrong, and so a pregnancy following a miscarriage is unlikely to be the same as a pregnancy without that previous experience. However much you feel that this one is different and you feel confident that it will be successful, you have the knowledge that it may not work out. The 'rosy glow' that you may have experienced before seems rather innocent and unobtainable. It is natural to be worried when you are pregnant but miscarriage seems to heighten these anxieties because it is a possibility, if an unlikely one, for most women. It can be difficult to keep your anxiety in proportion and many women find they are constantly on the look out for tell-tale symptoms.

Every wind pain and rumble is treated with fear and suspicion.

I never really breathed easy until I held him in my arms; every time I went to the toilet I dreaded seeing the sight of blood, every little twinge I imagined the worst.

Many women find once the first and most vulnerable third of the pregnancy is over, or the date when they last miscarried is reached, they can relax and enjoy the pregnancy. Frances felt very positive about her pregnancy and although she was anxious in the early weeks, as the pregnancy progressed and she passed the eleven-week hurdle (the time she miscarried before), she felt increasingly optimistic and found she did not worry about miscarrying at all. For Caroline the anxiety that it would go wrong again carried on way past the time of her previous miscarriage.

I was terrified all the way through: I had horrific dreams of a baby with a head or an arm or leg missing. The worry never went away. It just changed its form. I worried about miscarriage, then about stillbirth and then about cot death.

Until the birth of her daughter, she feared she would not have a baby.

Three weeks before she was born my mother came down to be with me, and she brought a suitcase of things she'd knitted. I remember sitting there in the front bedroom, just looking at everything and just crying, thinking, what if I haven't got something to put these things on? I think with the miscarriages first, it was as if I wasn't going to have a baby this time either.

At the time of her miscarriage at twenty-three weeks, Bethan was told she would need a stitch in her next pregnancy. She was nineteen weeks into her next pregnancy when she wrote this:

They have now said I don't need a stitch – we'll soon see. Life at the moment is a nightmare. At present I don't worry about the baby, just what I'll have to go through. Sometimes I can't believe I've put myself in such a situation that it could happen again. If things do go wrong now, it'll be my last baby: I could never go through this again. As I get near twenty plus weeks I don't sleep well, and dread going to the toilet. Every backache, every little ache and pain – I think, it's going to happen. You can't do anything to take your mind off it, as I'm supposed to take things easy. I don't talk to anyone about this. They ask about when I have the baby etc. I don't even dare to think about it.

Coping with the Anxiety

Protecting yourself from the reality of the pregnancy, pretending it is not happening is how some women cope.

> I coped by switching off to the pregnancy completely. I didn't talk about it to anyone, not even my husband – I got on with life and did everything I had to do. I made plans assuming as much as I could that I wouldn't be pregnant. I decided if I was still pregnant at Christmas I'd tell people. It was a bit difficult because although I wanted to forget about it, I was still feeling sick and needed to eat small amounts, frequently. I relaxed once I'd got to fourteen weeks, and didn't worry then.

Cathy had had several miscarriages. She coped with her last and successful pregnancy by distancing herself from the baby throughout her pregnancy, but adjusting to the birth was difficult for her.

> We managed to keep our feelings under control by seeing it as a medical problem which would resolve itself, so I didn't allow myself to develop any loving feelings towards the baby – I didn't talk to it or refer to it, but we both just talked about 'afterwards'. I couldn't enjoy being pregnant. We didn't have any baby items at all and I feel really sorry that I couldn't plan and buy in advance.

Alice found she developed her own way of coping with her anxiety.

> I gave myself time limits to break up the duration of the

pregnancy and help me cope with the anxiety I felt. If I got to twelve weeks, that was better than last time, fourteen weeks then the placenta was working properly, sixteen weeks then I had a scan and saw the baby moving.

Support from someone close to you through the anxious stages of the pregnancy can be vital. Many women comment on their partners' long-suffering support, through the trials and tribulations of the next pregnancy, and miscarriage support groups can provide an invaluable source of support once you are pregnant again. It can be a relief to be in the company of other women who instinctively understand your anxieties and do not expect you to be overjoyed at the prospect. The company of other pregnant women who appear to be having trouble-free pregnancies can be hard to take, as Caroline found at her antenatal class.

> I couldn't believe it that all these women took it for granted that they were going to get pregnant, have a baby and everything was going to be all right. I used to think, how can you all sit there so calm? All I wanted to say was I'm worried if something's wrong.

Medical Care

Supportive medical care in the early stages, and through the anxious times of the next pregnancy, can turn a worrying nightmare into a manageable problem. Doctors and midwives, who recognise that a miscarriage can influence your feelings in a subsequent pregnancy and who understand that it is perfectly normal to be anxious and worried, can make all the difference. Jane had had several miscarriages and was very anxious.

> I was a neurotic wreck all the way through. My GP was a saint. The times I went to see her, because I'd got back-ache and was convinced I was in labour, and another time I

hadn't felt the baby move for a while so she arranged a scan to ease my mind. Needless to say the baby started moving as soon as I got to the hospital. And not once did she tell me I was being silly or paranoid, she treated my every worry with understanding. I felt as though she was carrying the baby with me.

Cathy found her consultant very helpful. She too had had several miscarriages.

During the pregnancy which ended in our son, she saw me every four weeks until six months, then every fortnight and was there to deliver him at the birth. I think she was as excited as we were and was determined not to miss it!

When your confidence has been undermined and you cannot trust the signs from your own body, or the pregnancy is still in the very early states and you are very worried, a scan can be immensely reassuring. The benefit must be weighed against the slight risk that there might be some side-effects (see page 16), and not everyone welcomes the technological intervention. Elaine said she enjoyed her scans enormously and they gave her the confidence she needed.

Up to four to five months I was still convinced I was going to lose the pregnancy, and so to see him alive on the screen and to see his heartbeat and what little there was of his spine – that was very important to me: to know that he was alive inside me, even though he was so small that I couldn't really feel it yet. Until I felt him move at fourteen weeks I relied heavily on the clinic appointments to tell me whether his heart was beating.

Julia's GP sent her for a scan when she was eight weeks pregnant as she was very upset and felt she wasn't pregnant any more.

This time I saw a heartbeat. Believe me this really was the

best moment of my life, even better than when my son was born.

These women were fortunate in getting appropriate help at the right time. Based on the fact that most miscarriages occur in the first third of pregnancy, antenatal care does not usually start until the pregnancy is well established. By then many women feel more relaxed about their pregnancy. Most need help before they are pregnant, and in the early stages of the next pregnancy, rather than once they are twelve weeks or so into it. Even then antenatal care can be sadly lacking. When Caroline booked in for her antenatal care at the hospital she was surprised by the lack of significance attributed to the miscarriage. It had been of immense importance to her.

At antenatal at the hospital you fill in a form. The midwife said, 'You've had a miscarriage?' 'Yes.' So they put *0 + 1* and that was it. It was never mentioned again. It just seemed so normal to them. I suppose they hear it every day so it doesn't really mean anything. Nought plus one sounds like minus one.

It can be very distressing when your anxiety about your pregnancy is dismissed as neurotic, especially if you experience symptoms similar to those at the start of your miscarriage. Penny was admitted to hospital with slight bleeding.

The registrar on the ward accused me of panicking. He didn't seem to understand that I had every right to panic. All was well after a couple of days.

Ginny's GP was trying to ensure she got appropriate help. Unfortunately the hospital failed to respond.

My GP sent me to the antenatal clinic when I was eight weeks, so that I could be helped from the start. I saw the consultant: he gave me an internal examination, confirmed I was eight weeks pregnant – then said he would see me when I was twenty weeks. I explained to him my GP had sent me so early because I had suffered two previous miscarriages around twelve weeks. He said that there was nothing he could do for me. If I was still pregnant he would see me at twenty weeks and he decided there and then that the majority of my problems were probably due to the termination of a pregnancy I had had in 1979.

In focusing entirely on her physical needs and ignoring her emotional needs, the consultant failed to reciprocate the GP's good intentions. Perhaps it would have been more helpful to refer her to a sympathetic midwife. Cathy had this to say about the help she needed during her most recent pregnancy.

> I needed a counsellor. Our tension got higher and higher. The thought of losing what became a small bump and then a large bump at a point before it could survive was dreadful.

However sympathetic your GP or consultant, antenatal care will focus primarily on physical and medical rather than emotional needs and time will normally be very limited. Many doctors seem to underestimate the need for counselling, seeing it as something they can do themselves when they have the time, and if they are nice to the patient, rather than a skilled and time-consuming business for which they may not have the necessary expertise. Many women who have been anxious in their pregnancy, either because they have suffered recurrent miscarriage or because their miscarriage was particularly traumatic, have said how much they would have valued a health professional they could turn to to express their deep-felt worries about the pregnancy and the effect it was having on them. Few women have this opportunity.

In some areas community midwives can fulfil this role and can provide excellent care through the pregnancy, birth and early days of the baby's life. The help from her community midwife made all the difference to Kim.

I was booked for a domino-delivery so saw the community midwife from quite early on. She was very sympathetic and spent over an hour with me on her first visit, listening to my history. I really felt she understood why I wasn't enjoying the pregnancy at all and how this spilled over into the rest of my life and into worries about the birth. She visited a few more times before the birth and then delivered my daughter. She was wonderful, a real anchor in it all.

꒜

A Baby at Last

From the moment my daughter was born I felt an enormous weight lift from my shoulders. I felt a different person. All that worry, unhappiness and utter misery vanished and there was this beautiful, calm, little girl with pink rosy cheeks. I will never forget that moment. With her, my confidence flooded back and I began to enjoy life again.

For many women the birth of their baby heralds the end of an anxious and unhappy time. Kim clearly saw her daughter's birth as a turning point in her life. Claire was also overjoyed with the birth of her son. His arrival put her worries into proportion and she felt very happy with the way things worked out.

I had wanted a girl but it just didn't seem to matter. He had this huge double chin which everyone seemed to joke about and I thought, well, how irrelevant – who cares. He was a good baby which seemed a real bonus and worth waiting for. And it's a really nice age gap [4-and-a-quarter years] once you've given up on the idea of having a pair that are very close. It's been much easier for my elder son – he's not over-jealous and seems to genuinely like his brother. I've been able to enjoy the baby because the elder one's more separate and independent. In the end I got the gap I really wanted. I was ready for a baby by the time I had him. I wouldn't have been before. And now I've thought an awful lot about having another – I've not been put off.

After several miscarriages Jenny was expecting twins, which to her seemed an added bonus.

The joy was overwhelming when the babies were born, as all through the pregnancy I couldn't really believe there would be a baby at the end of it.

That there actually is a baby at the end of it all can come as a bit of a shock. The disbelief that you will ever achieve it and the defences you have built to protect yourself from further loss can make it hard to relate to your baby and, if it is your first, makes the adjustment to motherhood even more of an upheaval. Cathy, who had had several miscarriages, describes her feelings after the birth of her son.

When he was born our biggest feeling was relief that the pregnancy was over, disbelief that he was alive and healthy, and utter shock that we had him for keeps. I enjoyed breastfeeding – I'm glad about that because I hadn't been able to enjoy the pregnancy. I had so much love for him but how could I let myself feel that love when it might (probably would) end before long? In some ways I felt as if he had been loaned to us, like a library book, and while I looked after him physically, there was a feeling that he would be reclaimed again soon and life with him at home wasn't quite real – like playing at 'house' when I was a little girl. I think in some ways our feelings and reactions must have been very similar to adoptive parents – they live with the fear that the natural parents will change their mind and we had the fear that he would be taken from us.

Cathy felt the experience of recurrent miscarriage made her adjustment to first-time motherhood harder for her. It took her many months fully to get used to being a mother, to realise her son was there to stay. Mary felt her experience of three miscarriages contributed to her experience of postnatal depression after the birth of her daughter. Other people told her she was so lucky to have her baby.

> Lucky was actually the last thing I felt at the time. She was a beautiful baby and very easy to look after. I had no problems with feeding, no sleepless nights, yet still felt terrible. I spent long periods of every day crying, but didn't feel I could share it with anyone, even my husband, so nearly wore myself out with the pretence. I was very frightened that if he knew I was so depressed, he wouldn't love me so much, and I thought that if anyone else, like the health visitor or GP knew, they would make me take pills which would interfere with my looking after my daughter. Eventually the health visitor picked up on how bad I was feeling. I was put on anti-depressants which I took for a year and they did help. I did feel that a lot of what I was feeling was put down to 'hormones', which I don't deny, but do feel that the unresolved grief from three miscarriages had a lot to do with it.

Women who recurrently miscarry will spend far, far longer than nine months anticipating the birth of a child. After waiting so long there can be immense pressure to enjoy the baby. While babies can be enjoyable, they are also immensely demanding and stretch most women's resources near to their limits. It is not only women who have miscarriages who find it difficult to relate to their babies, or who suffer postnatal depression. They are relatively common problems, but it does seem that the physical and emotional strain of recurrent miscarriage can make you vulnerable and the stress of prolonged disappointment on a relationship may mean the support you need from your partner is not there.

The birth of your baby can also bring a new realisation of

the potential nature of the previous loss and feelings about the miscarriage are reawakened.

> He is my second child and will always be. I don't believe one baby cancels out another. I didn't get pregnant with Andrew to help me forget my first baby. My love for Andrew, and the good feelings I have for him, bring this loss home for me.

The birth of a child after a miscarriage or miscarriages can seem extra special. That the child was especially wanted makes him or her particularly treasured.

> It has made me very emotional about my baby daughter. I'm overwhelmed sometimes.

> Almost every day since he was born we mention to each other how wonderful it is to have him, how blessed and lucky we are and how special he is to us. We will never be able to take him for granted, nor resent him for removing a little of our own former freedom – he will always be, in our eyes, a sort of miracle.

A realisation of how fragile life can be makes you more fearful of losing them.

> I am a 'happy-ending' story with two beautiful children – I shall never take them for granted and always have a fear of losing them. Miscarriages make you very insecure.

꒰

Acceptance

For many women it is only when they finally have their baby that the miscarriage is more in the past than the present. One woman described how the birth of her baby had taken the sting out of her miscarriage, and another described how she felt the emotional effects of her miscarriage would have been far more permanent had she not been one of the 'lucky ones who went on to be successful'. If you miscarry before you have a child, your ability to have a child and to become a mother are at stake. For some women it is only when motherhood has been successfully achieved that the miscarriage becomes less significant.

It wasn't until I had my own child successfully that you can say it was something that happened, an illness, a bereavement, it's in the past. But while it's still going on, and you still haven't tried your body out to see if it can carry a pregnancy to term, you feel as though you haven't established yourself as a mother. I feel able to talk about it now but if you'd asked me before I had a child I might not have been so willing.

Miscarriage is not something you get over, as a child gets over the chicken pox, but something you come to accept; that it has happened to you, you experienced it, it had an impact on your life but gradually has become less painful. A successful pregnancy is often part of that process.

Jean's story – part three

Jean wrote this when she was
sixteen weeks pregnant.

'When I first thought I was pregnant I wouldn't do a pregnancy test, if I was going to lose it early I wanted to think of it as a bad, late period, not another miscarriage. I am always expecting to see the worst – every time I go to the loo I still expect to see blood. I heaved a sigh of relief as first six and then eleven weeks passed by uneventfully. The GP let me hear the heartbeat last week and I must say there was a feeling of relief that the baby was still there and still showing signs of activity. I dare not plan more than a few weeks ahead. I'm frightened to let myself get excited, I can't bear to buy anything or knit anything for the baby. I sit and hope that in six months' time all this anguish will seem worth it.'

It was worth it, and a year later she wrote this:

'Forty weeks seemed an eternity. I counted the weeks gone and regarded each week as another hurdle overcome. I was always so aware of all the things that could go wrong. I listened with envy to the other expectant mothers, with all their hopes and aspirations for the future, all excitedly buying things for the baby. I couldn't get excited, nor plan for the future and I bought only bare essentials. I couldn't really relate to the growing bump actually being a baby. When I felt the baby kick

249

the first time I was frightened to let myself get attached to this little bundle of life. If the baby kicked too much I was frightened, if it didn't move for a while, panic set in. I could not have survived the stress of those forty weeks without the support of my husband and GP. I am so grateful to them.

'When Ben was born I had expected to cry, instead I stared in wonder and amazement at this little bundle placed on my tummy – no words can really express the joy we felt! Now when I look at him I am so in awe of the miracle of life. He is a very special baby and I know my emotions for him are deeper than they would have been without all the problems. I have not forgotten my lost babies but somehow they have taken a different place in my life for, without them, Ben would not have been. I cannot imagine a dearer baby who never ceases to give me joy. I can now think and talk about my lost babies with tranquillity, although I still shed tears at times.'

Notes

Chapter 1
1. Ann Oakley, Ann McPherson, Helen Roberts, *Miscarriage*, Fontana, Glasgow, 1984, p. 168.
2. K. M. Swanson-Kauffman, *The Unborn One: A Profile of the Human Experience of Miscarriage*, doctoral dissertation, University of Colorado, 1983.
3. Ros Kane: *The Cervical Stitch: What it's like*, Ros Kane, Miscarriage Association, 1986.

Chapter 2
1. H. J. Huijes, *Spontaneous Abortion*, Churchill Livingstone, 1984, p. 44.
2. W. Vlaanderen, Euro Teratogenic Soc 1984 Conference Proceedings pp. 30–31.

Chapter 3
1. Association of Radical Midwives *Newsletter*, no 22.

Chapter 5
1. P. Alderson (ed), *Saying goodbye to your baby*, SANDS.
2. Details of a memorial service available from the Miscarriage Association.

Chapter 6
1. C. Everett, H. Ashurst, I. Chalmers, 'Reported management of threatened miscarriage by general practitioners in Wessex', *British Medical Journal*, vol 295, 5th Sept 1987, pp. 583–6.

Chapter 8
1. Association of Radical Midwives *Newsletter*, no 22.
2. T. Friedman, 'Women's Perceptions of General Practice

Management of Miscarriage', *Journal of Royal College of General Practitioners*, Nov 1989, vol 39, no 328, pp. 456–8.
3. Dr Paul Gill, 'A study into the Emotional Sequelae of Miscarriage', unpublished study.

Chapter 10
1. H. J. Huisjes, *Spontaneous Abortion*, Churchill Livingstone 1984, p. 154. M. H. Houwert-de Jong, *Habitual Abortion: views and fact-finding*, PhD thesis, University of Utrecht 1988.
2. L. Regan, P. R. Braude, P. Trembath, 'Influence of past reproductive peformance on risk of spontaneous abortion' (1989) *BMJ* vol 299 p. 541.
3. B. Stray-Pedersen, S. Stray-Pedersen, 'Etiologic Factors and subsequent reproductive performance in 195 couples with a prior history of habitual abortion'. *Am J. Obst and Gynae* vol 148 no. 2 Jan 84.

Chapter 12
1. Association of Radical Midwives *Newsletter* no 22.

Chapter 14
1. Dora Black, 'What happens to bereaved children?' *Proc Royal Soc Med*, vol 69, Nov 1976.
2. B. Kane, 'Children's concepts of death', *The Journal of Genetic Psychology*, 1970, 134, p. 141–153.
3. R. Lansdown & G. Benjamin, 'The development of the concept of death in children', *Childcare Health and Development*, 1985, 11, p. 13–20.

Chapter 15
1. W. Vlaanderen, L. M. Fabriek and C. van Tuyll Serooskerken, 'Abortion risk and pregnancy interval', *Acta Obstet Gynecol Scand* 67: 139–40, 1988.
2. Association of Radical Midwives *Newsletter* no 22.

The guidelines for good practice

The quality of health care crucially affects a woman's experience of miscarriage. Good health care minimises the trauma and assists a woman in her recovery; poor health care can add to the distress. These guidelines outline what it would be desirable to offer women who miscarry, based on women's experience of what is helpful and the good professional practice that already exists. More detailed information in support of these recommendations will be found in the relevant sections of the text. It is not intended as a definitive document but as a basis for discussion – a starting point for health professionals who want to assess and improve the care they offer women who miscarry, and for women who want to negotiate with them.

The Basic Principles

There are two ideas which are central to these guidelines.

1 Women are individuals with different needs and reactions. A choice of alternative courses of action, where possible, is helpful. Good care, in allowing and enabling a woman to express her needs and work out the meaning of her own experience – rather than defining it for her – is sensitive to her as an individual.

2 Pregnancy loss is a continuum of experience. Gestational age does not determine how a woman feels about her loss, and the needs she has. Most women, from a very early stage, think of their pregnancy in terms of a baby and therefore to them, if to no one else, they have lost their baby when their pregnancy ends. The emotional experience is not necessarily in tune with the physical reality. Gestational age may influence the degree of attachment or the extent to which the baby is perceived as a separate entity but not that the attachment exists.

This does not mean that a miscarriage at 10 weeks is the same as one at 22 weeks, it obviously is not, nor that two women who miscarry at 12 weeks have identical reactions, they will not, but that miscarriage at any gestational age should be treated as a significant event, and that all women should be offered care that is appropriate to the meaning the miscarriage has for them.

Women's Needs

In order to offer good health care it is essential to understand, from a woman's point of view, what it is like to miscarry and therefore what her needs are.

1 The need to be looked after

Miscarriage is usually, at the least, a physically unpleasant, upsetting and confusing experience. Women feel vulnerable, sometimes frightened, in need of good physical care, prompt medical attention and protection. Emotionally women need to be looked after in an accepting environment where they can discover and express their feelings.

2   The need for acknowledgement and legitimation

Women often feel their experience is minimised. It is of great benefit if health workers acknowledge what has happened, say they are sorry, talk about it, and communicate that what has happened is something that matters.

3 The need for respect and dignity

It is helpful if a woman feels there is respect for her experience and for her and her partner's feelings, if the miscarriage can take place with some dignity in an appropriate place and that what is lost, baby, fetus or products of conception, is handled with respect.

4   The need for information

Most women know little about miscarriage until it happens to them and ignorance can make an experience worse than it need be. It is helpful for women to have information throughout the miscarriage about what has happened, what is happening and to be prepared for what might happen next. It is impossible for a woman to make sense of her experience unless she has as full a grasp as possible about what has happened to her and her baby. If a woman wants this information it should be made readily available. If questions cannot be answered, it is acceptable to say so and to explain why. It is difficult to take in information at a time of stress and it may be necessary for it to be repeated. It is also helpful if it can be written down.

The Guidelines

These fundamental needs and ideas form the principles on which the specific proposals that follow are based. The guidelines are a summary of the practical recommendations made in the text. They are not necessarily new ideas, but they bring together the elements of good practice to illustrate the pattern of care it is helpful to offer. There are various solutions to the issues raised, different ways of implementing these ideas which are sensitive to local needs and the particular, practical restraints that impinge on any public service, and which, in practice, turn the desirable into the possible.

1 When a miscarriage threatens

A threatened miscarriage brings uncertainty and anxiety. A woman needs:

- contact with her GP or midwife – a visit, if at all possible
- reassurance that her feelings are natural
- information about what can or cannot be done to save the baby
- an accurate diagnosis if this is possible, or a clear time limit for when a diagnosis can be made, for example organising a scan appointment
- preparation for what may happen, the physical process and the nature of the loss, as far as this can be predicted
- information about miscarriage.

2 When hospital admission is unnecessary

While many women would prefer to stay at home and avoid hospital admission and an ERPC, if possible, that does not mean that professional help is unnecessary. A woman needs:

- support, regular contact with her GP and midwife, if one is available
- preparation for the physical process and the nature of the loss
- information about the length of time normal bleeding will continue, the nature of more serious symptoms and what to do if they develop
- the opportunity to discuss her feelings
- if she already has children, recognition that she may need help in looking after them
- follow-up care (see page 261).

3 The management of scans

The use of ultrasound is an increasingly routine part of medical care for women who miscarry. It is helpful if:

- scans take place within 24 hours of referral, earlier if at all possible

- a woman is allowed to have her partner, friend or relative present if she wishes
- the scan operator is allowed to communicate the result to the woman, followed up by a more detailed discussion with a doctor
- there is an agreed system of obtaining a second opinion

4   Timing

Once a miscarriage is confirmed, either by ultrasound or by clinical assessment, a woman should not be rushed into having an ERPC or sent away for it to happen naturally unless that is what she wants. Some women need time to take in the information and discuss it before having an ERPC, while others will want to have an ERPC as soon as possible. It is helpful if individual wishes can be respected.

5   Admission to hospital

Hospital staff can play a vital role in how women feel about their miscarriage. It is helpful if:

- information is given about what is happening and what will happen next
- preparation is given for the physical process and the nature of the loss. Many women will worry about this but be unable to ask questions.
- accurate information is given about procedures and when they are likely to happen. A definite timescale can make the unknown more manageable.
- if alternative courses of action are possible they are discussed and as much choice as possible is given
- her partner or relative or close friend can be with her if she wishes
- adequate pain relief is given if requested and the alternatives and implications discussed with the woman
- physical needs are met: supplies of pads in the bedside locker, clean draw sheets readily available, location of toilet and washing facilities explained

- there is a sensitive use of language. For example, words such as 'abortion', 'the scrape' and referring to the fetus as 'bits and pieces' are unacceptable. Women use the words 'baby' and 'miscarriage' and wish others would too. Finding words that both women and professionals are comfortable with is an essential basis for easy communication.

6   Place in hospital

It is up to each hospital to create a caring environment for women who miscarry. There is not an obvious best place for women to go. Different hospitals may choose different locations and it is likely that women with early and late miscarriages will be cared for in different places. It does not have to be a ward which only cares for miscarriage patients. Women are most likely to feel well cared for when:

- they are admitted to a ward where they are expected, where all women who miscarry go, where staff are prepared for them and understand why they are there, where procedures are known or information about them at hand, and the issues that miscarriage poses have been thought about
- they are not in close proximity to pregnant women, women having induced abortions, or newborn babies
- there is a choice about privacy, if at all possible. Women vary in the amount of privacy they need and this may vary over the duration of the miscarriage.

7   The products of conception/fetus/baby

When a woman miscarries she may not understand the precise nature of her loss. To some women this will be unimportant while to others it will be of great significance, and it should not be something that is thought about when it is too late to do anything about. Regardless of whether there is a completely-formed baby or only the products of conception, it is helpful if:

- women have the opportunity to know what they have lost if they wish. Some may want to see, others will want to be told. Others will not want to know at the time, but will want to later. Some will not want to know about the loss.

- an adequate explanation is given for the nature of the loss and if there is no fetus a woman understand why
- a detailed description of the loss is recorded in the medical notes and forwarded to the GP. Women who did not think about this at the time may want to know later.
- where there is a complete baby, of whatever size or gestational age, a woman and her partner have the opportunity to see and hold their baby if they wish. If there are obvious abnormalities or maceration this should be sensitively explained and a woman and her partner prepared. It may be helpful if the baby is wrapped. The offer should be repeated on several occasions, over a period of time.
- the sex of the baby, when it is known, is clearly recorded in the notes and the woman told.

8 Disposal

Most women will not have thought about the issues that disposal poses before they miscarry. For many it is not a matter of great concern but for some it is, particularly when there is a complete fetus or when the miscarriage is late in pregnancy. While not wanting to overstate the case by attributing an importance to her loss that it does not have for her, a woman's burden should not be increased by insensitive disposal arrangements. The important considerations are that:

- women are informed of the options open to them and the time limit within which a decision has to be made
- where there is a complete fetus it should be kept for a period of time (six weeks maximum) to allow the parents to make their own disposal arrangements if they wish
- if parents wish to make their own arrangements they are helped to do so. In Britain a medical statement from a doctor or midwife confirming that the baby was less than 24 weeks gestation and showed no signs of life is necessary to arrange a burial or cremation. There is no legal restraint to burial in the garden at home.

- the hospital arrangements for disposal are sensitive and respectful. It is unacceptable to most women that the baby or remains are disposed of in the hospital incinerator, along with the rest of the hospital waste. As awareness of these issues grows so practice is improving. Some hospitals make arrangements with their local crematorium and others arrange for all miscarried babies and remains to be incinerated together in the hospital incinerator, or a special incinerator, at regular intervals. The hospital chaplain organises a regular memorial service.

9   Creating memories

Miscarriage can be a very intangible event. It is helpful in the aftermath to have memories to cherish. Hospital staff can help in various ways, by:

- talking about the miscarriage, the baby, if there was one, and the hopes and expectations for that child
- suggesting to parents that they name their baby, write about their experience, organise a memorial service or make some memorial of their own
- when there is a baby, taking a photo (with a good quality camera) to give to the parents or to remain on file until asked for. A footprint can also be something to remember with.
- some formal recognition of a miscarriage – there is no certificate as there is with a stillbirth. A letter or certificate from the hospital confirming that the pregnancy took place and that the baby existed, however briefly, would be very helpful.

10   Discharge from hospital

The hospital stay is usually brief. It is helpful if:

- women are not rushed out of hospital too quickly. It confirms feelings of being abandoned and unwanted, of being a misfit and having done something untoward. Some women will of course want to get home as soon as possible.

- before leaving a woman has an opportunity to discuss her miscarriage with a senior doctor and to ask questions
- for women who miscarry later in pregnancy (from about 16 weeks but it varies) advice is given about milk coming in and the alternative ways of handling it (expressing a little, cold compresses, well-supporting bra, drugs, homeopathic treatment). Emotional support is essential.
- women are advised to return to work when they feel ready and that it may take longer than is generally realised before they feel both physically and emotionally up to work again. Taking time after the miscarriage is one way of marking the significance of the event.
- written information should be given to every woman covering: basic causes of miscarriage; the physical and emotional after-effects; the implications for partner and family; advice about resuming sexual intercourse, use of tampons, and bathing; advice about preconceptual care and trying again; and details of relevant local support groups
- arrangements for follow-up appointments are given before she leaves hospital
- antenatal and scan appointments are cancelled and the GP, health visitor and midwife are informed of the miscarriage.

11   Follow-up care

Professional follow-up care after a miscarriage, at whatever gestation of pregnancy, is essential. Every woman should be offered the opportunity to discuss her individual case with an informed health professional. Not all will take up the offer but it should be offered rather than asked for. It is very difficult to ask for help when you most need it, and the experts give the impression that you are not supposed to. The follow-up should include:

- detailed information about the process and possible causes of the miscarriage
- the results of any tests that have been done, and if no tests have been done the reasons why not should be explained. If

tests are to be done, their purpose and process to be fully explained.

- discussion about the woman's physical health and an examination if necessary. Most women would wish to avoid a physical examination unless it is essential.
- acknowledgement of the sadness of the loss and the normality of grief. An opportunity for the woman to talk about her feelings if she wishes.
- an opportunity to ask questions
- advice about a future pregnancy – 'when you feel ready but don't rush it unless you really feel up to it', is better advice than a specific number of months which will undoubtedly conflict with someone else's advice and cause confusion. Advice on preconception care and antenatal care that should be available in a subsequent pregnancy.
- involving the woman's partner without question if the woman wishes.

There is a distinction between the need for specific medical information and the need for support, the expression and exploration of feelings and the offering of advice. It may not be possible for one health professional to offer all these things. For women who miscarry after 16 weeks a follow-up appointment with a senior hospital doctor should always be given, preferably with the doctor the woman had most dealings with in hospital and in a comfortable place, not the antenatal clinic. This does not mean they will not need further help in the community. Women who miscarry early may gain as much, if not more, from an appointment with a community midwife or hospital midwife, running a follow-up clinic, for example, or from their GP, if he or she is sympathetic. It is important to be flexible to the needs of individual women and to the strengths of local provision, but it is essential that women are not abandoned once they have left hospital knowing little about their miscarriage or their baby.

Self-help groups can be a source of information and advice and they provide an opportunity for a woman to express and explore her feelings with other women with similar experiences – an invaluable source of support, when it is needed. Support groups are not a substitute for professional follow-up appointments.

12   Antenatal care in the next pregnancy

Many women who have miscarried are naturally anxious they will miscarry again. They often feel that too little antenatal care is offered too late. It is helpful if:

- a woman is encouraged to seek professional help early in her next pregnancy
- regular and frequent appointments are offered, either with the GP or midwife, providing the opportunity for her to share her anxieties and ask questions, and to seek support and reassurance
- an early scan is arranged if the woman is very anxious, so that she knows if the pregnancy is viable or not.

Conclusion

Providing this sort of care is emotionally demanding on all staff, while working in a pressured, under-resourced system stretches their ingenuity. Health service staff are only human, like the women they are there to care for. Women are most likely to get the sort of care they need when staff work closely together in a team, when they discuss policy, share problems, are free to express the emotional burden they will at times carry and have sympathetic managers. These guidelines are not meant to suggest unobtainable goals but to provide a model of care for miscarrying women to compare with the existing service. Many places are already attending to these issues, but many are not. Clearly this could be discouraging for services which fall short of these ideals, but hopefully it could provide an agenda of improvements to work towards.

Glossary of terms

Blighted ovum
An abnormal conception; the placenta and membranes are formed but no embryo. You feel pregnant because the placenta is developing and making the right hormones but without the baby the placenta will eventually stop growing and the miscarriage will occur, usually about 6-10 weeks after your last period.

Cervical stitch/cervical suture
A stitch that is inserted, under general anaesthetic, into the neck of the womb after about 14-16 weeks of pregnancy when it is known or suspected that the cervix is weak and will open too early (incompetent cervix). It is called the Shirodkar or MacDonald suture and is often compared to a purse string. It is usually removed during the thirty eighth week of pregnancy. (See Ros Kane: *The Cervical Stitch: What it's like*, Miscarriage Association 1986.)

Complete miscarriage (abortion)
A miscarriage when all the tissue from the pregnancy has been passed.

Dilettation and curettage (D and C)
Under general anaesthetic the cervix is gently opened and the lining of the womb is scraped clean using a currette.

Ectopic pregnancy
A pregnancy that starts to grow outside the womb, usually in the fallopian tube (see page 36).

Epidural anaesthetic
A form of anaesthetic often used in later miscarriages. It is given into the epidural space surrounding the spinal chord. It numbs all sensation around the womb but you are conscious and therefore aware of what is going on.

Evacuation of the Retained Products of Conception (ERPC)
The correct medical term for a D and C when it is required after you have been pregnant. Sometimes suction apparatus is used to empty the womb instead of scraping it clean.

Fallopian tubes
The tube that connects the ovary to the womb – often the place of an ectopic pregnancy.

Histology
The study of organic tissue.

Hydatidiform mole/Molar pregnancy
A pregnancy in which an abnormal placenta develops made up of small grape-like blobs. Can become cancerous. See page 35.

Hysterosalpingogram
An x-ray of the womb. A liquid is injected into the womb which shows up on x-ray so the outline of the shape of the womb can be seen.

Immunotherapy/Immunological treatment
Offered to couples who suffer recurrent miscarriage and immunological problems are suspected as being the cause (see page 157). The woman is immunised with white blood cells taken from her partner's blood. It is thought that this enables

the woman to develop the necessary protective factor which will prevent her from rejecting the growing embryo.

Incompetent cervix
Weakness in the neck of the womb which means it opens too early in pregnancy, usually after the fourth month, before the baby is mature enough to survive. The cervix may be naturally weak or it may have been caused by a difficult birth or previous surgical intervention. (See Ros Kane: *The Cervical Stitch*)

Incomplete miscarriage (abortion)
The miscarriage is inevitable but not all the tissue from the pregnancy has come away. It is likely that you will continue to bleed until all the tissue is passed and so to curtail the bleeding an ERPC is usually advised.

Inevitable miscarriage (abortion)
A miscarriage becomes inevitable once the neck of the womb opens.

Laparotomy
Incision in lower abdomen through which remains of tubal pregnancy are removed.

Maceration
When the fetus has died sometime before the miscarriage it begins to waste away or disintegrate. Macerate is the medical term that is used.

Missed abortion
The pregnancy has ended, either the baby died and the process of disintegration and re-absorption has begun or the embryo never developed (blighted ovum) but you have not expelled the pregnancy. You may begin to feel less pregnant but you will have no bleeding or cramps. In time you would miscarry naturally but this could take months. It is usual for an ERPC to be performed when a missed abortion is detected because it can cause an infection or a disturbance in the clot-

ting mechanism of the mother's blood. An ultrasound scan can detect a missed abortion.

Salpingectomy
Surgery to remove the fallopian tube.

Threatened miscarriage (abortion)
When the cervix remains closed but there have been symptoms of miscarriage, bleeding and cramps.

Ultrasound scan
High frequency soundwaves are beamed onto the uterus and as they bounce back are used to build up a picture on the video of the baby and placenta in the womb. The picture is often very blurred and needs expert interpretation. Early in pregnancy you may need to drink a lot so that your bladder is full, which will push your womb higher and make it easier to see. Later in pregnancy you may need to have an empty bladder. Ultrasound can date a pregnancy quite accurately and can show the heartbeat, abnormalities in the shape of the womb and the position of the placenta.

Further reading

This list of books, pamphlets and articles is not intended as a comprehensive bibliography but as a guide to where to find additional information on particular topics.

Miscarriage
Allen, M. and Marks S. *Miscarriage: Sharing from the Heart*, Wiley, 1993.
One hundred women interviewed after miscarriage share their experiences and thoughts.
Borg, S. and Lassker, J. *When Pregnancy Fails*, Routledge Kegan Paul, London, 1983.
An American book, good on the emotional aspects of losing a baby late in pregnancy.
Cruttenden, P. *Angels of the Heart*. Available from Paula Cruttenden, 24 Rockcliffe Avenue, Bath BA2 6QP (£5.99).
A collection of poetry by parents who have lost a child through miscarriage, illness or accident.
Hey, V., Itzin, C., Saunders, L. and Speakman, M. A. *Hidden Loss*, The Women's Press, 1989.
Accounts of individuals' experiences, medical information and chapters on emotional significance and recovery.
Hill, S. *Family*, Michael Joseph, London, 1989.
Susan Hill gives a moving personal account of miscarriage, infertility and baby loss following a premature birth, and finally a healthy pregnancy.
Ilse, S. and Hammer Burns, L. *Empty Arms: Coping with Miscarriage, Stillbirth and Infant Death*, P. Wintergreen (USA), 1990.
Sensitively written with a real insight into the feelings that are often very hard for people to express.
Kane, R. *The Cervical Stitch: What it's like*, The Miscarriage Association, 1986.

Available from the Miscarriage Association. Draws on medical research and the experience of women who have had the stitch.

Kohner, N. and Henley, A. *When a Baby Dies: The experience of late miscarriage, stillbirth and neonatal death*, Pandora, London, 1991.

Lachelin, G. C. L. *Miscarriage: The Facts*, Oxford University Press, Oxford, 1985.
Written by an obstetrician, it gives clear information about the medical aspects of miscarriage.

Leroy, M. *Miscarriage*, Optima, in co-operation with The Miscarriage Association, 1988.
Easy to read and informative on medical and emotional aspects of miscarriage. The author draws on her own and others' experiences.

Lovell, A. 'When a baby dies', *New Society*, 4 August 1983, p. 167.

Oakley, A., McPherson, A. and Roberts, H. *Miscarriage*, Penguin, 1990 (revised from 1984 Fontana edition).
The authors have had miscarriages themselves and address the meaning of miscarriage and review the medical research, drawing on the experience of women who completed their questionnaire.

Pfeiffer, N. and Woollett, A. *The Experience of Infertility*, Virago, London, 1983.
Chapter 8 is on miscarriage.

Pizer, H. and Palinski, C. O'Brien. *Coping with Miscarriage*, Jill Norman, London, 1980.
An American book written by a woman who had three miscarriages, and her doctor friend.

Books for children
Harper, A. *Remembering Michael*, SANDS, 1994.
A story about a family where a baby brother dies at birth.

Medical texts
Bennett, M. J. and Edmonds, D. K. (eds). *Spontaneous and Recurrent Abortion*, Blackwell Scientific Publications, 1987.
A series of articles on recent research, including abnormalities in conception, the stitch, immunology and recurrent miscarriage.

Huisjes, H. J. *Spontaneous Abortion*, Churchill Livingstone, Edinburgh, 1984.
An academic textbook reviewing research on the causes of miscarriage and implications for treatment. Well worth ploughing through if you want detailed information.

Grief and depression
Nairne, K. and Smith G. *Dealing with Depression*, The Women's Press, London, 1983.
Written by two women, both clinical psychologists, about women's

experience of depression and sources of help.

Parkes, C. M. *Bereavement: Studies of Grief in Adult Life*, Penguin, 1983.
Written by a psychiatrist, it describes in detail the process of grief, based on his clinical experience and extensive research.

Peppers, L. G. and Knapp, R. J. *Motherhood and Mourning: Perinatal Death*, Praeger, New York, 1980.
Based on research interviews with couples who experienced perinatal death. Draws on individuals' experience and looks at the implications for health care.

Schiff, H. S. *The Bereaved Parent*, Souvenir Press, Human Horizon Series, 1977.
Written by the parent of a 10-year-old boy who died, it deals with the feelings of grief, guilt and hopelessness which afflict many bereaved parents and the impact on their relationship. Draws on author's own and others' experiences.

Stack, J. M. 'The psychodynamics of spontaneous abortion', *Am. J. Orthopsychiatry*, 54(1) January 1984.

Assertion

Dickson, A. *A Woman in Your Own Right: Assertiveness and You*, Quartet Books, London, 1982.
A self-help book aimed at enabling women to learn how to become more assertive.

Planning for a future pregnancy

Brewer, G. S. and Brewer, T. *What Every Pregnant Woman Should Know*, Penguin, Harmondsworth, 1985.

Elkington, J. *The Poisoned Womb*, Penguin, Harmondsworth, 1986.

Foresight. *Guidelines for Future Parents*, and other leaflets. Available from 28 The Paddock, Godalming GU7 1XD. Send C5 size envelope.

Maternity Alliance. *Pregnant at Work, Getting Fit for Pregnancy* and *A Bibliography on Health before Pregnancy*. Leaflets available from The Maternity Alliance, 15 Britannia Street, London WC1X 9JP. Send SAE.

Philips, A. and Rakusen, J. (eds). *The New Our Bodies, Ourselves*, Penguin, Harmondsworth, 1989 (revised edition).

Pickard, B. *Are You Fit Enough to Become Pregnant? Be Fit and Healthy Before You Start a Baby*, 1983.
Available from The Miscarriage Association, c/o Clayton Hospital, Northgate, Wakefield, West Yorkshire WF1 3JS; 50 pence.

Pickard, B. *Eating Well For a Healthy Pregnancy*, Sheldon, London, 1984.

Further reading

Professional care and service provision
These articles may be of interest to those concerned with the quality of both personal care and the management of miscarriage.

Batcup, G., Clarke, J. P. and Purdie, D. W. 'Disposal arrangements for fetuses lost in the second trimester', *Brit. J. Obs. & Gynae*, vol. 95, June 1988, pp. 547–50.

Hutti, M. H. 'A Quick Reference Table of Interventions to Assist Families to Cope with Pregnancy Loss or Neonatal Death', *Birth*, 15: March 1988.

Institute of Burial and Cremation Administration. *A Policy Document on the Care and Disposal of Foetal Remains*, available from Ian Hussein, National Secretary, I.B.C.A., The Gatehouse, Kew Meadow Path, Richmond, Surrey TW9 4EN. Please send large SAE. Tel: 0181 392 9487.

Joint Committee for Hospital Chaplaincy. 'Miscarriage, Stillbirth and Neo-natal Death', *Guidelines in Pastoral Care for Hospital Chaplains*, available from Church House Bookshop, 31 Great Smith Street, London SW1P 3BN.

Knapp, R. J. and Peppers, L. G. 'Doctor–Patient Relationships in Fetal/Infant Death Encounters', *J. of Medical Education*, vol. 54, Oct. 1979.

Lovell, A. 'Mothers and babies in Limbo', *Nursing Mirror*, 3 November 1982.

Peppers, L. G. and Knapp, R. J. 'Maternal Reactions to Involuntary Fetal/Infant Death', *Psychiatry*, vol. 43, May 1980.

Proctor, E. 'Too young to live', *Nursing Mirror*, vol. 160, no. 20, 15 May 1985.

SANDS. *Miscarriage, Stillbirth and Neonatal Death: Guidelines for Professionals*, Stillbirth and Neonatal Death Society, 1991.

SANDS. *A Dignified Ending*, Stillbirth and Neonatal Death Society, 1992.

Research into the experience of miscarriage
I found the following particularly helpful in researching this book.

Hutti,. M. H. 'An Exploratory Study of the Miscarriage Experience', *Health Care for Women International*, 7: 1986, pp. 371–89.

Journal of Reproductive and Infant Psychology, Special Issue on 'Understanding the Experience and Emotional Consequences of Miscarriage', vol. 12 (1) 1994, pp. 1–68.
Contains a series of articles reporting recent research into different aspects of miscarriage.

Lovell, A. 'Some Questions of Identity: Late Miscarriage, Stillbirth, and Perinatal Loss', *Soc Sci Med*, 17 (11) 1983, pp. 325–7.

Lovell, A. 'A Bereavement with a Difference: A Study of Late

Miscarriage, Stillbirth and Perinatal Death', South Bank Sociology: Occasional Paper 4, 1983, Social Science Department, Polytechnic of the South Bank, London SE1 0AA.

Swanson-Kaufman, K. 'The Unborn One: A profile of the Human Experience of Miscarriage', unpublished doctoral dissertation, University of Colorado, 1983.

Useful addresses

Pregnancy loss
Child Bereavement Trust
1 Millside, Riversdale, Bourne End, Buckinghamshire SL8 5EB
Resources for bereaved families and for professionals.

Miscarriage Association (MA)
c/o Clayton Hospital, Northgate, Wakefield, West Yorks. WF1 3JS
Tel: 01924 200799 (9 a.m.–3.30 p.m. Mon–Fri; answering machine out of hours, which gives another number should you want to speak to someone urgently)
Publishes quarterly newsletter and information leaflets; network of support groups and contacts throughout the country; will try to put women with similar experiences in touch with each other. Phone or write sending SAE.

SANDS (Stillbirth and Neonatal Death Society)
28 Portland Place, London W1N 3DE
Helpline: 0171 436 5881
Admin: 0171 436 7940
Offers support for those whose baby dies after 24 weeks of pregnancy or in the early days of life. Support groups and contacts throughout the country. Publishes various information leaflets.

SATFA (Support around Termination for Abnormality)
29–30 Soho Square, London W1V 6JB
Helpline: 0171 439 6124
Admin: 0171 287 3753
For women who consider or decide on a termination of pregnancy after an abnormality has been detected. Offers information, befriending and contacts. Phone or send SAE.

Twins and Multiple Births Association (TAMBA) Bereavement Support
Groups
PO Box 30, Little Sutton, South Wirral L66 1TH
Tel: 0151 348 0020
For parents who have lost one or both twins, or babies from a multiple
birth.

Pregnancy – general
Association for Improvements in the Maternity Services (AIMS)
21 Iver Lane, Iver, Buckinghamshire SL0 9LH
Tel: 01753 652 781
Advice on rights, complaints procedures and choices in maternity care.

Child–Infertility Research, Education and Counselling
Suite 219, Caledonia House, 98 The Centre, Feltham, Middlesex
TW13 4BH
Tel: 0181 893 7110
Support and information for families with infertility problems.

Family Planning Information Service (FPIS)
27–35 Mortimer Street, London W1N 7RJ
Tel: 0171 636 7866
Information on infertility and sexual difficulties. Referral to local
sources of help.

Foresight Association
(The Association for the Promotion of Preceonceptual Care)
28 The Paddock, Godalming, Surrey GU7 1XD
Provides a wide range of booklets on preconception care and informa-
tion on preconception clinics. Write with history of problems, sending
C5 size SAE.

ISSUE – The National Fertility Association
509 Aldridge Road, Great Barr, Birmingham B44 8NA
Tel: 0121 344 4414
Advice, information and counselling for people with infertility and
related problems. Registration fee.

The Maternity Alliance
15 Brittannia Street, London WC1X 9JP
Tel: 0171 837 1265
Produces leaflets including 'Getting fit for pregnancy' and 'Thinking
about a baby: A man's guide to preconception care'. Campaigns on
maternity issues.

National Childbirth Trust
Alexandra House, Oldham Terrace, Acton, London W3 6NH
Tel: 0181 992 8637 (closed 1 p.m.–2 p.m.)
Publishes a leaflet on miscarriage and runs several support groups
around the country.

WHRRIC – (Women's Health and Reproductive Rights Information
Centre)
2–4 Featherstone Street, London EC1Y 8RT
Tel: 0171 251 6580 (10 a.m.–4 p.m., Mon, Weds, Thurs and Fri;
answering machine out of hours)
Provides information on most aspects of women's health and reproduction, publishes a quarterly newsletter and a range of information leaflets
on particular topics, including miscarriage. Phone for information or
send SAE and 60 pence for miscarriage leaflets. Reference library.

Help and advice with specific problems
Association for Spina Bifida and Hydrocephalus
42 Park Road, Peterborough PE1 2UQ
Tel: 01733 555988 (Mon–Fri, 9 a.m.–5 p.m.; answering machine out of
hours)
Offers general advice as well as support for couples offered termination
after aminocentesis.

Cytomegalovirus Support Group
69 The Leasowes, Ford, Shrewsbury, Shropshire SY5 9LU
Tel: 01743 850 055
For parents whose babies have been damaged by cytomegalovirus
(CMV).

Lupus UK
51 North Street, Romford, Essex RM1 1BA
Tel: 01708 731 251
For people with lupus (systematic lupus erythematosis or SLE). There is
also a lupus adviser in the Welfare Department of Arthritis Care, 18
Stephenson Way, London NW1 2HD (0171 916 1550).

National Endometriosis Society
35 Belgrave Square, London SW1X 8OB
Tel: 0171 235 4137 (10.30 a.m.–4.00 p.m., Mon–Fri, out-of-hours
answering machine with name and number of person on helpline duty)
Phone or write sending SAE for an information pack with details of the
Society, endometriosis and how to join. Membership fee currently £12,
which includes three newsletters per year, access to group contact lists,
publications and workshops.

SOFT UK (Support Organisation for Trisomy 13/18 and related disorders)
National co-ordinator for Trisomy 13 (Patau's syndrome):
Tudor Lodge, Redwood, Ross-on-Wye, Herefordshire HR9 5UD
Tel: 01989 567 480
National co-ordinator for Trisomy 18 (Edward's syndrome):
48 Froggatt's Ride, Walmley, Sutton Coldfield, West Midlands B76 8TQ
Tel: 0121 351 3122
For parents of children born with Trisomy 13 (Patau's syndrome), Trisomy 18 (Edward's syndrome) or related chromosomal disorders.

The Stitch Network
Tel: Julie 01926 843223
For women who have an incompetent cervix and need the stitch. Puts them in touch with one another. For written information on the cervical stitch please contact the Miscarriage Association (address and phone number as above).

Toxoplasmosis Trust
61–71 Collier Street, London N1 9BE
Tel: 0171 713 0599 (9.30 a.m.–5.30 p.m.)
Provides information about toxoplasmosis, counselling and advice. Send A4 SAE for fact sheet, or telephone for advice. Answering machine when office unmanned.

Turner's Syndrome Society
2 Mayfield Avenue, Chiswick, London W4 1PW
Tel: 0181 994 7625
For parents of children with Turner's Syndrome.

Counselling and therapeutic help
British Association for Counselling
1 Regent Place, Rugby CV21 2PJ
Tel: 01788 578 328 (answering machine)
Information on where to get counselling locally. Send A4 SAE.

British Association of Psychotherapists
37 Mapesbury Road, London NW2 4HJ
Tel: 0181 452 9823
Phone or write for name and phone number of local assessor who will help you find therapist. Assessor's fee currently £38. Therapy sessions start at £20 per session.

Catholic Marriage Advisory Council
Clitherow House, 1 Blythe Mews, Blythe Road, London W14 0NW
Tel: 0171 371 1341
Education and counselling for marriages and relationships.

Guild of Psychotherapists
47 Nelson Square, London SE1 0QA
Tel: 0181 947 0730 (Tues, Weds, Thurs 10 a.m.–1 p.m.)
Will take your details and find a therapist in your area. Fees vary.

Perinatal Bereavement Unit
Tavistock Clinic, 120 Belsize Park, London NW3
Tel: 0171 435 7111
A group of therapists and analysts with a special interest in late miscarriage, stillbirth and neonatal death. Available as a resource for practitioners and researchers. Able to take some referrals (via GP) for women
living in the London area.

Cruse
Cruse House, 126 Sheen Road, Richmond, Surrey TW9 1UR
Helpline: 0181 332 7227 (Mon–Fri 9.30 a.m.–5.00 p.m.)
Admin: 0181 940 4818 (closed 1–2 p.m.)
Support and advice for bereaved people.

Jewish Bereavement Counselling Service
1 Cyprus Gardens, London N3 1SP
Tel: 0171 387 4300 x 227 (also 24-hour answering machine 0181 349
0839)
Offers parents bereavement counselling.

London Association of Bereavement Services
356 Holloway Road, London N7 6PN
Tel: 0171 700 8134
Counselling and support for anyone who is bereaved.

National Association of Bereavement Services
20 Norton Folgate, Bishopsgate, London E1 6DB
Tel: 0171 247 0617
Counselling enquiries: 0171 247 1080
Counselling and support for anyone who is bereaved. Referral to a local
bereavement service.

RELATE – National Marriage Guidance Council
Hubert Gray College, Little Church Street, Rugby, Warwickshire
CV21 3AP

Tel: 01788 573241
Offers help to couples experiencing difficulties. The phone number of your local branch should be in your local phone directory under Relate, or you can ring the headquarters.

Samaritans
10 The Grove, Slough, Berkshire SL1 1QP
Tel: 01753 532713 (or see under Samaritans in the local telephone book)
24-hour confidential telephone help for people who are in despair, some of whom feel suicidal.

Westminster Pastoral Foundation
23 Kensington Square, London W8 5HN
Tel: 0171 937 6956
Individual, marital and family counselling. Information on similar services in other parts of the UK.

Sources of further advice and support
Action for Victims of Medical Accidents (AVMA)
Banks Chambers, 1 London Road, Forest Hill, London SE23 2TP
Tel: 0181 291 2793

Association of Community Health Councils for England and Wales (ACHCEW)
30 Drayton Park, London N5 1PB
Tel: 0171 609 8405
Community Health Councils (Local Health Councils in Scotland, Area Health and Social Services Councils in Northern Ireland) are independent watchdogs over local health services and can support people who wish to complain about the care they or members of their family have received. See the local telephone book for the address and telephone number of the local Community Health Council or equivalent.

The Scottish Association of Health Councils
5 Leamington Terrace, Edinburgh EH10 4JW
Tel: 0131 229 2344

Eastern and Social Services Council
19 Bedford Street, Belfast, Northern Ireland BT2 7EJ
Tel: 01232 321 230

Bereavement Training Consortium
Stapley Mill, Stapley, Churchstanton, Taunton, Somerset TA3 7QA
Tel: 01823 601106

Useful addresses

Training for health-care and other professionals in all aspects of pregnancy loss and the death of a baby.

AUSTRALIA
Association for Improvement of Maternity Services
Tel: Janet Hutchinson: 06 2589230

Family Planning Australia, PO Box 26, West Deakin ACT 2600
Tel: 062 85 1244
Provides pregnancy counselling and an advice and referral service for women. Offers information on full range of reproductive and sexual health issues. Contact for local branch.

Maternity Alliance
Sydney: 02 987447
Blue Mts: 047 822008

SANDS (Stillbirth and Neonatal Death Society)
Sue Walker: 06 2888109
Kim Hanson: 06 2924330

NEW ZEALAND
Miscarriage Support Group
c/o Parent & Family Resource Centre, PO Box 46140, Herne Bay, Auckland
Tel: 09 631 5644
Phone for address and phone number of contact in your area.

USA
The Compassionate Friends
PO Box 3367, Oak Brook, IL 60522–3696
Tel: 708 990 0010

Pregnancy & Infant Loss Center of Minnesota
1415 E. Wayzata Boulevard # 22, Wayzata, MN 55391
Tel: 612 473 9372
Educational resources and information.

SHARE
St Joseph Health Center, 330 First Capitol, Saint Charles, MO 63301–2893

CANADA
Compassionate Friends
Winnipeg, Manitoba
Tel: 204 787 4896
Voluntary self-help group for parents grieving the death of a child of any age.

Pattylou Bryant
Empty Cradle Support Group
Pen-Parents of Canada
1102–2829 Barnet Highway, Coquitlam, BC V3B 7JW
Tel: 604 469 1272

Index

Miscarriage

postnatal 173, 246; symptoms of 124

diagnosis: of ectopic pregnancy 36; of miscarriage 1, 10–11, 84

disbelief, feelings of 16, 171

discharge from hospital 55, 114, 260–61

disposal 43–5, 57, 69–71, 80, 259–60

doctors: changing 163; consultants 95, 96, 156–64; general practitioners (GPs) 33–4, 43, 50, 91, 95–6, 103, 148, 158–64, 170, 199, 218, 241–3; hospital doctors 46–7, 96–8, 199

dreams about miscarriage 40, 238

due date 130, 232

ectopic pregnancy 37–8, 265

emotional attachment to your baby 1, 60, 64, 245, 249

endometriosis 275

epidural anaesthetic 55, 265

ERPC (evacuation of the products of conception) 25, 30–34, 52, 91, 106, 184, 265; after late miscarriage 55; anxieties about 32; routine procedure 29–34; timing of 31–2

ergometrine 27

explanation of miscarriage, the need for 92–3, 98, 126, 156, 257

failure, feeling a 125

fallopian tubes 37, 265

family, effect of miscarriage on 143–5, 191–3; see also children

Family Practitioner Committee 163

fear, feelings of 2–3, 11, 24–5, 88, 125, 174

fetal sac 33

fetus: examination of 46; loss of complete 8, 23, 43–5, 50–57, 258; respect for 47, 258; status of 61, 81

follow-up care 41, 59, 91, 94–9, 161–2, 261–3; after molar

pregnancy 35

friends: impact of miscarriage on relationships with 189–91; support from 146

funeral 69–71

GP see doctors

grief 42, 88, 95, 103–5, 113–31, 143, 147, 154, 169, 172–4, 180; expression of 115–16, 120–21, 135–6; permission for 81, 90, 121–2; unresolved 173

guilt 49, 93, 116–17, 126–9, 167–9, 189, 221

habitual miscarriage see recurrent miscarriage

haemorrhage, risk of 30, 34

health professionals 79–99; attitudes to miscarriage 80–81, 88–90, 96, 99

health visitor 95, 148, 218, 246

helpless, feeling 3, 19, 24–5, 91, 123, 171; see also loss of control

histology 41, 265

homeopath 149

hormone treatment 158–9

hospital care 83–90; admission to 31, 256–8; conflict with community care 83; discharge from 55, 114, 260–61; location of miscarrying women 85–7, 258

husband see partner

hydatidiform mole see molar pregnancy

hysterosalpingogram 265

immunological problems 157, 161–2, 265

identity, feminine xiii, 229

incompetent cervix 50–51, 156, 158, 169, 266

induction 52–3

infection, risk of 30, 34, 53, 106–7, 110, 184

infertility and miscarriage 166, 171